$8.50

P9-CRN-567

Twentieth-Century Music

The Sense Behind the Sound

Twentieth-Century Music

The Sense Behind the Sound

by JOAN PEYSER

SCHIRMER BOOKS
A Division of Macmillan Publishing Co., Inc.
NEW YORK

Collier Macmillan Publishers
LONDON

I am indebted to my friend Patricia Carpenter, Professor of Music at Barnard College, for her illuminating thoughts on music, and to the psychiatrist Dr. Herbert S. Peyser, for the knowledge that underlies the general approach of this book.

For reading the manuscript and making helpful suggestions, I thank Milton Babbitt and Luciano Berio. Finally, I am grateful to Stanley H. Brown for teaching me how to say what I mean.

Copyright © 1971, 1980 by Katomo Ltd.
Copyright © 1970 by Joan Peyser

All rights reserved. No part of this book may be reproduced or transmitted in any form or by any means, electronic or mechanical, including photocopying, recording, or by any information storage and retrieval system, without permission in writing from the Publisher.

Schirmer Books
A Division of Macmillan Publishing Co., Inc.
866 Third Avenue, New York, N.Y. 10022

Collier Macmillan Canada, Ltd.

Library of Congress Catalog Card Number: 79-57286

Printed in the United States of America

printing number

1 2 3 4 5 6 7 8 9 10

Library of Congress Cataloging in Publication Data

Peyser, Joan.
    Twentieth-century music.

    Reprint of the 1971 ed. published by Delacorte Press, New York, under title: The new music.
    Bibliography: p.
    Includes index.
    1. Music—History and criticism—20th century. 2. Schönberg, Arnold, 1874-1951. 3. Stravinskiĭ, Igorʹ Fedorovich, 1882-1971. 4. Varèse, Edgard, 1883-1965. I. Title.
[ML197.P42   1980]   780'.904   79-57286
ISBN 0-02-871880-1

Contents

PREFACE   vii

PROLOGUE   xi

I. SCHOENBERG, WEBERN AND THE
AUSTRO-GERMAN TRADITION   1

II. STRAVINSKY AND THE FRANCO-
RUSSIAN STYLE   81

III. VARÈSE AND OTHER
MUSICAL CURRENTS   139

EPILOGUE   185

GLOSSARY   189

BIBLIOGRAPHY   193

INDEX   197

Preface

The original title of this book was *The New Music: the Sense behind the Sound*. But Schoenberg, Stravinsky and Varèse can no longer be identified as "new." Therefore I have changed the title to *Twentieth-Century Music*.

When I wrote this book in the late 1960's, I ended it on an optimistic note. Rock had developed into a sophisticated genre that had its effect on the serious avant-garde. Composers were allowing more freedom to performers, multi-media happenings proliferated, and Luciano Berio actually composed a major work for large orchestra and The Swingle Singers, a pop-vocal group. The pedantry and self-consciousness that had set the tone for much of the art music through the 1950's had evolved into something new, and I responded with enthusiasm. But today one fact is incontrovertible: the style and syntax that had crystallized in the early part of the century never succeeded in being accepted into the ears, heads or hearts of most audiences.

Although I am no more certain now than I was ten years ago of the direction in which music will move, I would not change my cast of characters if I were writing this book today. For through the personalities, works and reputations of Schoenberg, Stravinsky and Varèse, we capture an important cultural situation. Still, the fact that the activities described in this book led to an end, rather than to a fresh start, calls for some explanation.

To what can we attribute the consistently diminishing transmitting power of music over the course of this century? Consider the music of the generation of Schoenberg, Webern, Berg, Stravinsky, Bartók, Prokofiev, Hindemith and Varèse. Then consider that of the next generation: Babbitt, Boulez, Carter, Stockhausen, Berio, Feldman and Cage. Finally call to mind the work of the present-day minimalists—Philip Glass, Steve Reich, Gordon Mumma, Pauline Oliveros—who reject melody, harmony, rhythm and form in favor of the creation of a static, trancelike state. The point of this current music is to extend or repeat a single idea until it and the listener are exhausted.

What finally can be described only as the lessening of greatness in the music of modern times results, I believe, from the ideas of Darwin, Marx, Einstein and Freud. The dissemination and popularization of their theories propelled everything hidden into the light: Analysis annihilates mystery. In place of intimacy we have calculation. In place of belief we have self-promotion. In place of God we have unbridled narcissism. Bach's purpose in composing cantatas is light years removed from today's composer's aim to see his or her face on the cover of *Newsweek*. Since art, above all, mirrors civilization and reinforces what it finds, it is not surprising that a silent piece by John Cage should have become the touchstone for the composer of our time.

Many composers, of course, have turned their backs on modernism. They seem content to reinvestigate well-traveled roads, as if searching for a way out of the modern music dilemma. But to compose in an old syntax or form strips genuine art of its power, a power which can only be felt if the artist responds to the exigencies of the moment, using the specific tools of his own time. And art must possess power—power to transform or at least clarify one's perception of the world—if it is to be worthy of its name.

In the Preface to *The Waning of the Middle Ages*, Jan Huizinga writes: "In history, as in nature, birth and death are equally balanced. The decay of an over-ripe civilization is as suggestive a spectacle as the growth of new ones. And it occasionally happens that a period in which one had, hitherto, been mainly looking for the coming of the birth of new things, suddenly reveals itself as an epoch of fading and decay."

But fading and decay are not death. They are not irreversible. And just as it took about one hundred and fifty years for the Middle Ages to evolve into the Renaissance, so it may take one hundred and fifty years for the present period to evolve into the succeeding one.

So, in the spring of 1980, I do not reject what I wrote in 1970. The present book—together with its sequel, *Boulez*—traces the death of the beautiful, life-enhancing music that has characterized the art during the past half-millennium. But this narrative should not be viewed as grim. On the contrary, it is celebratory. It celebrates unpredictability, that greatest and most terrifying aspect of life. It celebrates talent and flexibility. It even celebrates the possibility that technology can be harnessed, intuitively and humanistically, to serve a presently unimagineable but distinctly new art.

Prologue

The story of twentieth-century music is in great part the story of how different composers coped with the annihilation of tonality, that particular system of organizing tones that was assumed after several centuries to be the natural law in music.

Tonality, as it evolved in the seventeenth century, is a system of seven-note scales in which one note is the focal point or tonic key. The function of each of the other notes in this scale is determined by its relationship to that key. This dynamic hierarchy dominated all Western music in the eighteenth and nineteenth centuries.

Yet even at its most pervasive and unassailable, the system contained the seeds of its own decay. Between the notes of the seven-note scale there are, of course, half or chromatic notes. At first these chromatic tones served the auxiliary function for which they were named; they added "color" to a musical work. But as time passed, chromatic notes assumed more significance. In his Dissonance Quartet, Mozart bypassed certain rules of tonal logic and thus elevated "disagreeable" sounds at the expense of agreeable ones.

Several decades later, Beethoven almost burst the tonal seams. But as chromatic as his writing became, all the parts were still resolved in a smooth, orthodox way. Tonality remained a guiding principle.

The trend toward atonality—music without this tonal center or key—accelerated in the late nineteenth century. Debussy turned his back on the seven-note scale with its five whole tones and two halftones in favor of a five-note scale of whole tones. Wagner developed a form of modulation—changing key within a work—that went far beyond even the unconventional relationships of the late Beethoven works and made for a pervasive tonal restlessness. His perpetual shifting of key centers undermined tonality. Wagner's intellectual protagonist, Hans Sachs, sings of the situation in *Die Meistersinger*:

> Your closing key is not the same,
> This gives the Masters pain;
> But Hans Sachs draws a rule from this:
> In Spring, it must be so! 'Tis plain!

Arnold Schoenberg quotes these very lines in an essay and adds his own ethical interpretation: "In Spring! In the development of art it must always be as it is in Spring!"

Schoenberg's first keyless movement ushered in the atonal period in Vienna in 1908. After writing several extraordinary, expressionist atonal works between 1908 and 1912, Schoenberg sought a set of musical commandments which would lead his people out of the chaos of atonality. When he was fifty years old, Schoenberg revealed this new law, referring to it as "the method of composing with twelve tones," now commonly known as the "12-tone technique" or "dodecaphony." Repudiating the omnipotence of the tonic, he asserted the equal importance of all twelve notes of the chromatic scale. The composer arranged the twelve notes in a particular order, the "tone row." It was this row or "series" of pitches—whether in its original position, inverted, reversed or with its inversion reversed—that determined the structure of the entire work. Schoenberg compared the row to a hat, identifiable as a hat independent of the angle from which it was viewed. Thus the composer attempted to formulate a 12-tone, melodic technique which would supply the unity formerly provided by the tonal, harmonic one.

Schoenberg attracted a corps of disciples in Vienna and Berlin. Webern, his most famous pupil, went further than his teacher and extended the serial principle beyond just pitch to that of the duration of notes. Inspired by Webern, members of the next generation adopted the serial idea, applying it to still other attributes of the musical tone—like dynamics, timbre, attack and decay. Many post-Webern serialists have since moved away from this tight application of the serial idea. Pursuing an ideal which depends upon the absence of any focus at all, they strive, paradoxically, for a sense of discontinuity and unpredictability around a unifying principle.

Schoenberg's revolution of 1923 not only was difficult for many listeners to accept but impossible for many composers to adopt. Musicians—especially those outside Austria and Germany—resented the imposition of a new set of rules far more stringent than any imposed by tonality. Those opposed to dodecaphony, including such disparate composers as Stravinsky, Hindemith, Bartók, Milhaud and most Americans in the thirties and forties, found themselves thrust together under the large amorphous umbrella labeled "neoclassicism."

In its broadest meaning, neoclassicism implied a rejection of the 12-tone technique and a revival of interest in eighteenth-century forms. This led not only to the use of such traditional forms as the concerto, opera buffa and oratorio but also to a reexploration of tonality. Stravinsky composed with tonal centers without reverting to the sonata form, that particular formal structure that was an organic outgrowth of harmonic tonality. Stravinsky often balanced two key centers at once, and Milhaud went further in this direction; the French composer promulgated "polytonality," balancing four or five different tonalities at the same time.

Each of the two major schools in the first half of the twentieth century—dodecaphony and neoclassicism—was presided over by a God-like figure: Schoenberg over the 12-tone school and Stravinsky over the neoclassicists. Both created a formidable kind of idolatry; neither questioned the correctness of his way.

Edgard Varèse, the pioneer of electronic music, by contrast enjoyed no comparable following. His case is a lonely one. In 1965, after he died, Pierre Boulez wrote in the *Domain Musical* that he loved Varèse because he was "marginal" and "solitaire," possessing the "rarété d'un diamant unique." Varèse did not interest himself in dodecaphony and despised the apparent retrogression of neoclassicism. He dismissed polytonality as the "simultaneous sounding of parts each of which is inane, one of which has been transposed into another key to help disguise the lack of substance. We get the impression, usually, of a dirty chord in C Major."

Producing increasingly vertically dense scores, Varèse created a nonmelodic fabric that depended on rhythm and sonority. Until after World War II he had neither the technology nor the audience he so desperately needed. But today his work has been vindicated: electronic media and pitchless sounds produced by conventional instruments are integral aspects of the new music.

In *Eminent Victorians*, Lytton Strachey examines the lives of only four people to throw light upon the entire era he had just lived through. In his Preface he explains this method:

> It is not by direct method of scrupulous narration that the explorer of the past can hope to depict that singular epoch. If he is wise he will adopt a subtler strategy: He will fall upon the flank and the rear. . . . He will row out over that great ocean of material and lower down into it, here and there, a little bucket which will bring to the light of day some characteristic specimen, from these far depths, to be examined with careful curiosity.

In adopting a similar approach, I have focused on only three men—Schoenberg, Stravinsky and Varèse—plus those musicians who influenced, opposed or followed them. Each was born at the height of the Romantic movement and each lived well into our own time. Each emerged from a different musical culture and transferred that culture to the United States. By following their lengthy careers, one can follow the inexorable path of twentieth-century music.

In order to pursue this specific task, I have omitted great composers, whole nations and popular genres that have contributed to the vitality of music in this century. Béla Bartók, as original a composer as those examined, is omitted because he stood alone. In assimilating his scholarly study of Magyar, Romanian, Serbo-Croatian, Turkish and Arabic music into his musical work, Bartók created a new compositional idiom but one that held little relevance to other musicians. Again, Italy is notable for its absence. Entrenched in an operatic tradition that functioned through tonality, Italians were still committed to Puccini when composers in other countries had long since moved on. Finally, jazz and rock are barely mentioned. Jazz stimulated art musicians in their search for new rhythms, but its influence was soon dissipated. And although rock has contributed a loosening of shape to the art music of the 1960's, the Beatles and other rock musicians have taken more from art music than they have given. Jazz and rock flirted with intellectual music but both are rooted in the tonality of an earlier time.

By confining my history of twentieth-century music to the minds of the most influential figures of our time, I have tried to translate an alien phenomenon into an understandable and estimable human endeavor. I hope that, on the completion of this book, the reader will recognize that today's "difficult" music is inevitable and that composers are not hostile men, bent on displeasing an audience, but artists who could go no other way.

Twentieth-Century Music

The Sense Behind the Sound

Twentieth-Century Music

The Sense Behind the Sound

> History is not something that inexorably marches on regardless of mankind. On the contrary, it is composed of the history of individual creeds, passions, follies, heroisms in contrast with a universe that knows it not and goes its own way.
>
> BERNARD BERENSON,
> *The Passionate Sightseer*, 1960

Chapter 1

It was inevitable that tonality would outlive its usefulness. But it was an accident that at the very time this happened—during the first decades of the twentieth century—a man emerged who not only had an insight into the aesthetic requirements of the time, but also the unshakable faith that he was put on earth to proclaim these requirements to the world. Arnold Schoenberg (1874–1951) was convinced of his destiny as lawgiver: "I am the slave of an internal power stronger than my education; it compels me to obey a conception which, inborn, has greater power over me than any elemental artistic formation."

Schoenberg regarded himself as the figure whose duty it was to reestablish the formerly undisputed hegemony of Austro-German music. Born in Vienna, a direct descendant of Wagner and Brahms, Schoenberg viewed this goal in mystical terms. But his sense of destiny: "I have a mission . . . I have a task . . . I am but the loudspeaker of an idea. . . ." is not to be interpreted merely as a symptom of megalomaniacal thinking; it should be considered in the context of the milieu in which he grew up.

Friedrich Nietzsche, hovering about his compatriots, had repudiated nineteenth-century ideology and demanded the reorganization
of human society under the guidance of exceptional leaders. Richard
Wagner (1813–1883) answered the call. Arrogant beyond measure, Wagner became the German superhero, the embodiment of
the Dionysiac ideal for which Nietzsche yearned. Schoenberg, by
the age of twenty-five, had heard each of Wagner's operas between twenty and thirty times and inherited Wagner's tryrannical
mien.

Yet Schoenberg was also a confirmed Brahmsian. This appears to
be a paradox, for the conflict between Wagner and Brahms re-
volved around such crucial artistic principles that any conciliation
seemed, in Schoenberg's youth, to be impossible. Brahms was considered a conservative; Wagner a revolutionary. Brahms chose the
classic molds of the piano sonata, string quartet and symphony,
rather than the popular "moments musicales" and symphonic tone
poems of other contemporaries. Wagner experimented with a musical idiom that moved away from diatonicism and toward an all-
embracing chromaticism totally theatening to the tonal system.
Brahms did not play with notes for their sensuous effect; tonality
was not an inhibiting force for him.

The balance of power was divided. On the one hand the critic
Eduard Hanslick defended the classicist; on the other hand a host
of imposing figures rallied for the musical revolution. Richard
Strauss, ten years older than Schoenberg, started as a strict Brahmsian and became a confirmed Wagnerian, and Anton Bruckner
consistently praised the new in music. Hugo Wolf, song composer
and music critic of the fashionable journal the Viennese *Salonblatt*,
expressed disdain for Brahms's conservatism: "The leaders of the
revolutionary movement in music after Beethoven (in which Schumann indeed expected a Messiah and thought he had found one
in Brahms) have passed our symphonist by without leaving a trace
on him. Brahms writes symphonies regardless of what has happened in the meantime."

Yet Schoenberg clearly perceived a common factor in the work
of both classicist and rebel; each exhibited a linear, horizontal
orientation in his compositional procedures which was, in a most
conscious sense, derived from the late works of Beethoven. It is this
polyphonic emphasis—the musical realization of a germinal motive
—that Schoenberg inherited, via Brahms and Wagner, from the
late Beethoven. In an analysis of Beethoven's String Quartet in
F Major, Opus 135, Schoenberg articulated his debt to Beethoven.

He used the work to illustrate his belief that its composition was not motivated by divisions into architectonic tonal areas, but that it was derived from the first three notes of the first theme of the first movement. In another essay, "Brahms, the Progressive," Schoenberg cited a number of examples in which Brahms subjected a single germinal motive to the technique of perpetual variation and gave examples to illustrate what he considered to be Brahms's sense of "unitary perception." He points out that the primary melodic idea in Brahms's First Symphony is not restricted to the usual single movement but binds all four.

It is less easy at first to see Wagner's debt to Beethoven than to see Brahms's, for Wagner was devoted to opera while Beethoven, like Brahms, shunned the genre. (Beethoven wrote one; Brahms none.) But on closer inspection the affinity between Beethoven and Wagner becomes clear. Despite the fact that Wagner wrote opera, his focus was centered on what was played by the orchestra—not what was sung on the stage. The popularity of the orchestral version of the "Love-Death" duet from *Tristan und Isolde*—to cite one example—attests to the importance of the purely musical in Wagner's work. His musical fabric is a complex one, held together by *leitmotifs* which not only identify particular characters and situations in the drama but unify the purely musical texture the way the thematic material unifies a symphony or chamber work. Wagner recognized the essentially abstract nature of his music. He claimed that he was not continuing the tradition of Gluck, Mozart or Carl Maria von Weber. Instead, his music-dramas stemmed directly from Beethoven's Ninth Symphony. In fact, Wagner considered Beethoven his immediate precursor; he viewed Beethoven's inclusion of voices in the last movement of this symphony as the first step in the revival of the Greek ideal, the all-inclusive art work embracing the whole compass of arts and letters, Wagner's Romantic creation, the *Gesamtkunstwerk*.

Thus the musical idea, an intellectual concept that had its genesis in Beethoven's art, developed through both Brahms and Wagner. Because of the importance accorded "theme" in Brahms's instrumental works and Wagner's sensuous music-dramas, and despite the different styles of the two Romantic men (Wagner snidely referred to Brahms as the "chaste Johannes,"), Schoenberg drew lavishly from both and repudiated everything outside of Austro-German composition. One of his earliest pupils has reported that the composer once said to him: "Either what *we* do is music or what the French do is music. But both cannot be music." And when

Schoenberg wrote to Josef Stransky, conductor of the New York Philharmonic, suggesting he perform works by his two most gifted pupils, Schoenberg asked: "Would you not like to look at scores of works by Dr. Anton von Webern and Alban Berg, two real musicians—not Bolshevik illiterates, but men with a musically educated ear!"

The attitude that excluded France and Russia from the center of Schoenberg's musical orbit was founded not only on traditional German prejudice, but on what were for him the most valid artistic principles: "Today the majority strive for 'style, technique and sound,' meaning thereby something purely external and striking in character, for the sake of which all old culture displayed in presenting a thought is neglected." Casting aside with contempt the Stravinsky-inspired music that received so much attention during the 1920's, thirties and forties, Schoenberg, in both his writing and teaching, continued to stress the old German masters. Throughout his life he never thought of himself as a radical, but as a traditionalist in the classic sense. In 1937 he wrote to Nicolas Slonimsky: "I personally hate to be called a revolutionist, which I am not."

"The Method of Composing with Twelve Tones Related Only to Each Other," which Schoenberg formulated when he was fifty years old, dramatically altered the course of composition in the twentieth century. Schoenberg never "taught" the technique, which he regarded as a private affair. But Anton Webern, his most famous pupil, described both its genesis and its nature with clarity in lectures he gave in Vienna during the early 1930's:

> Just as the church modes disappeared and made way for major and minor, so these two have disappeared and made way for a single series, the chromatic scale. Relation to a keynote, tonality, has been lost . . . Schoenberg expressed this in an analogy: double gender has given rise to higher race. . . .
>
> Now I'm asked: "How do I arrive at this row?" Not arbitrarily, but according to certain secret laws. (A tie of this kind is very strict, so that one must consider very carefully and seriously, just as one enters into marriage—the choice is hard!) How does it come about . . . speaking from my own experience, I've mostly come to it in association with what in productive people we call "inspiration." What we establish is the law. Earlier, when one wrote in C Major, one also felt "tied" to it; otherwise the result was a mess. One was obliged to return to the tonic, one was tied to the nature of this

scale. Now we base our invention on a scale that has not seven notes but twelve, and moreover in a particular order. That's 'composition with twelve notes related only to each other.'

. . . The basic shape, the course of the twelve notes, can give rise to variants—we also use the twelve notes back to front—that's cancrizans—and then inverted—as if we were looking in a mirror—and also the cancrizans of the inversion. That makes four forms. But then what can one do with these? We can base them on every degree of the scale. Twelve times four makes forty-eight forms. Enough to choose from! Until now we've found these forty-eight forms sufficient, these forty-eight forms that are the same thing throughout. Just as earlier composition was in C Major, we write in these forty-eight forms.

As applied in the 1950's and early 1960's, the 12-tone technique was a numerical, proportional one, with no extramusical elements. Yet Schoenberg was a Romantic composer who wrote such grand and lavish pieces as the *Gurrelieder* and *Pelleas und Melisande* at the beginning of his career and the expressive String Trio, Opus 45, at the end of it. Schoenberg was aware of the public image of him as abstract philosopher but he was unconcerned:

"A problematic relationship between the science of mathematics as expressed by Einstein and the science of music as developed by myself has been suggested. There may be a relationship between the two fields of endeavor but I have no idea what it is. . . ."

Several of Schoenberg's original group became disenchanted in the 1920's after Schoenberg proclaimed the 12-tone technique. Alfredo Casella accused the Viennese master of confining music in a narrow prison, and the Marxist Hanns Eisler, shifting to the principle of socialist realism, commented that his teacher had gone to the trouble of bringing about a revolution in order to be a reactionary. But Schoenberg did not develop dodecaphony to be perverse; the technique was indissoluble from what he considered to be the well-expressed idea: "Music essentially consists of ideas. Beethoven called himself a 'brain proprietor.' It is no use to rail at new music because it contains too many ideas. Music without ideas is unthinkable."

In the following conversation with the music critic José Rodriguez, Schoenberg elucidated his point:

SCHOENBERG: We all have technical difficulties which arise not from the inability to handle the material, but from some inherent quality in the idea. And it is this first idea, the first thought, that must dictate the structure and texture of the work.

RODRIGUEZ: In the beginning was the Word. . . .

SCHOENBERG: What else? What else can I do but express the original Word, which to me is a human thought, a human idea or a human aspiration?

Thus it can be seen that Schoenberg's theme was a musical translation of an idea which, in its origin, was the Word of God. Schoenberg was a profoundly religious man and his most ambitious works were religious subjects. His last great opera, *Moses und Aron*, which he worked on throughout his life, ends: "But even in the wasteland you shall be victorious and achieve the goal: unity with God."

Although in conversation and in his letters, Schoenberg frequently indicated a sense of despair at being chosen God's emissary on earth, he never questioned the fact that he was. He often repeated a story from his days in the army during World War I: a colonel asked him whether he was really *the* Arnold Schoenberg, and he replied: "Somebody had to be. Nobody wanted to. So in the end I agreed to take on the job." At other times he was far more mystical about his mission: "I was content when I wrote in the period of the Chamber Symphony. But I hardly had written so when I began to compose in a new style without knowing it. In the time of the Chamber Symphony I understood better what I had written and had more personal pleasure with that than with the music that followed. Then to compose was a great pleasure. In a later time it was a duty against myself. It was not a question of pleasure. . . ."

But Schoenberg's sense of mission was not only a burden; it brought moments of supreme inspiration. "I am," he wrote in an essay, *Heart and Brain*, "the creature of inspiration. I compose and paint instinctively. When I am not in the mood I cannot even write a good harmony example for my pupils. There are times when I write with the greatest fluency and ease. My third quartet was composed in six weeks. They say I am a mathematician. Mathematics goes more slowly."

The actual speed with which he composed confirms his claims; except when a psychological block interrupted the course of a work, which generally occurred while he was at work on a religious text— only *Die Jakobsleiter*, *Moses und Aron*, and *Modern Psalms* were uncompleted—Schoenberg claimed that he would spend one week writing a sonata movement, ten days on a short opera, and between one and three hours on a song. His students have said that his teaching was also affected by these periods of inspiration. One reports that several lessons could be prosaic. "Then, suddenly, Schoenberg would get up, pace back and forth with his hands clasped tightly behind his back, and with eyes that were frightening in the force they had, begin to explain something in a very special way. It was intuition that made the whole thing tick."

Schoenberg held his mystical convictions in concrete terms. An American interviewer asked him, toward the end of his life, whether he thought he would have become as good a painter as he was a composer. Schoenberg answered yes—because he could paint a perfect circle without the aid of a compass. He was, in fact, a most precise painter and executed a portrait of Mahler which Mahler's widow claimed surpassed any photograph in realistic detail. He also painted a self-portrait from the back, with the aid of a mirror, which friends report portrays his bald spot and crooked stance with deadly accuracy.

The literal characteristics that played a role in his painting were in evidence in his approach to composition. Whether writing in a chromatically embellished tonal framework, or in a thoroughly atonal one, specific programs determined many of the works he wrote before 1912. Not only were *Gurrelieder* and *Pelleas und Melisande* program works; *Verklärte Nacht, Das Buch der hängenden Gärten, Erwartung, Die glückliche Hand* and *Pierrot Lunaire* were also organized around nonmusical material. Even at the end of his life this penchant for literalism returned: Thomas Mann has written that Schoenberg told him that the seemingly abstract Trio, Opus 45, depicted a recent illness and included musical references to a male nurse and hypodermic needle.

Schoenberg's emphasis on form rather than literal content after 1912—when he began to evolve the 12-tone technique—concealed his own experience and emotion; thus the method should be considered in the context of Schoenberg's tendency to withdraw: "There are some things I have not finished," he wrote on his fiftieth birthday in *Die Musikblätter des Anbruch*. "Thus, I have published less than I have written and written less than I have thought."

His revolutionary method of composing music may be interpreted, as Hans Keller has suggested, as a method to hide rather than to communicate the deepest emotional responses of its creator. That this was his objective is borne out in an essay published in the collection *Style and Idea*; in it Schoenberg refers to music as a "language in which a musician unconsciously gives himself away." The composer predicts that "one day the children's children of our psychologists will have deciphered the language of music. Woe, then, to the incautious who thought his innermost secrets carefully hidden and who must now allow tactless men to besmirch his most personal possessions with their own impurities. Woe, then, to Beethoven, Brahms, Schumann—when they fall into such hands— these men who used their human right of free speech in order to conceal their true thoughts. Is the right to keep silent not worthy of protection?"

The 12-tone technique put an end to a several-hundred-year period in which music was devoted to a dramatic-expressive ideal. The technique, as extended by Schoenberg's musical descendants of the 1950's and 1960's, developed into an abstract language devoid of extramusical implications. Music was not alone, among the arts, in developing along a more abstract path. It was a logical counterpart of that movement in the development of art in which its function, as Arnold Hauser has stated, "of being true to life and faithful to nature has been questioned for the first time since the Middle Ages."

Although some of the developments of dodecaphony provide a kind of music appropriate for a scientific, technologic age, the roots of that system lay in one man's way of viewing the world and his compelling manner of systematizing that view. The method which solidified Schoenberg's position in the history of music can best be understood—in terms of the personal dynamics that motivated it— by investigating the life that Schoenberg began to give to letters and numbers about 1912, just before he set about creating his new system.

Before 1912, Schoenberg's ritualistic behavior was not apparent. The names of his first two children, Gertrude and George, appear to have been chosen on an arbitrary basis. Several decades later, after Schoenberg married a second time, he chose Ronald as the name of his first son by this marriage and Roland as the name of the second, both anagrams of his first name. Upon discovering adverse numerological implications in the name Roland, he changed the child's name to Lawrence Adam, which contains all the letters of Arnold except the o.

In symbolism, numbers are not merely expressions of quantities, but idea forces, each with a particular character of its own. The actual digits are only the outer garments. The most generally accepted symbolic meaning of the number 13, one which figured prominently in Schoenberg's life, is that of death. And to the composer, 13 did represent the height of malevolent magic. Born on

September 13, he considered this to be an evil portent and was so convinced of the inherent destructive power of the number that he claimed if he interrupted a composition and left it for a week or two, he invariably found that he stopped on a measure that was a multiple of 13. This prompted him to number his measures, later in life, as 12, 12A and 14. "It is not superstition," he often said, "it is belief."

The belief was of such an overpowering nature that the composer feared he would die during a year that was a multiple of 13. He so dreaded his sixty-fifth birthday that a friend asked composer and astrologist Dane Rudhyar to prepare Schoenberg's horoscope. Rudhyar did this and told Schoenberg that although the year was dangerous, it was not necessarily fatal. Schoenberg survived it. But in 1951, on his seventy-sixth birthday, the Viennese musician and astrologist Oscar Adler wrote Schoenberg a note warning him that the year was a critical one: 7 plus 6 equals 13. This stunned and depressed the composer, for up to that point he had only been wary of multiples of 13 and never considered adding the digits of his age. He became obsessed with this idea and many friends report that he frequently said: "If I can only pull through this year I shall be safe."

On Friday, July 13, of his seventy-sixth year, Arnold Schoenberg stayed in bed—sick, anxious and depressed. Shortly before midnight his wife leaned over and whispered, "You see, the day is almost over. All that worry was for nothing."

He looked at her and died.

Placing a musical note held as much magical significance to Schoenberg as placing a letter or number. He admitted that shortly after he evolved the 12-tone technique, he wanted to destroy the Chamber Symphony because he could see no relationship between the two themes. But then he made a happy discovery. He saw that the fourth, twelfth, thirteenth, fourteenth, and eighteenth notes of the first theme, when altered in rhythm and inverted, gave him his second theme. As far-fetched as this relationship may appear to an outsider, it caused Schoenberg's agony about the piece to abate.

Schoenberg identified his ways with God's, and was as impatient with critics who questioned him as he was with anyone questioning God's ways. "Everything which we do not understand we take for error," he wrote. "Everything which makes us uncomfortable we take for a mistake of its creator. And we do not stop to think that since we do not understand the meaning, silence, respectful silence, would be the only fitting response. And admiration—boundless admiration."

Viewing Schoenberg's mystical beliefs in light of the fact that he was not attached to a single religion throughout his life (Schoenberg converted from Judaism to Lutheranism back to Judaism, and the children from his second marriage were educated in Jesuit schools), one is struck with what psychiatry would consider to be obsessional behavior, a carefully ordered system that influences one's every thought and action. Psychiatrists generally attribute such behavior to the belief that one has the power to control events. Drawn to a belief in this kind of magic Schoenberg attempted to control his powerful inner drives as well as what happened during the course of his life and possibly even the moment of his death.

How meaningful it must have been to this man that the number of semitones into which the scale is divided is 12—that celestial number preceding 13! And how fortuitous for the history of music that this compelling, self-pronounced emissary of God arrived at the appropriate moment and ordered into being what composer Ernst Křenek has described as "the only method by which the idiom of atonality could be brought clearly and unmistakably under control."

Chapter 2

"We shall not have our hero in a housecoat."

Thus Felix Greissle, Schoenberg's son-in-law, articulated why members of Schoenberg's family and close circle of friends have maintained Schoenberg's obsession with secrecy beyond the grave.

Although little personal biographical information is available, it is known that Samuel Schoenberg, the composer's father, came from Pressburg, a stronghold of Jewish orthodoxy in Hungary. A nephew, Hans Nachod, has described him as a "genius, a dreamer, a thinker, a sort of anarchistic idealist." Schoenberg's mother, Pauline Nachod, came from Prague where her family had been cantors for several hundred years. Arnold's parents arrived in Vienna shortly after the enactment of the 1867 Constitution which removed the legal inequities against the Jews.

But anti-Semitism continued unabated. Sigmund Freud, for instance, was denied the post of associate professor at the University of Vienna although he had been teaching for seventeen years without a formal appointment. The world of music was also closed to Jews: Mahler had to renounce Judaism and be baptized in order to be eligible for the director's post of the Vienna Court Opera, a powerful organization administered by the Court Chamberlain.

Although anti-Semitism persisted in Vienna, the city was the birthplace of Haydn, Mozart, Beethoven and Schubert. After the Napoleonic Wars, it had become the center of the musical life of Europe. Aristocratic families gave concerts in their palaces, patrician families held recitals in their homes, concert halls opened, and the Viennese press began to exert considerable influence on musical events, with the music critic achieving an unprecedented position in the life of the art.

Arnold Schoenberg, oldest son of Samuel (then a shopkeeper in Vienna), has been described by his cousin Nachod as wild, energetic, witty and brash. At eight he began to study the violin and a little later learned to play the cello. Young Schoenberg taught himself to compose duets, trios and quartets so that he would have chamber music to play with his friends.

When Arnold was sixteen, his father died poor. The boy left school at the end of the year in order to help support his mother. He took a job which a friend, David Joseph Bach, has described as that of an "underpaid clerk in a tenth-rate bank." Bach reports that one day Schoenberg entered the name of Beethoven in the principal ledger instead of the name of his client and announced to his friends: "I am so happy to have lost my job. The firm is insolvent anyhow and no one will ever drag me into another office."

Thus, at twenty-one, Schoenberg committed himself to a life of music and all of its consequences, including little prospect of making a living. He couldn't play any one instrument well although he made an effort to play them all. He took a job conducting a chorus of metal workers in Stockerau, a community just outside Vienna, but had difficulty with it because he had trouble playing the piano. Nevertheless, he got them to sing Brahms.

Schoenberg joined an orchestral society, the Polyhymnia, where he met Alexander von Zemlinsky, conductor and well-known avant-garde musician. Zemlinsky persuaded him to study music seriously and became his one and only teacher, instructing him in counterpoint for several months. Zemlinsky told friends and colleagues that Schoenberg learned everything quickly and with little apparent effort.

In 1895 and 1896, the years during which Schoenberg was conducting the workers in the suburbs, he became involved in progressive music circles in the city. In the Cafés Landtmann and Griensteidl, where he and his contemporaries gathered, conversation focused on *Tristan und Isolde*, the Wagnerian music-drama that had used an advanced harmonic language steeped in sensuous chromaticism. During these years the programs of the Vienna Philharmonic included Bruckner's symphonies, Richard Strauss's tone poems and Max Reger's orchestral works, all richly chromatic and polyphonic in the Austro-German tradition.

In 1897, while on a summer holiday with Zemlinsky, Schoenberg wrote the piano score for Zemlinsky's opera, *Sarema*, and composed a string quartet which, operating in the familiar vocabulary of its time, was well received at its first performance in Vienna. But in 1897 Johannes Brahms died, and his death may have freed Schoenberg to move in a new path, for his work immediately took on a different cast. He composed his first mature works, a group of lieder. Recognizing them as such, he gave them the opus numbers 1, 2 and 3. About that time he left Judaism to become a Lutheran.

The Opus 1, 2 and 3 Lieder, performed at a recital with Zemlinsky at the piano, got a hostile reception. The clean and contrapuntal texture of the songs heightened the intensity of the dissonances. These dissonances were not qualitatively different from Wagner's, but they were more obvious, because they were not obscured by lush orchestrations. Secondly, the melody startled; notes were used to create intervals (an interval being the distance between any two notes) that were not only difficult to sing but often very unfamiliar to the ear. Major and minor seconds alternated with leaps of sixths and sevenths. Thirdly, the rhythmic treatment was new; notes no longer depended upon the bar line. These harmonic, melodic and rhythmic devices, which were to become hallmarks of Schoenberg's later style, shocked the Viennese audience. Schoenberg's own response proved characteristic. He proudly proclaimed to his pupil René Leibowitz—reportedly with a smile— that "ever since this performance the riots have never stopped."

Thus 1898, the year after the death of his "conservative" idol, Brahms, Schoenberg found his own modern sound, which was, at the least, unpalatable to the public. At the same time he adopted a new religion which would help him make his way in the world.

"He believed in his mission very strongly," Greissle said. "I know it sounds swollen but it was completely natural to him."

Verklärte Nacht, Schoenberg's first major large-scale work, composed in 1899, fulfilled the composer's desire for recognition only after an initial hostile response. He introduced the American recording of the work in 1950 with the following notes:

> At the end of the nineteenth century, the foremost representatives of the Zeitgeist in poetry were Detlov von Liliencron, Hugo von Hofmannsthal, and Richard Dehmel. But in music, after Brahms' death, many young composers followed the model of Richard Strauss by composing program music. This explains the origin of *Verklärte Nacht*; it is program music, illustrating and expressing the poem of Richard Dehmel.
>
> My composition was, perhaps, somewhat different from other illustrative compositions firstly, by not being for orchestra but for chamber group, and secondly, because it does not illustrate any action or drama but was restricted to portray nature and express human feelings. It seemed that, due to this attitude, my composition has gained qualities which can also satisfy if one does not know what it illustrates or, in other words, it offers the possibility to be appreciated as "pure music." Thus it can make you forget the poem which many a person today might call rather repulsive.

Schoenberg ends his notes with the following admonition: "It shall not be forgotten that this work, at its first performance in Vienna, was hissed and caused riots and fist fights. But very soon it was successful."

Verklärte Nacht, Opus 4, is a sextet for strings, written during a three-week holiday spent with Zemlinsky during the summer of 1899. The poem, taken from Richard Dehmel's novel *Zwei Menschen*, tells the story of a man's forgiveness of the sin committed by the woman he loves and of how, by this forgiveness, the world appears transfigured. The work is a literal one, despite Schoenberg's claims to the contrary. There are five sections: the first, third and fifth portray the couple wandering in the moonlight; the second contains a confession by the woman, the fourth the lover's response. The dialogue between the man and the woman is expressed by cello and violin.

The difference between *Verklärte Nacht*'s delicate chamber structure and Wagner's gigantic stage apparatus should not obscure the fact that the musical language of Schoenberg's early work is similar to that of Wagner. There is one harmonic innovation in *Verklärte Nacht*: an inversion of a ninth chord in which the ninth is in the bass position. A concert society refused permission to perform the piece on the basis of the inclusion of this "forbidden" chord. Later Schoenberg facetiously explained: "It is self-evident; there is no such thing as an inversion of a ninth chord; therefore there is no such thing as a performance of it; for one cannot perform something that does not exist. So I had to wait for several years."

The year after completing *Verklärte Nacht*, Schoenberg began to work on his monumental *Gurrelieder*. He completed it in the spring of 1901 but took another decade to finish the orchestration. The reason for the delay lay in the nature of the score. Responding, most likely, to the influence of Mahler's overwhelmingly large symphonies, Schoenberg called for a huge complement of performers: an orchestra of 140 players, five vocal soloists, one speaker, three male choirs and one mixed choir. He even specified "heavy iron chains," motivated, perhaps, by Mahler's use of cowbells in his Sixth Symphony. Schoenberg ordered specially made music paper—with 48 staves—twice the size of the usual paper.

In 1901, Schoenberg married Zemlinsky's sister, Mathilde. In order to make a living he left Vienna and moved to Berlin, where he had been offered a job scoring and conducting light music in an artistic cabaret. The position was probably not as offensive to him as many scholars assume it to have been. In his youth Schoenberg admired Franz Lehar and Leo Fall and later he frequently expressed admiration for Gilbert and Sullivan. Nevertheless, the scoring of some 6,000 pages of operetta interfered considerably with his serious work.

Schoenberg took *Gurrelieder* with him when he went to Berlin. The exuberant, emotional Romantic work, a cantata set to a text by Danish poet Jens Peter Jacobsen, tells a typical story: King Waldemar of Denmark, passionately in love with Tove, is forced, for political reasons, to marry Helvig. Wild with jealousy, Queen Helvig causes Tove's death. The program note continues: "The grief of Waldemar was terrible to witness. He uttered many fearful blasphemies, which provoked Divine punishment and Waldemar was condemned to death to hunt nightly from dusk to dawn, galloping with his henchmen in a wild chase across the skies." But love proved to be stronger than death and Waldemar was reunited with his beloved Tove.

Gurrelieder is a three-part work. The first section contains an Orchestral Prelude, the statements of the lovers' passion and Tove's death. The second portrays Waldemar's curse and the third the tale of the nightly hunt. Although *Gurrelieder* is divided into these sections in its most apparent form, it is, as George Perle has pointed out, "entirely novel in form, a cycle of songs that are individually self-contained numbers in the tradition of the German lied but collectively a single large-scale work based on the Wagnerian technique of the leitmotif." Even in this very early work, Schoenberg focuses on what becomes the *idée fixe* of his life in music: the perpetual variation of a melodic idea. Waldemar's opening theme is related to material originally heard in the Orchestral Prelude, and Tove's theme, heard when she first expresses her love, becomes the major motive of the work, appearing in countless manifestations as leading melodic idea and subsidiary material as well.

Shortly after he arrived in Berlin, Schoenberg met Richard Strauss and showed him the first two sections of this formidable work. On the basis of what he saw, Strauss recommended Schoenberg to the Sterne Conservatory as a teacher and to the Liszt Foundation for a scholarship. Schoenberg was grateful for the position and the grant, for the cabaret had closed and his wife was pregnant. Their first child, Gertrude, was born in 1902.

At the same time that Schoenberg began teaching at Sterne, he began to work on a project suggested to him by Strauss, the setting of Maurice Maeterlinck's *Pelléas et Mélisande*. Debussy's opera, based on the same poem, was performed in Paris in 1902, the year that Schoenberg began work on the theme. Years later Schoenberg evaluated the difference between his *Pelleas* and Debussy's:

> I had first planned to convert *Pelléas et Mélisande* into an opera, but I gave up this plan, although I did not know that Debussy was working on this opera at the same time. I still regret that I did not carry out my initial intention. It would have differed from Debussy's. I might have missed the wonderful perfume of the poem, but I would have made my characters more singing.

The program approach to music characteristic of *Verklärte Nacht* and *Gurrelieder* is pushed to extremes in *Pelleas*. In the notes he prepared for the American recording, Schoenberg wrote: "I tried to mirror every detail of it . . . the three main characters are presented in the manner of Wagner's leitmotifs." Not only are people represented by musical motives but "Golaud's jealousy" is pictured by one melodic idea and "destiny" by another. The story echoes the romantic legend of the doomed lovers. It centers on a beautiful young woman, lured into marriage with a much older man whom she does not love. Golo, the husband, and Pelleas, the lover, are half brothers. Thus the final catastrophe is inevitable; Melisande must die.

Schoenberg's *Pelleas*, Opus 5, orchestrated for a very large ensemble, is densely polyphonic, with every melodic idea surrounded by numerous other melodies. Despite the fact that this work, like *Verklärte Nacht*, begins and ends in the same key and is, therefore, a "tonal" composition, Schoenberg moves farther away from tonality than he ever did before. For the first time he builds chords on fourths, thus devastating the harmonic scheme of superimposed thirds. The new vertical arrangement of notes heralded the end of tonal organization.

In 1946, in a lecture at the University of Chicago, Schoenberg said: "I always attempted to produce something conventional and it always, against my will, became something unusual."

Whether or not the composer consciously tried to be conventional is irrelevant; the fact is that he always did produce something unusual. Even in these early days of his career, when he was still steeped in the Romantic tradition, Schoenberg introduced at least one radical procedure into each of his works. In *Verklärte Nacht* he transferred the program idea from orchestral music to the chamber idiom for the first time. In *Gurrelieder* he strung together twenty German art songs as though they were individual movements in a cyclic symphony. And in *Pelleas* he introduced chords built on fourths. The searching quality and restless energy manifested in these works were reflected in his life as well. In July, 1903, Schoenberg left Berlin with his wife and child and returned to Vienna, the city that had been so unfriendly to him.

During their first year there—while living in Zemlinsky's house—Schoenberg met Gustav Mahler. The renowned composer-conductor, having heard his brother-in-law Arnold Rosé conduct a rehearsal of *Verklärte Nacht*, asked Zemlinsky to introduce him to Schoenberg. Dika Newlin, one of Schoenberg's American disciples, writes of a curious relationship that developed, in which Mahler referred to Zemlinsky and Schoenberg by the diminutives "Eisele and Beisele." At first Schoenberg expressed extreme irritation at Mahler's condescending manner but soon he became utterly devoted to him and courted his attention in a most impassioned way. He orchestrated *Gurrelieder* in a characteristically Mahlerian manner, and in 1904, wrote to Mahler:

> Honored Herr Direktor: In order to do any justice to the unheard of impressions which I received from your symphony, I must speak, not as musician to musician, but as man to man. For I have seen your soul naked, stark naked. It lay before me like a wild, mysterious landscape with its frightening crevasses and abysses. . . .

And in the summer of 1906: "Nothing would please me more than your saying we had come closer together."

The evidence is that they had. Rosé's quartet performed Schoenberg's Quartet No. 1 in February, 1907, and Alma Mahler described the event:

"The critic yelled 'Stop it!' when the audience was registering quiet but unanimous amusement. An unpardonable error! For his shouts were followed by such a whistling and racket as I have never heard before or since. A fellow parked himself in front of the first row and hissed at Schoenberg, who insisted on coming back for innumerable bows, cocking his head—the head of a Jewish Bruckner—this way and that, as though asking pardon and at the same time unobtrusively pleading for consideration. Mahler jumped up, stood beside the man, and said, 'I'd just like to get a good look at a fellow who hisses.' "

Later, after a performance of Schoenberg's Chamber Symphony which was attended by as unruly an audience as the one attending the First Quartet, Mahler stood up ostentatiously in his box and applauded loudly until the last of the hostile demonstrators had left the hall. Despite this enthusiastic behavior toward Schoenberg, Mahler privately admitted to him that he did not understand the Opus 7: "I'm accustomed to reading thirty-voiced scores, but the four voices of your quartet give me at least twice as much trouble."

In 1903 Rosé conducted *Verklärte Nacht* in Vienna for the first time. The audience response was predictably unpleasant. It was after this occasion that a formidable decision was made: for what may have been the first time in history, a group of composers decided to organize a society, the Union of Creative Musicians, to educate listeners and critics. Mahler was the honorary president; among its members were such avant-garde composers as Schoenberg, Zemlinsky and Bruno Walter. Under these auspices Schoenberg conducted the first performance of his *Pelleas und Melisande* and Mahler directed the premier of his own *Kindertotenlieder* and Strauss's *Sinfonia Domestica*. Forty years later Schoenberg described the reaction to *Pelleas*:

"The first performance, under my direction, provoked great riots among the audience and even the critics. Reviews were unusually violent and one of the music critics even suggested putting me in an insane asylum and keeping music paper out of my reach."

After his return to Vienna, Schoenberg avoided the program format and began to order his music along classic lines. His String Quartet No. 1, Opus 7, in D Minor, finished in 1905, shows the composer's affinity for Mahler, with sudden shifts of tempo, interrupted tunes and abrupt modulations. But Brahms still affected his work; a four-beat rhythm combined with triplets in the viola and cello is reminiscent of Brahms.

In 1906, the year in which a second child was born, Schoenberg wrote his Chamber Symphony, Opus 9. In this work for fifteen solo instruments, the composer used the whole-tone scale, almost completely negating the E Major signature. Chords which had formerly been used simply as passing harmonies were now allowed to stand quite alone. Another important aspect of the work lay in the fact that it started the trend toward the chamber form in Germany, six years before Stravinsky began to score for groups of solo instruments. Schoenberg's reaction against the superorchestra was one of the factors that led the way to the overwhelming concern for instrumental color which has characterized much twentieth-century work.

In 1906, Webern, according to his own later testimony, showed Schoenberg a movement of a new work inspired by the Chamber Symphony. (Webern, Alban Berg, Erwin Stein and Heinrich Jalowitz all began to study under Schoenberg in 1904.) Its tones were not related to any particular key. It was, in effect, an "atonal" piece. Schoenberg finally rejected it and Webern wrote his next piece in the key of C Major, but it is probable that his experiment affected Schoenberg's own next work, the String Quartet No. 2, Opus 10, in F Sharp Minor. The first three movements bear the traditional key signatures, but the fourth enters into another domain, which Schoenberg characterized as having been inspired by Mahler's "pantonal" realms of composition.

In his writing Schoenberg demonstrated pantonality as one of Mahler's particular contributions to composition, by contrasting the classic symphony, which begins and ends in the same key or begins in a minor key and ends in the relative major, with Mahler's symphonies. The First begins in D Minor and ends in F Minor; the Fourth begins in G Major and ends in E Major; the Fifth begins in C sharp Minor and ends in D Major. Thus Schoenberg considered the fourth movement of his quartet to have been derived from Mahler. Schoenberg's attempted break-up of the tonal system in this movement is actually more closely related to Mahler's post-Romantic tonal experiments than to Webern's more radical compositional thinking. The conductor Robert Craft has written: "It is interesting today to listen to parts of Schoenberg's Second Quartet and mark the stray excursions into atonality and the rather sheeplike return to the tonal fold whose border is, of course, as arbitrary as the ear's education."

To specify his gratitude to Mahler, Schoenberg used two of Mahler's most striking devices in the F Sharp Minor Quartet. He introduced a soprano into the third and fourth movements, as Mahler introduced the human voice into his symphonies. And he quoted the folk tune, "Ach, du lieber Augustin," in the Scherzo movement as Mahler had quoted another folk tune in his First Symphony. Schoenberg's choice of this particular tune might have had some additional significance of a more personal nature. In an interview Mahler had with Freud, he told the psychoanalyst that once, having witnessed a bitter fight between his parents, he ran into the street and heard an organ grinder playing this song. The juxtaposition of pathos and bathos, Mahler said, came back to him at every moment of emotional tension to "twist his inspiration" and prevent him from reaching his ideal as a composer. This intimate vignette may have been confided to Schoenberg as well as to Freud. In any event, the tune's banal qualities stand out in sharp relief against the context of Schoenberg's otherwise difficult, angular writing.

It should be noted that the Quartet, Opus 10, was the work that followed the Chamber Symphony; Schoenberg himself described the transition: "In the time of the Chamber Symphony I understood better what I had written and had more personal pleasure with that than with the music that followed. Then to compose was a great pleasure. In a later time it was a duty against myself. . . ." The emotion that lay behind this crucial, revolutionary, atonal movement was accurately reflected by the soprano's words. The piece is set to a poem by Stefan George:

> I feel the air of other spheres . . .
> I dissolve into tones, circling, wreathing . . .
> yielding involuntarily to the great breathing . . .
> The earth shakes, white and soft as foam.
> I climb across huge chasms.
> I feel as if I were swimming beyond the farthest
> cloud in a sea of crystalline brilliance.
> I am only a flicker of the sacred fire.
> I am only a mumbling of the sacred voice.

Chapter 3

Theodor W. Adorno, the late German philosopher, sociologist and composition student of Alban Berg, has written that the Quartet No. 2 was an "echo of a crisis in personal life whose sorrow, hardly ever mastered, brought to Schoenberg's work its full creative weight."

The crisis is not revealed by any of Schoenberg's biographers. Its genesis took place in 1906, when Zemlinsky introduced Schoenberg to Richard Gerstl, a painter nine years younger than Schoenberg and a man so withdrawn that he did not sign the front of his paintings, nor did he ever exhibit. Alma Mahler has said that although she knew Gerstl well, she never saw anything of his work. Gerstl lived with the Schoenberg family during the summers of 1907 and 1908; under his guidance, Schoenberg began to paint.

Gerstl began a love affair with Mathilde Schoenberg and revealed the pain of the ensuing relationship in a number of wild, Kokoschka-like works. Paintings of Arnold, Mathilde, and the couple with their children were followed by a naked self-portrait and finally by a portrayal of his face in a grotesque state of laughter. This was

*Mathilde Schoenberg
by Richard Gerstl*
OTTO BREICHA

The Schoenberg Family by Richard Gerstl
OTTO BREICHA

Richard Gerstl: Self-portrait
OTTO BREICHA

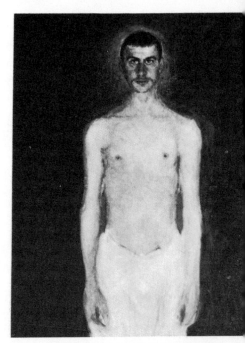

Richard Gerstl: Self-portrait
OTTO BREICHA

Gerstl's last work, clearly the painting of a deeply disturbed man. In the fall of 1908, Mathilde left her husband to live with her lover. Several days later, Gerstl gathered his paintings together in a pile on the floor, set his studio on fire, plunged a kitchen knife into his heart, and hanged himself over the burning débris. (Gerstl's family salvaged fifteen paintings and stored them in a cellar in Vienna where they were discovered in 1931.)

Gerstl's tortured relationship with Schoenberg, whom he adored, was similar to Schoenberg's relationship with Mahler and consistent with the cult of suffering implicit in the Romantic agony that had been cultivated by Byron, Berlioz, and Wagner's *Tristan*. Coincident with the Gerstl affair, Mahler left Vienna for New York. It was during this highly traumatic time that Schoenberg tentatively entered the atonal world with the last movement of his Second Quartet.

Schoenberg's next and crucial work is a cycle of songs set to Stefan George's *Das Buch der hängenden Gärten*. Schoenberg's notes indicate his awareness of the profundity of his own stylistic change:

> In the *Georgelieder* I have succeeded for the first time in approaching an ideal of expression and form that has hovered about me for some years. Hitherto I had not sufficient strength and sureness to realize the ideal. Now, however, I have definitely started on a new journey, I may confess to have broken off the bonds of a bygone aesthetic; and, if I am striving towards a goal that seems to me to be certain, nevertheless, I always feel the opposition I shall have to overcome.

It is in the thirteenth song of the cycle, "Du lehnest wider eine Silberweide," that there is no key signature at all; it is the first literally "atonal" piece. As the number 13 marked the birth and death of Schoenberg, it also marked the birth of atonality and the death of the tonal scheme. In all the other songs of the cycle, the principle of tonality is simply suspended. Composed in 1908, immediately after Gerstl's death, it is Schoenberg's most extended work for voice and piano. (The composer Milton Babbitt, according it a position with the song cycles of Beethoven, Schubert and Schumann, points out that it combines the human voice—the most restrictive instrument in register—with the piano—the most restrictive instrument in timbre—and marvels at the diversity which the composer was, nevertheless, able to achieve.)

Schoenberg disclaimed responsibility for the term "atonal," noting that it was as absurd to call music atonal as to call painting aspectral. He preferred the term "atonical," implying an absence of a tonic center, or "pantonal," referring to a merging of all the keys.

Thus music entered a state of crisis in 1908. The breakdown of the tonal system confirmed the annihilation of law and order in the Austro-German musical world. The absence of all formal restrictions in the non-harmonically conceived works that followed permitted a great discharge of emotional tension. An era of highly expressionistic music began that paralleled the art of Kokoschka and Kandinsky.

The Gerstl affair not only precipitated Schoenberg's move into the atonal world; according to a member of the Schoenberg family, it also generated his involvement in painting and he entered the field as a full professional. Between 1908 and 1910 Schoenberg produced about sixty paintings and drawings. In a letter to his publisher, Emil Hertzka, in which he sought Hertzka's aid in obtaining commissions for portraits, he displayed the same arrogant, defensive attitude that characterized his dealings in the world of music:

> It is much more interesting to have one's portrait done or to own a painting by a musician of my reputation than to be painted by some mere practitioner of painting whose name will be forgotten in twenty years whereas even now my name belongs to the history of music. For a life-size portrait I want from two to six sittings and from two hundred to four hundred kronen. That is really very cheap considering that in twenty years people will pay ten times as much for these paintings. I am quite sure you realize this, and I hope you won't make any feeble jokes about a matter as serious as this, but will treat it as seriously as it deserves.

Art was a serious business for Schoenberg. His interest in painting led him to Wassily Kandinsky, the Russian abstract expressionist who was living in Munich, and Schoenberg became a member of the famous Blaue Reiter group. His paintings were exhibited in 1910 at the bookstore and art gallery of Hugo Heller. Kandinsky commented on his work:

> Schoenberg's pictures fall into two categories: on the one hand the portraits and landscapes painted directly from nature; on the other hand, heads imagined intuitively, which he calls "visions." The former Schoenberg designates as finger exercises, which he feels he needs, but which he does not particularly value, and which he does not like to exhibit. The others he paints (just as rarely as the first sort) to express emotions that find no musical form. These two categories are extremely different. Internally they stem from one and

the same soul, caused to vibrate in one case by external nature and in the other by nature within. . . .

Schoenberg and Kandinsky followed remarkably similar paths in their moves away from representation to abstraction and from the single focuses of perspective and tonality in painting and music to the subsequent afocal attributes of both. Both artists had received the initial impulses in these directions as early as the last years of the nineteenth century, and neither one achieved the full realization of his purpose until many years later.

As Kandinsky formulated the principles of an abstract style for the first time in 1910 in his treatise *On the Spiritual in Art*, so Schoenberg first set down the theory of the emancipation of the dissonance in his *Theory of Harmony* (*Harmonielehre*) published in 1911. In this work Schoenberg analyzes what he refers to as the "function of tonality":

> Tonality does not serve; on the contrary it demands to be served. . . . It has always been the referring of all results to a center, to an emanating point of tonality, which rendered important service to the composer in matters of form. All the tonal successions, chords, and chord successions in a piece achieve a unified meaning through their definite relation to a tonal center and also through their mutual ties. That is the unifying function of tonality. . . .

Schoenberg asks whether one could "write a piece which does not use the advantages offered by tonality and yet unifies all other elements so that their succession and relation are logically comprehensible." He answers yes, if the composer substitutes melodic motive for tonal structure:

> It could be easily shown that a work might have tonal unity, but nevertheless still be confused in content, incoherent, superficial, external, yes, even without sense. . . . I am rather inclined to believe that one may sooner sacrifice logic and unity in the harmony than in the thematic substance, in the motives, in the thought-content.

In this treatise Schoenberg defined "consonance" as the clearer and simpler relation with the ground note, and "dissonance" as the more remote and complicated, holding a quantitative rather than a qualitative distinction between the two. Removing the qualitative distinction between consonance and dissonance eliminates the concept of the one being beautiful and the other ugly. The physical basis that Schoenberg thus provided for atonal composition resulted in the "emancipation of the dissonance," a process that was taking place in the most advanced composition in France (Debussy) and Russia (Scriabine) but without the accompanying verbal justification. The freeing of tones from "tonal" obligations implies that the historic process of adding chords to the harmonic vocabulary had finally come to an end. Schoenberg's important 500-page treatise was dedicated to Mahler, who died at the age of fifty just before the book was completed:

> This book is dedicated to the memory of Gustav Mahler. It was hoped that the dedication might give him some small joy while he still lived. It was intended, thereby, to do honor to his immortal compositions and to show that his work, at which cultivated musicians in their superiority shrugged their shoulders and which they even passed by with contempt, was revered by one who, perhaps, to some extent understood it.

During his last illness, Mahler asked his wife to take care of Schoenberg after his death. She carried out his wish, setting up a fund to serve this purpose.

Between 1908 and 1912, Schoenberg produced at least three of the great pieces from which, as Stravinsky has claimed, subsequent generations of composers have taken their bearings. Although Richard Strauss was, at the time, the most important Establishment figure, Schoenberg was the central creative musician around whom all advanced musical activity in Germany took place. With *Der Rosenkavalier*, which Strauss composed in 1911, the latter repudiated the advances he had made in *Salome* (1905) and the wildly dissonant *Elektra* (1909). At the same time Schoenberg continued to move ahead, increasing the harmonic complexities as he decreased his instrumental forces.

The striking reduction in size from his earlier, grandiose program works to the atonal, short, nonprogram pieces indicates the power that tonality—however much extended—had been able to provide in Schoenberg's Romantic works. Once having abandoned the tonal framework, the composer relied on the musical motive alone as the source of unity for his composition. This is clearly in evidence in the first of these works, the *Piano Pieces*, Opus 11, and, most particularly, in the second of these pieces. Here an initial idea, a swift upbeat followed by a melodic tritone, is introduced in the first four measures and sustains the rest of the short composition. The "theme" is Schoenberg's *Grundgestalt*, the creative idea which undergoes perpetual variation but never repetition. It was in the Preface to Opus 11 that Schoenberg wrote that he was following "an inner compulsion that is stronger than my education, stronger than my artistic training." The move into the atonal world had extramusical implications for him.

Schoenberg then moved away from the piano, the instrument on which he first applied his most radical ideas, and composed an "atonal" work for orchestra, the Five Orchestral Pieces, Opus 16, the only purely orchestral work of this period.* That each of these pieces bears a poetic title should not, however, misdirect the listener. In an entry in his diary just before the publication of the work in 1912, Schoenberg wrote:

> Letter from Peters, making an appointment with me for Wednesday in Berlin, in order to get to know me personally. Wants titles for the orchestral pieces—for publisher's reasons. Maybe I'll give in, for I've found that titles are at least possible. On the whole, unsympathetic to the idea. For the wonderful thing about music is that one can say everything in it, so that he who knows understands everything; and yet one hasn't given away one's secrets—the things one doesn't even admit to oneself. But titles give you away! Besides—whatever was to be said has been said, by the music. Why, then, words as well? If words were necessary they would be there in the first place. But art says more than words. Now, the titles which I may provide give nothing away, because some of them are very obscure and others highly technical. To wit:

I.	Premonitions	(everybody has those)
II.	The Past	(everybody has that, too)
III.	Chord-Colors	(technical)
IV.	Peripetia	(general enough, I think)
V.	The obbligato	(perhaps better the "fully developed" or the "endless recitative")

> However, there should be a note that these titles were added for the technical reasons of publication and not to give a poetic content.

The Five Pieces for Orchestra, together with the Three Piano Pieces, represent a clean break with the past. In each of the orchestral pieces an original cell gives rise to the whole. In one, Schoenberg's *Grundgestalt* is only a five-part chord; he achieves variety through a constantly shifting instrumentation. Schoenberg wrote of the importance of tone color in his *Treatise on Harmony*, predicting its growth as a structural element in composition:

---

* In a program note to Opus 16, Webern wrote that these pieces contained the "experience of Schoenberg's emotional life."

I cannot unreservedly agree with the distinction between color and pitch. I find that a note is perceived by its color, one of whose dimensions is pitch. Color, then, is the great realm, pitch one of its provinces. . . . If the ear could discriminate between differences of color, it might be feasible to invent melodies that are built of colors (*klangfarbenmelodien*). But who dares to develop such theories?

Not grounded in tonality, the Opus 16 pieces were not encased in the formal framework that serves to articulate tonal areas. These instrumental pieces are revolutionary in their free formal structure as well as in the soloistic treatment of instruments within the orchestral fabric. They were not performed until 1912, and then not in Germany but in London under the direction of Sir Henry Wood. The work received a bad press in London. *The Times* described it as "incomprehensible as a Tibetan poem," and Berlin musicologist Hugo Leichentritt wrote: "How poor our descendants will be if they take this joyless, careworn Schoenberg as the sensibility of our age."

Both sets of abstract, atonal works, the Opus 11 and Opus 16, contained only very short pieces. Schoenberg found, at the beginning of 1910, that the perpetual variation of a melodic motive could not alone sustain more extended works. The composer later described the predicament which he faced and how he came to depend on extramusical sources to provide the unity which he sought: "Formerly the harmony had served not only as a source of beauty, but, more important, as a means of distinguishing the features of the form. . . . Hence it seemed at first impossible to compose pieces of complicated organization or of great length. A little later I discovered how to construct larger forms by following a text or a poem."

The first of the large, atonal works was *Erwartung*, a monodrama set to a text by Marie Pappenheim, the wife of a Viennese psychiatrist. (This was the golden age of psychoanalysis in Vienna.) The piece, written in the strikingly short span of seventeen days, describes a hysterical woman's terrified thoughts. The angular melodies and profusion of dissonances mirror the anxiety, depression, love and hate which she experiences as she searches for her lover on a dark and moonlit night. In *Erwartung* Schoenberg uses ten- and eleven-note chords which destroy any trace of traditional consonance. No musical idea is ever repeated in exactly the same way; the text is what holds the work together.

Schoenberg composed his next piece, *Die glückliche Hand*, in the same atonal idiom as *Erwartung*, only this time he wrote the libretto as well, a strongly autobiographical one. The Man is obviously Schoenberg who, at the beginning, lies prone on the stage with the monster of dissatisfaction gnawing at his back. A Greek chorus unbraids him for desiring worldly things—recognition and acclaim —when he knows that fulfillment can only come to him through spiritual and intellectual paths.

The women of the chorus begin the work, intoning:

> Be still, won't you,
> You know how it always is,
> and yet you remain blind.
> So many times already! And once again?
> Once again the same ending.
> Once again trusting in the same dream.
> Once again you fix your
> longing on the unattainable.
> Once again you give yourself up
> to the sirens of your thoughts,
> thoughts that are unworldly
> but thirst for worldly fulfillment.
> You poor fool—worldly fulfillment!
> You, who have the divine in you,
> and covet the worldly!

The humiliation which Schoenberg, who had "the divine in him," must perpetually suffer is the theme of this curious musico-dramatic work. Schoenberg's involvement in the visual arts profoundly affected his realization of *Die glückliche Hand*, for he specified the lighting effects in the score. Color, both instrumental and spectral, was of primary importance during these expressionistic, productive years.

Around 1910 Schoenberg's career began to improve. The Union of Art and Culture in Vienna produced part of *Gurrelieder* with piano accompaniment, and Oscar Fried, champion of new music, conducted *Pelleas und Melisande* in Berlin. In 1910 Schoenberg began making carbon copies of his letters, obviously intending them for posterity.

In 1911, Schoenberg received the news of Mahler's death. He expressed his reaction verbally in an essay in the journal *Der Merker* and musically in the Six Little Piano Pieces, Opus 19. The most notable characteristic of these pieces is their brevity and musical concentration: the longest is eighteen measures and the shortest only nine. In the last piece Schoenberg records his·impressions at Mahler's funeral by setting an angular five-note melody against a series of bell-like chords (built upon the still unconventional fourths).

During the summer of 1911, Schoenberg and his family moved back to Berlin. His situation in Vienna had not improved; he had only a few pupils and no chance for a steady position. The fact that he was "permitted" but not engaged to teach at the Academy was particularly humiliating to him. Financial prospects in Berlin were not much better. He had only two pupils waiting for him there, but the progressive atmosphere in general and Fried's performance in particular, motivated him into making the change.

Shortly after his arrival in Berlin, his two pupils there—Eduard Steuermann and Edward Clarke—arranged for him to give a series of public lectures. When his Five Orchestral Pieces was published in an inexpensive edition, the scores sold well, indicating that the lectures were exerting a profound effect. Schoenberg's first Berlin composition, the lied "Herzgewächse," Opus 20, was a setting of the Maeterlinck poem to the unusual combination of high coloratura soprano, celeste, harmonium and harp, with the voice covering the enormous range from F above high C to G sharp below middle C. The work provides a beautiful connecting link between the *Piano Pieces*, Opus 11—about which he wrote that he was following an "inner compulsion" and which heralded his atonal period—and *Pierrot Lunaire*, which culminated this most productive era in Schoenberg's life.

In March, 1912, Schoenberg started *Pierrot Lunaire*. Like the Man in *Die glückliche Hand*, Pierrot, with his tormented soul, clearly reflects Schoenberg's picture of himself. The composer chose to set a cycle of poems by Albert Giraud which had been published in 1884. Of the fifty poems in the cycle, he chose only twenty-one, but that number corresponds to the opus number of the work and is a reversal of the digits of the year of its appearance. Schoenberg grouped these pieces into three parts of seven poems each, and to ensure that no one should miss the number mysticism which had seriously begun to affect his life, he entitled the piece "Dreimal sieben Gedichte aus Albert Girauds Pierrot Lunaire."

Schoenberg's Pierrot is a far cry from the clown of the commedia dell'arte. This Pierrot presents many apparently psychotic features whose significance was being brought to light by psychoanalytic psychology. Stravinsky, whose *Petrushka*, composed the previous year, was an altogether simpler kind of clown, heard a rehearsal of

Pierrot Lunaire. Although he reported different reactions to this hearing at various times, he consistently praised the instrumentation. Written for piano, flute, piccolo, clarinet, double bass clarinet, violin, viola and cello, the work also celebrates *Sprechstimme*, a technique Schoenberg introduced into the chorus of *Die glückliche Hand.*

Reciting a text to instrumental accompaniment was not new. The spoken word, given a relatively free range within a certain allocation of bars, had been used during the eighteenth and nineteenth centuries. But, in *Pierrot Lunaire*, Schoenberg assures that the recitation will take place in strict time by using traditional notation. He places crosses on note heads to indicate the particular line of speech melody. This speaking voice is not only notated rhythmically, but with sharps, flats and returns to naturals. Schoenberg directed: "The sung note keeps to the level of the note without changing; the spoken note gives it, yet immediately leaves it to fall or rise."

In its musical form, *Pierrot Lunaire* represents a shift from Schoenberg's recent expressive compositions to a new emphasis on form. Piece No. 1 is based on a rigid ostinato, while some others are strictly canonic. Schoenberg displays a virtuoso handling of polyphonic procedures; in the piece "Moonspot," when Pierrot looks around and discovers a white spot on his back, his action is accompanied by the piano playing a three-part fugue, the clarinet and piccolo forming canons in diminution with the first two voices of the fugue, and a third canon, independent of the others, handled by the violin and cello. Halfway through the piece, the clarinet and piccolo, proceeding at twice the speed of the canonic partners, run out of notes and begin running backwards, an auditory parallel for Pierrot frantically trying to rub the moonspot off his back.

Each of the stanzas contains thirteen lines; the seventh and last lines repeat the first and the eighth repeats the second. Both in the text and the music, strictness of form is combined with freedom of content. The musical content is tonally free although, as is apparent in the use of canons and fugues, the forms in which the content is contained are frequently very strict.

Thus in 1912 Schoenberg had complete tonal freedom and used it in *Pierrot Lunaire*. At the same time he knew he had not found a purely musical way to sustain works with large dimensions. It was perhaps in the context of this stylistic crisis that Schoenberg chose the following verse as the last in the cycle, and underscored the

attraction of "days of yore" with the use of parallel thirds and a recurring E Major triad, nostalgic reminiscences of an earlier, more
comfortable musical time.

> O fragrance old from days of yore,
> Once more you intoxicate my senses.
> A prankish troop of rogueries
> Is swirling through the air.
>
> A cheerful longing makes me hope
> For joys which I have long despised;
> O fragrance old from days of yore
> Once more you intoxicate me.
>
> I have abandoned all my gloom
> And from my window framed in sunlight
> I freely gaze on the dear world
> And dream beyond in boundless transport—
> O fragrance old from days of yore.

After *Pierrot Lunaire,* Schoenberg's compositional pace slowed
down dramatically. In the decade that followed he completed only
one work, the Orchestral Songs, Opus 22, of 1914 and early 1915.
As World War I began, his position and that of Austria and
Germany were threatened by the spectacular artistic production of
the French. Marcel Proust finished his monumental novel *À la
Recherche du Temps Perdu,* Debussy composed the great and
revolutionary ballet *Jeux,* and in Paris, the Ballet Russe presented
Stravinsky's colossal *Le Sacre du Printemps.*

"Vorgefühl" (Premonition), one of the Opus 22 songs with a text
by Rainer Maria Rilke, articulates the anxiety Schoenberg must
have felt:

> I feel the winds that come, and must endure them.
> While things on earth must rest in utter stillness.
> The doors close softly, in the room is silence;
> The windows yet unmoved, the dust is heavy.
> But I live the storm—I am stirred like the sea—
> I stretch forth my arms—am thrown back on myself—
> I cast myself forth—and remain all alone
> In the greatest of storms.

Chapter 4

During the next decade, Schoenberg evolved the 12-tone technique. He began working out the method in an oratorio, *Die Jakobsleiter*, which he never completed.

The project originated in 1912, when poet Richard Dehmel wrote Schoenberg a letter: "Last night I heard *Verklärte Nacht* and I should feel it a sin of omission if I did not send you a word of thanks for your wonderful sextet." Schoenberg replied to Dehmel, thanking him and requesting him to serve as librettist once again, this time for an oratorio which he described the following way:

> Modern man, having passed through materialism, socialism, and anarchy, and despite having been an atheist, still having in him some residue of ancient faith (in the form of superstition) wrestles with God (see also Strindberg's *Jacob Wrestling*) and finally succeeds in finding God and becoming religious, learning to pray! It is *not* through any action, any blows of fate, least of all through any love of woman, that this change of heart is to come about.

Dehmel would not agree to the project, so Schoenberg wrote the libretto himself. Like the Man in *Die glückliche Hand*, and the tortured clown in *Pierrot Lunaire*, Gabriel, the protagonist for *Die*

Jakobsleiter, is clearly identifiable as the martyred composer, the sole human being called upon to proclaim the new to the world, the ultimate musical lawgiver of our time.

Die Jakobsleiter, which Schoenberg worked on intermittently during the second decade of the twentieth century (he was in and out of the Austrian army twice), is, as Bertold Viertel has written, an allegory of his mission as an artist. The work opens with a group of dissatisfied people wandering about in considerable confusion. They are tired but strive on, not knowing where the journey leads. Gabriel is among them, giving help and advice, judging and leading them.

Although Schoenberg structured the work as an oratorio, the language is far from traditional and indicates the curious, pathological nature of his relationship with God and man: "Union with Him awakes magnetically the currents of the mind by induction," is interwoven with "My Word I leave here; make what you can of it. My form I take with me. In any case it must remain beyond you until it reappears in your midst with new words—the old ones over again—to be newly misunderstood."

Between 1915 and 1923, Schoenberg did not publish a single composition. He appears to have been exclusively concerned with the development of the dodecaphonic principle which he desperately hoped would reestablish Germany as the undisputed center of the musical world and himself as its sole redeemer.

The first measures of *Die Jakobsleiter*, written in 1917, reveal the nature of the 12-tone technique. Karl Rankl, Schoenberg's student during that year, has pointed out that the first half of the 12-note scale is played by cellos, which repeat the same six notes six times in succession. The other six are built up vertically, from the second bar onward, and are handled by brass and woodwinds. "These bars clearly show," Rankl writes, "the exposition of a 12-tone scale divided into two halves." Schoenberg, in what appears to be a strikingly ingenious double-entendre, described the nature of the technique in the opening words of the oratorio:

> Whether right or left,
> Forwards or backwards,
> Uphill or downhill,
> We have to go on without asking
> What lies beyond or ahead.
> It will remain hidden from you.
> You should, you must forget it
> To fulfill your task.

Egon Wellesz, another early Schoenberg pupil, tells an interesting story about the development of the 12-tone technique in an August, 1961 issue of The Listener:

> It was in 1915 that a private in the Austrian army was sent to me because the military psychiatrists found that he was so neurotic and talked about music in such a peculiar way that they did not know what to do with him and wanted my advice. The man was Josef Hauer. Hauer had developed in his compositions the idea of 12-note rows which, according to his theory, had the same function as the *nomoi*, the type-melodies in Greek music. Though Hauer expressed his views in a very amateurish way, I found his ideas very interesting and his attitude toward music reminded me of Erik Satie. I think that my favorable report helped to get Hauer released from his work in an army office. Reti, of whose judgment Schoenberg thought highly, told him about Hauer's theories and compositions, and Schoenberg began to develop these ideas which led him to introduce the system of composition with twelve tones.
>
> There can be no doubt that Hauer was the first to construct rows of twelve notes—rather haphazardly—and to choose which one of them suited him best for a composition.

Hauer, in fact, did not choose a single row for a musical work nor did he work with the "row" as we know it. Unlike Schoenberg, who insisted that one row provide all the material and thus ensure a sense of unitary perception, Hauer allowed that any number of 12-tone melodies could be combined within a single movement.

In 1920, Hauer published an essay, "On the Nature of Music," in which he argued that the notion of equal temperament, the division of the scale into twelve equal parts, which had developed during the nineteenth century (as opposed to the division of the scale into unequal intervals, which pulled all the notes to a single tonic) necessitated a new compositional system. In describing what he had in mind, Hauer used the word "atonal" for what we generally designate as 12-tone:

> In atonal music . . . which stems from "totalities," intervals alone are relevant. Music expression is no longer achieved through the use of major and minor keys and of specific instruments with a single timbre: it is founded on the totality of intervals and timbre, and this is best and most clearly realized by using one single, tempered instrument. . . . The "law" or "nomos" is that all twelve notes of the temperament are to be repeated over and over again.

The question of priority—of who conceived the 12-tone idea first—is not the crucial one. What is interesting is Schoenberg's desire to be first in announcing the technique in light of the fact that he postponed publishing any 12-tone work until 1923, years after he began using the method. A letter Schoenberg wrote to Hauer in December, 1923, gives such a full picture of the uses to which Schoenberg put his theory that it is here quoted in full:

Modling, 1 December, 1923

Dear Herr Hauer:

Your letter gave me very, very great pleasure. And I can give you proof of this. The fact is that about 1½ or 2 years ago I saw from one of your publications that you were trying to do something similar to me, in a similar way. After coming to terms with the painful feeling that someone else, by also being engaged in something I had been thinking about for pretty well fifteen years, was jeopardizing my reputation for originality, which might cause me to renounce putting my ideas into practice if I did not want to pass for a plagiarist—a painful feeling, you will admit—after having come to terms with this feeling and having come to see wherein we differ from each other and that I was in a position to prove the independence of my ideas, I resolved to make the following suggestion to you:

"Let us write a book together, a book in which one chapter will be written by one of us, the next by the other and so on. In it let us state our ideas, exactly defining the distinctive elements, by means of objective but courteous argument trying to collaborate a little bit in spite of these differences: because of what there is in common a basis can surely be found on which we can get along smoothly and with each other."

And I meant to say also: "Let us show that *music*, if nothing else, would not have advanced if it had not been for the Austrians, and that *we* know what the next step must be."

Then, however, I had qualms (there are always mischief-makers and gossips) lest I would be exposing myself to a refusal, and so the letter was never written. Perhaps now, your suggestion of a school is even better. Above all, because in that way an exchange of ideas would come about spontaneously, more frequently, and without the agitatory contributions of a public maliciously looking on and provoking one to stubbornness. But the idea of the book, for the purpose of establishing the present point of view, should not be completely rejected either.

We are perhaps both in search of the same thing and have probably found related things. My point of departure was the attempt to replace the no longer applicable principle of tonality by a new principle relevant to the changed conditions: that is, in theory. I am definitely concerned with no other theories but the methods of "twelve-note composition" as—after many errors and deviations—I now (and I hope definitively) call it. I believe—for the first time again in fifteen years—that I have found a key. Probably the book to be entitled *The Theory of Musical Unity* originally planned about ten years ago, often sketched out and just as often scrapped, time and again newly delimited and then enlarged, will in the end have just the modest title: *Composition with Twelve Notes*. This is as far as I have got in the last approximately two years, and frankly, I have so far—for the first time—found no mistake and the system keeps on growing of its own accord, without my doing anything about it. This I consider a good sign. In this way I find myself positively enabled to compose as freely and fantastically as one otherwise does only in one's youth, and am nevertheless subject to a precisely definable aesthetic discipline. It is now more precise than it has ever been. For I can provide rules for almost everything. Admittedly, I have not yet taught this method, because I must still test it in some more compositions and expand it in some directions. But in the introductory course for my pupils I have been using a great deal of it for some years in order to define forms and formal elements and in particular to explain musical technique.

Please do believe that my wish to reach an understanding with you springs above all from the urge to recognize achievement. This is something I have proved often enough; among other cases, also where you were concerned (I mention this in order to show you that the two occasions when you tried to find an approach to me were, after all, not wasted), in my *Theory of Harmony* I argue (on page 488 of the new edition) against the term "atonality" and then continue with an appreciation of you personally: you will realize that I did this for no one's sake but my own, out of the need to be fair: and this makes the value of my praise objectively even greater! My friends will be able to confirm, too, that although I have put my head down and charged like a bull at what I am opposed to in your ideas, in conversation I have acknowledged your achievements at least as much as I have done in my book.

It is a pleasure to give you proof of all this, for your amicable advance is of a kind that should remove all misunderstanding and all grudges; and so I shall gladly contribute a share as large as yours. I should be very pleased if we could now soon also have a further discussion about further details. It is in particular the project of the school that I have a good deal to say about, having long been turning over the idea of starting a school for the development of style. Perhaps you will yourself name some afternoon next week when you would care to visit me (excepting Tuesday and Friday). Although I may be in Vienna next week, I do not know whether I shall have the time then.

I am looking forward very much to the further development of our understanding and remain, with kindest regards, yours sincerely,

ARNOLD SCHOENBERG

N.B. This letter was not dictated, but written by me personally on the typewriter, thus respecting your wish that for the present I should not mention our discussions to any third person.

Neither the book nor the school materialized.

Schoenberg and Hauer were not the only two musicians independently to formulate the 12-tone technique; Webern later claimed that he was composing 12-tone music as early as 1911 but was not then conscious of the underlying law. What made dodecaphony such an extraordinary innovation in the history of music in Western civilization was that the man who first *did* become conscious of the law and its importance in a generative sense, had a special arrogance of manner stemming from a mystical conviction that he had been chosen by God to proclaim it to the world. Until Mahler's death, Schoenberg played the role of the follower, an idolator of the great Viennese musician. But after Mahler's death Schoenberg stepped into a new role, the adored leader, the subject of idolatry on the part of a group of utterly devoted disciples.

As he proceeded to develop his system during these years, he institutionalized his leadership by establishing—directly after the Armistice—the Society for Private Musical Performances in Vienna. Webern and Berg were both members and the latter has described the aims of the society: "The Society was founded in November, 1918, for the purpose of enabling Arnold Schoenberg to carry out his plan and give artists and music lovers a real and exact knowledge of modern music." At these meetings, experienced musicians played exceptionally well-rehearsed works by a diversity of composers including Berg, Debussy, Webern, Zemlinsky, Stravinsky, Scriabine, Strauss, Max Reger, Hans Pfitzner, Josef Hauer and Schoenberg. Those entering the group were aware of its stringent regulations: "Upon joining this Society, members must fill in and mail the appended form, declaring knowledge and willingness to abide by the Statutes. February 16, 1919, Arnold Schoenberg." The statutes cited that "a completely free hand in the direction of the Society, and all decisions of the General Assembly including elections, changes in statutes, dissolution of the Society, require for their validity the consent of the President."

Schoenberg's growing megalomania and paranoid manner of thinking manifest themselves not only in the authoritarian nature of the society but in the suspicious nature of the regulations. The most striking one is that each member come to each performance armed not only with an identification card but with an accompanying photograph as well, so that no hostile outsider could slip into the hall unnoticed.

In a collection of articles published by Schirmer in 1937, César Searchinger described Schoenberg's personality during these years in which he was completing the formulation of the 12-tone technique:

> My first experience with Schoenberg was in Amsterdam at the Mahler Festival of 1921. Here, surrounded by his disciples, Schoenberg went around, revered as a musical prophet. . . .
>
> A few months later I saw Schoenberg again in Vienna, ruling with the iron hand of the musical pedant, the concerts of the Society for Private Musical Performances, insisting on innumerable rehearsals and the strictest precision and perfection in the delivery of the works of his contemporaries of all nationalities—an artistic tyranny such as I have never witnessed before or since.

The society dissolved in 1922, primarily because of the devastating devaluation of Austrian currency. The short-lived history of this miniscule dictatorship has never been revealed.

Schoenberg's tyrannical manner during these critical years just before the release of his 12-tone technique is understable in the light of his sense of possession and mystical convictions concerning the system. Then how curious it is that although he began to formulate the technique during the writing of the libretto to *Die Jakobsleiter* in 1915, and developed it further in various sketches and movements composed after that, he kept all of this music under wraps until 1923 when the firm of Wilhelm Hansen in Copenhagen published the Five Piano Pieces, Opus 23. One would expect that his desire to preempt Hauer, whose article on 12-tone composition appeared in 1920, and anyone else working in a similar vein would have motivated him into releasing his first 12-tone piece almost as soon as it was written.

Yet, clearly, this was not the case.

A study by Jan Maegaard published in 1962 in the *Dansk Aarbog for Musikforskning* reveals all of the dates of composition of the various movements included in Schoenberg's first three 12-tone works: Five Piano Pieces, Opus 23, Serenade, Opus 24, and Suite for Piano, Opus 25. Schoenberg's care to date his finished drafts, his hesitancy to throw anything away and the fact that his handwriting changed recognizably all facilitated Maegaard in identifying the manuscripts.

From this study one learns these facts: Schoenberg completed the first and third of the Five Piano Pieces in July, 1920, but did not publish them until 1923. He finished the last piece of Opus 24 in April, 1923, but did not publish the work until 1924. And he completed the last movements of the Opus 25, the Trio and Gigue, on March 3 and March 2 of 1923, but the Suite was not published until 1925.

In a letter to Nicolas Slonimsky, Schoenberg described his early attempts to formulate the 12-tone technique:

> As an example of such attempts (i.e., to base the structure consciously on a unifying idea) I may mention the Piano Pieces, Opus 23. Here I arrived at a technique which I called for myself "composition with tones," a vague term, but it meant something to me. . . .
>
> The fourth movement, "Sonett," (i.e., of the Serenade, Opus 24) is a real composition with twelve tones. The technique is here relatively primitive, because it is one of the first works written strictly in harmony with this method, though it was not the very first. There were some movements of the Suite for Piano which I composed in the fall of 1921.

Schoenberg informs Slonimsky that he had actually composed various kinds of 12-tone works between 1914 and 1923. One of them, he wrote, was an uncompleted symphony which included a Scherzo written in late 1914 or early 1915 that was built on a 12-note theme; but he adds that other themes were used in the work. "My conscious aim," he claimed, "was always to build up my musical structures from one unifying idea which was the source of all the other ideas and also governed the accompaniment and chords or the 'harmonies.' I made many attempts to achieve this. But few of them were completed or published."

Why were they not completed or published? In 1909, Schoenberg had concluded his first agreement with Universal Edition, the worldwide publishing house which handled the most important composers in Vienna. Yet, as late as 1921, no work of Schoenberg's written after 1915 appeared in their catalogues. Schoenberg's biographer, H. H. Stuckenschmidt, says of these curious circumstances: "Even the pupils and friends of Schoenberg's closest circle did not know how to explain this fact. Some of them had been allowed a glimpse of *Die Jakobsleiter*—the work of the war years 1915–1917. After that Schoenberg's inspiration seemed to have dried up."

It was during the summer of 1922, almost five years after he had begun the score for *Die Jakobsleiter*, that Schoenberg confided to his close friend Josef Rufer: "I have discovered something that will guarantee the supremacy of German music for the next hundred years." In relating this incident, Stuckenschmidt goes on: "There followed an indication of the 'method of composing with twelve notes.' At the time he had written a number of works in which the method had been consciously used. Schoenberg had not made any of them public: he hesitated for years before he spoke of a discovery and before showing its results, which he knew would take the technique of composition along quite new lines."

The composer's obsession with numbers, so evident by now, must have caused him to wait until 1923 to publish his Opus 23, 1924 to publish his Opus 24, and 1925 to publish his Opus 25, magically ensuring the success of the 12-tone technique by having the opus numbers of the first three works composed in that system coincide with their dates of publication.

In October, 1923, Mathilde Zemlinsky Schoenberg, who had betrayed Schoenberg with Gerstl sixteen years earlier, died alone in a hospital. Schoenberg refused to go to her. In August, 1924, the composer married Gertrude Kolisch. She was the sister of the violinist Rudolf Kolisch, who proved to be as much a friend and promoter of his brother-in-law's music as Alexander Zemlinsky had been.

The unity provided by the recently evolved 12-tone technique made it possible for Schoenberg to return to the use of larger forms without the aid of a text and thus permitted him to work with classic structures. The Piano Suite, Opus 25, an eighteenth-century suite with a Prelude, Gavotte, Musette, Intermezzo, Minuet and Gigue, is unified by a single row that provides constructional material for the whole work. The Woodwind Quintet, Opus 26, a forty-five-minute work, closely approaches the classic sonata with its Allegro, Scherzo, Adagio and Rondo. Maegaard considers this as the first thoroughly pervasive application of dodecaphony: "Here Schoenberg reached the goal for which he strives, since his music had been doomed to aphoristic shortness by the expressionistic style—viz. a method of composing large forms without sacrificing either atonality or the possibility of considerable tightness of expression."

At fifty, Schoenberg had found the solution he had sought. Certain basic tenets prevail:

(1) Each row represents an ordered arrangement of all twelve notes of the chromatic scale.

(2) The row may be presented in any or all of four ways: original, inverted, backwards or backwards and inverted.

(3) The row may be stated in any of these ways on any degree of the chromatic scale.

Schoenberg's half-century celebration, surely a notable occasion for a ritualistic man, marked a number of significant achievements. The composer had crystallized his compositional technique, published his first pieces written in this method, and married a young woman. To celebrate his birthday, friends and disciples published a dedicatory volume, *The Special Schoenberg Birthday Book*, in which adulatory articles appeared by Webern, Berg, Alfredo Casella and G. F. Malipiero. Universal Edition opened an Arnold Schoenberg Library of Modern Music available to students free of charge. And only a short time elapsed between the publication of a work of his and its first public performance. Unlike the Five Orchestral Pieces, which had to wait three years for its first performance, the Woodwind Quintet, Opus 26, a lengthy and complex work, was conducted by Webern soon after its completion. Schoenberg's fame was spreading beyond Austro-German borders for the first time. In Rome, the Saint Cecilia Academy conferred an honorary membership upon him.

Meanwhile in Paris Igor Stravinsky startled the public with his Octet, and in 1925, he successfully toured the United States, both as composer and pianist.

The revelation of the 12-tone technique had not secured for Schoenberg unequivocal control.

Chapter 5 The progressive conductor Hermann Scherchen and composer Paul Hindemith organized a major festival in Frankfurt-am-Main to honor Schoenberg's fiftieth birthday. After receiving notice of these plans, Schoenberg wrote Scherchen expressing his gratitude, admittedly a curious kind of gratitude:

> Now let me thank you again most warmly and ask you to tell Hindemith too that I am *extremely pleased with him*. By doing this he is making a splendid sign of a proper attitude towards his elders, a sign such as can be made only by a man with a genuine and justifiable sense of his own worth; only by one who has no need to fear for his own fame when another is being honored and who recognizes that precisely such an honor does honor also to him if he associates himself with it. I once said: "Only he can bestow honor who himself has a sense of honor and deserves honor. Such a man knows what is due to him and therefore what is due to his peers."

The festival and various published accolades succeeded in mellowing the fifty-year-old Schoenberg. He himself noticed the change. In the Introduction to *The Special Schoenberg Birthday Book*, he wrote: "I cannot hate any more the way I used to; and worse yet, I can sometimes understand things without holding them in contempt."

In June, 1930, a Berlin newspaper wrote to Schoenberg asking him to comment on the "musical life and the shift of the center of gravity from Vienna to Berlin."

Schoenberg replied:

> Even before the war people in Vienna were rightly and wrongly proud and ashamed of being less active than Berlin.
>
> Even at the time Berlin showed a lively and intense interest in recognizing and explaining the symptoms of a work of art, something that was missing in Vienna, thanks to centuries of experience in composing.
>
> Even in those days whatever was new was derided after several performances in Berlin, whereas in Vienna it needed only one performance. In extreme cases—in both places—no performance at all.
>
> Even in those days, in both cities, the public had discovered that there is always plenty of time to honor a great man after he is dead. Presumably it had been recognized even in those days that it can be done more effectively and decoratively, and, what is more to the point, more lucratively.
>
> The Society for Private Performances in Vienna had three hundred members, two hundred of them good ones. But they could not keep it afloat.
>
> 1/10,000 of 2 millions is 200.
>
> 1/10,000 of 4 millions is 400.
>
> Perhaps four hundred can keep an artistically pure enterprise going?
>
> I am looking for a center of *gravity* and find them all too light.
>
> What didn't get shiftily shifted in the inflation! Perhaps, behind my back, some lighter centers of gravity as well.

Berlin in the 1920's became the center of progressive activity in all of the arts. It not only supported the Berlin Philharmonic, under the direction of Wilhelm Furtwängler; it also housed two of the foremost opera houses in Europe, the International Society for Contemporary Music, and the Novembergruppe, the intellectual organization that enthusiastically supported new music. In 1920 Scherchen founded the periodical *Melos*, which spearheaded the cause of contemporary music, and in 1925 the Prussian State Academy of the Arts appointed Schoenberg a director of the master class in composition, a position left vacant by the death of Ferruccio

Busoni, whose revolutionary views on the aesthetics of music had made Berlin progressive two decades before.

Schoenberg accepted the appointment with delight. In a letter to the Prussian Minister for Science, Art and Education, he expressed his gratitude for the "great honor and distinction accorded me by this appointment to such an eminent position."

When Schoenberg arrived in Berlin in 1925, he was accompanied by several pupils and his long-time friend and colleague, Josef Rufer, who was to handle the more rudimentary teaching of harmony, counterpoint and form in order to provide Schoenberg with the free time he needed to compose. At this point in his career, Schoenberg could make stringent demands; in this case they included six months free each year so that he might spend the winters in the South. Schoenberg suffered severely from asthma.

During 1925, Erich Kleiber, in Berlin, conducted the world premiere of Alban Berg's *Wozzeck*, the most spectacular product to come from the Schoenberg school. The work received tremendous attention and Schoenberg was suddenly in great demand as a teacher. During the next few years he had among his pupils Winfried Zillig, Roberto Gerhard, Walter Goehr, Walter Gronostay, Peter Schacht, Adolphe Weiss, Joseph Zmigrod, Norbert von Hannenheim, Charilaos Perpessa, Erich Schmid, Niko Skalkottas, Rudolph Goehr, Fred Walter, Henry Cowell and Marc Blitzstein.

But just as his prestige grew and his work was performed more, a totally opposed movement, commonly labeled "neoclassicism," developed in other parts of Europe. Igor Stravinsky defined neoclassicism at precisely the time Schoenberg crystallized dodecaphony: the need for formal principles was felt at the same time by the leading figures of the musical world, despite their divergent backgrounds and different personalities.

Neoclassicism relied on key centers. In contrast to dodecaphony, which plunged into the future, neoclassicism drew from the past through its retention of some aspects of the old tonal system. Schoenberg expressed his disdain for this kind of composition in his *Satires for Mixed Chorus*, Opus 28, spelling out his aesthetic position in a Prologue in the unlikely event that any listener would miss the point of the music. The *Satires*, scored for viola, cello, piano, mixed chorus and tenor and bass solos, is a 12-tone work in which diatonic and dodecaphonic writing exists side by side. In the first two bars, the viola plays a seven-note scale while the cello plays the missing five notes—also diatonic—but seemingly in a different "key." At the same time the piano plays the twelve notes against the strings in an entirely different grouping. Schoenberg ends his fugue with a C after introducing all other eleven notes of the chromatic scale. Thus he mimics the neoclassic composer who, in Schoenberg's view, ends absurdly with a classic tonic chord after endless meaningless cacophonous music.

Perhaps in an effort to underscore the fact that he knew, only too well, where the true values of classicism lay, Schoenberg continued to compose a number of works which adhered quite closely to the classic forms, while using the 12-tone technique. The Suite, Opus 29, for E Flat Clarinet, B Flat Clarinet, Bass Clarinet, String Trio and Piano contains four movements: Overture, Tanzschritte, Langsam and Gigue. The first chord consists of the first six notes of the row while the piano figure that follows supplies the last six notes. Thus Schoenberg was able to superimpose his new discipline over broad, flowing, eighteenth-century forms. In doing this he confirmed his basic musical tenet: the presence of form in music does not depend on tonality.

Schoenberg's String Quartet No. 3, Opus 30, continues the practice of his Opus 29 Suite, rejecting the free forms of his atonal days and embracing the stricter, eighteenth-century structures. This work, composed at the request of the American patron Elizabeth Sprague Coolidge, was performed by the Kolisch Quartet in 1927. In it Schoenberg introduced a freer treatment of the row: five notes (not twelve)—G E D sharp A C—form an ostinato which continues for twelve measures.

Schoenberg had never denied the possibility of introducing such liberties into his method of composition. In the mid-1920's he told Roberto Gerhard:

"The reason why we must not use any of the traditional chords without the greatest precaution, why, in fact, I think we had better do without them altogether, is not difficult to discover. Our new musical language is in its early stage of development; promiscuity with elements of the older system could, at this stage, only obstruct and delay its natural growth. But when it consolidates itself the time will come, no doubt, for the reintegration of many elements of the older system which, for the present, we must firmly discard."

During 1927 and 1928 Schoenberg worked on his first 12-tone piece for orchestra, the densely polyphonic *Orchestral Variations,* Opus 31. It contains an Introduction, a thematic statement and nine Variations, as well as an important Coda. The work explores all the possibilities inherent in the variation technique within a dodecaphonic framework. Furtwängler and the Berlin Philharmonic first played it in December, 1928.

In this first work for orchestra in fifteen years, Schoenberg used the motif B A C H as his musical theme; Bach did the same in his *Art of the Fugue*. (In German musical nomenclature, B Flat is represented by H.) The composer's great respect for Bach, who he once said could be described as the first 12-tone composer, is reflected again in the work that followed, an instrumental transcription of Bach's E Flat Major Organ Prelude and Fugue.

During the 1920's, some of Schoenberg's disciples defected. Alfredo Casella abandoned him, accusing Schoenberg of being mad. Hindemith started on a more accessible path and Hanns Eisler left the fold to embrace socialist realism. In 1930 César Searchinger wrote: "The phrase 'professor of modernity' has probably been coined for him. Not radicalism but academicism is the charge leveled at Schoenberg by his colleagues today."

Schoenberg did not tolerate criticism. Eisler indicated his disenchantment with Schoenberg to Zemlinsky during a talk on a train. Zemlinsky reported the conversation to Schoenberg, who wrote Eisler two enraged letters during March, 1926, in which he made the following remarks:

> . . . Then this is the way it is: you hold opinions deviating from me, wherefore I shall presumably reject them out of hand, and on the basis of these opinions, as on the basis of everyone's right to freedom of speech, you spoke about them freely to Zemlinsky. . . . Views diverging from my own are something that I should never resent, as little as I resent anyone having any other disability! One short leg, a clumsy hand, etc. I could only be sorry for such a person, but I couldn't be angry with him. . . . I described your proceedings as treason. But now I consider it was not me you betrayed, it was *yourself* you betrayed in a "chat on the train"; in such chat, in fact, you were not capable of not betraying your opinion of me, you actually had to blazon it abroad.

The increasing opposition to Schoenberg's new formal principle affected the course of his own work. Only a short time after the radical and complex *Orchestral Variations*, he wrote a comic opera, *Von Heute auf Morgen*. Under the pseudonym Max Blonda, his wife created the libretto about the domestic entanglements of a bourgeois German couple. Such a dramatic departure can be understood in the light of the musical life of the time. American jazz had arrived in Europe and was captivating art composers. In Paris Stravinsky and Milhaud incorporated it into their work and in

Germany the enthusiasm of Kurt Weill was shared by other serious composers like Ernst Křenek and Hindemith. Schoenberg wrote *Von Heute auf Morgen*—the orchestra includes a saxophone—the year after Brecht and Weill wrote their *Three Penny Opera*. Křenek had just succeeded with *Jonny Spielt Auf* and Hindemith had written a light opera, *Neues vom Tage.*

Schoenberg's effort in this genre may justly be interpreted as his initial attempt to come to terms with a new aesthetic. But he failed completely. Although the plot was simple, the music was full of contrapuntal invention. Built on a 12-note row, canonic forms flowed; *Von Heute auf Morgen* was hardly light opera.

And in 1931, in response to a commission from a Magdeburg publishing house (Richard Strauss and others were similarly commissioned), Schoenberg made another effort to reach a large public through a 12-tone but programmatic approach. His *Accompaniment to a Film Scene*, Opus 34, depicts three different episodes: Imminent Danger, Fear and Catastrophe. (It accompanied no actual film.)

In an effort to work out a solution to his problems, Schoenberg went to work, once again, at the piano, where he handled his initial forays into both atonality (Piano Pieces, Opus 11) and dodecaphony (Piano Pieces, Opus 23). In his Opus 33 Piano Pieces, certain principles of combination govern the way in which the row is handled. One finds sections organized around different permutations of the row in much the same manner that sections in eighteenth- and nineteenth-century composition were organized around different tonal areas. The contemporary theorist George Perle writes that in these pieces the "composer has created a music in which the structure of the 12-tone set has the same total relevance as the diatonic scale and triadic harmonies have in the major-minor system. All the 12-tone works that Schoenberg wrote after his arrival in the United States are based on these principles."

In 1930 Schoenberg composed Six Pieces for Male Chorus, written for unaccompanied male voices. The last of the group, "Verbundenheit," seems to veer even more strongly toward the past. It includes conventional triads and even ends on a D Minor chord, although the chord is admittedly in an inverted position. The words reflect the composer's state of mind:

> Everything comes once, but what does it matter?
> One has luck, another has delusions.
> Is everything hopeless?
> Does it matter that one found luck and I found nothing?

Such a specific question must surely have been motivated by Stravinsky's rise in prestige and his own decline.

With national socialism on the rise, and the retrograde aesthetic of mass taste on the march, Schoenberg pleaded for recognition as a truly German artist who was determined to keep Germany the center of the musical world. In a document published in February, 1931, in the journal *National Music*, Schoenberg stated his curiously poignant case:

> It is strange that nobody has yet observed that my music, grown on German ground and untouched by foreign influences as it is, constitutes an art which has sprung entirely from the traditions of German music, and which effectively opposes the striving for hegemony on the part of the Romance and Slav schools.
>
> The general failure to perceive this is due not so much to the difficulty of my scores as to the indolence and arrogance of the observers. For the facts are self-evident.
>
> But let me, for once, recount them myself:
>
> My masters were in the first place Bach and Mozart, in the second Beethoven, Brahms, and Wagner.

Schoenberg then methodically listed each of the musical techniques he had learned from each of these eminent German musicians. He concluded:

> I have learned much from Schubert, too, and from Mahler, Strauss and Reger. . . . I am convinced that the time will come when people will realize how intimately my discoveries are related with the best that was handed down to us. I claim the distinction of having written truly new music which, based on tradition, as it is, is destined to become tradition.

But the Prussian Ministry of Culture did not respond to his plea. In May, 1933, Schoenberg was dismissed from his post at the Prussian State Academy of the Arts. With his wife and year-old daughter, he left Berlin and traveled first to France. There, in a Paris synagogue, he converted back to the religion of his birth.

This formality was not the first manifestation of Schoenberg's recommitment to Judaism; this had occurred as early as 1923, in an angry exchange with Kandinsky, who sought Schoenberg's entrance into the Bauhaus at Weimar. Schoenberg had heard the unlikely fact that some of its members were anti-Semitic and expressed his rage at those intellectuals who exempted him from the onus of being a Jew:

I have learned at last the lesson that has been forced upon me this year and I shall never forget it. It is that I am not a German, not a European, indeed, perhaps, scarcely a human being (at least, the Europeans prefer the worst of their race to me), but I am a Jew. I am content that it should be so! Today I no longer wish to be an exception. . . .

When I walk along the street and each person looks at me to see whether I'm a Christian or a Jew, I can't very well tell each of them that I'm the one that Kandinsky and some others make an exception of . . . and you join in that sort of thing and "reject me as a Jew"? Did I ever offer myself to you? Do you think someone like myself lets himself be rejected?

Schoenberg was rejected all his life. But he had supreme faith in his mission and his faith sustained him in the most difficult times. A few years before leaving Germany, Schoenberg began *Moses und Aron*, the work that occupied his attention for the rest of his life. In it he expresses his lifelong commitment: "My love is for the idea. I live just for it."

The words are sung by Moses, the biblical lawmaker and leader of his people who enforced upon them a discipline which they bitterly resented. Schoenberg clearly identified with Moses. It was not far-fetched for him to do so; there was much of Moses in Schoenberg's own nature.

Chapter 6

In the fall of 1933, Schoenberg and his family sailed for New York. He had accepted a position in a little known conservatory that had recently opened in Boston's Back Bay, the Malkin Conservatory of Music. Although the Malkin brothers had the foresight and courage to hire Schoenberg from abroad, they lacked the necessary funds to make his stay comfortable. They could not even afford a small orchestra. Then, too, Schoenberg found the climate disagreeable and the weekly trip between Boston and New York, where he also held classes, arduous. During his first winter in the United States, Schoenberg became ill and was forced to postpone conducting a performance of his *Pelleas* until the spring. The Juilliard School of Music finally offered him a teaching position, but he decided to leave the Northeast and settle in California.

Before moving West, the Schoenbergs spent the summer in Chautauqua, a resort that offers its guests recitals, music courses and orchestral concerts. There he met Martin Bernstein, music professor at New York University, who told him of the problems he had in finding good contemporary scores for his student orchestra. Bernstein mentioned that the orchestra had played works by Bloch, Porter, Ravel and Hindemith, and was continually in search of new material.

Before leaving Chautauqua, Schoenberg assured Bernstein that he would write a piece for the NYU group. Once in California, he wrote to Bernstein, saying that the work was not as easy as he had hoped it would be, but was very good nevertheless. The composer added that he would not send it to the publisher "on speculation"; he was, he proclaimed, "no amateur." Bernstein replied that the honorarium, during these Depression days, could only be the $50 which had been collected from the students themselves. Gertrude Schoenberg finally ended the affair with a note to Bernstein informing him that her husband had given the work to the Juilliard School and that Schirmer would publish it.

But the Juilliard School orchestra never performed the Suite in G Major. Otto Klemperer conducted the Los Angeles Philharmonic in one of the work's few performances during the spring of 1934. Schoenberg's piece of *Gebrauchsmusik* turned out not to be *Gebrauchsmusik* at all; in his negotiations the composer had defeated his own purpose. Because of its obvious tonal organization— it was Schoenberg's first piece with a key signature since 1907— and because it was also his first work written in the United States, it was widely interpreted (possibly correctly) as Schoenberg's attempt to join the "neotonal" movement that pervaded the country at that time.

Oscar Levant's view of Schoenberg's life in Hollywood is one of the rare glimpses we have of the man from someone outside his intimate circle of close friends and relatives:

> There is rarely a period in Hollywood when all the orchestrators and most of the movie composers are not studying with one or another of the prominent musicians who have come there to live. At one time the vogue was for Schoenberg, who came with a great reputation, of course, as a teacher. However, most of the boys wanted to take a six weeks' course and learn a handful of Schoenberg's tricks. They were sorely disappointed when they discovered that it was his intention to give them instruction in counterpoint, harmony, and chorale, which meant that they would have to expend considerable effort themselves in doing assigned work. . . .
>
> When Schoenberg arrived in California it was the desire of his friends to see him employed in the movies and well paid for it. He was invited to an important premiere, following which the producer

Schoenberg and Family
(with his second wife, Gertrude, and their child, Nuria)

intercepted him and asked what he thought of the score. Schoenberg replied that he hadn't noticed it, thus bearing out the average producer's theory of what constitutes a good score only in reverse. . . .

Schoenberg severed relations with the film community altogether when, at his wife's suggestion, he asked $50,000 and "not a note changed" in return for composing a score for a film. The price was so outrageous that, according to his own estimate of the incident, it saved him from "a destructive course of action."

Schoenberg complained during his California years that the United States had not proven the haven he expected. In 1936 the composer wrote to Hermann Scherchen:

> Artistically I am more dissatisfied than ever, and, as for what I am doing here, well, I have been teaching at one University [USC] and next year shall be teaching at the other of the two universities here [UCLA]. But unfortunately the material I get has had such an inadequate grounding that my work is as much a waste of time as if Einstein were having to teach mathematics at a secondary school.

Like other European composers, Schoenberg was confronted with the problem of writing music that satisfied his own criteria in a predominantly alien world. In the United States, Russia and other parts of Europe, retrogressive artistic movements took hold that were similar in principle to the idea held by the German National Socialist Party, that art was a weapon of the state. In the United States the musical results were very clear-cut: composers wrote simple, accessible and folklike works. Radio and movies contributed to the implementation of these ideas and the WPA commissioned such works. In 1937 the American composer Roger Sessions attributed the success of these reactionary artistic pressures to the "reaction of a public which, for the first time in musical history, had found itself completely out of touch with modern music itself." Sessions added that musicians desired a new and closer relationship with audiences.

Different composers, of course, responded differently. Some went along with the movement, inhibiting their advanced ideas. Some stopped composing altogether or, like Varèse, threw their scores into the wastebasket as they continued to produce them. Others, for example the Schoenberg-trained Blitzstein, motivated by a combination of social guilt and what he felt to be a genuine need of the society, went all the way and wrote simply structured, completely tonal, very tuneful music. Neoclassicism, with its enormous tonal umbrella, provided the "ism" into which all of this music could be drawn. In the late 1930's Schoenberg responded to the neotonal pressure; the Suite in G Major anticipated several impassioned program works which he composed in an idiom of extended tonality.

But immediately after the Suite in G Major, composed in 1934, he returned to the use of the 12-tone technique. Schoenberg's Violin Concerto, Opus 36, was published in 1936 and dedicated to Webern. It was the most important work of Schoenberg's early creative period in the United States. A 12-tone composition in three classic movements, it was practically unplayable. Even Schoenberg conceded that it needed a sixth finger. Louis Krasner, playing with the Philadelphia Orchestra under the direction of Leopold Stokowski, gave the work its first performance in 1941. The performance was not broadcast and Schoenberg did not hear his piece until shortly before his death when he heard a tape of a performance by the Cologne Radio Orchestra. Friends say he wept as he listened. Schoenberg said it was his favorite work.

The String Quartet No. 4, Opus 37, was completed before the 1936 Opus 36 Violin Concerto, again suggesting that Schoenberg manipulated events in order to give crucial works opus numbers corresponding to the years in which they were published. The Opus 37 String Quartet is a masterful 12-tone work written in the traditional four movements.

Kol Nidre, based on the ancient melody sung at the beginning of the Jewish Day of Atonement, is written in G Minor and ends in G Major. Nor is Schoenberg's next piece, Variations on a Recitative for Organ, a 12-tone work; there are notes in the harmony that create a distinctly tonal effect. The *Ode to Napoleon*, which Schoenberg composed immediately after he became a United States citizen, is constructed on a twelve-note row, but the notes are handled in such a manner that the listener can hear the tonalities of E flat Minor, G Minor and B Minor. The poem by Byron, written in sixteen verses of nine lines each, is a passionate denunciation of dictatorship scored for speaking voice, string quartet and piano. World War II moved even those most dedicated to form to compose music with a programmatic content.

Schoenberg, in his sixties, did more than compose and teach: he played tennis once a week on George Gershwin's courts; he liked chess and devised a new system requiring a hundred chessmen; and he opened his Brentwood house on Sunday afternoons to play music with his friends and colleagues. Among the musicians gathering there were Edgard Varèse, Henry Cowell, Roger Sessions, Darius Milhaud, David Diamond, René Leibowitz, Fritz Stiedry,

Eduard Steuermann, Rosalyn Tureck and Arthur Schnabel. Another friend who visited him was Thomas Mann, as well as his old friend Alma Mahler Werfel. Yet, in the fall of 1937, when invited to Denver to deliver a lecture at a festival in his honor, he chose a characteristic title: "How One Becomes Lonely."

In 1944, when Schoenberg celebrated his seventieth year, former pupil Heinrich Jalowetz and composer Darius Milhaud wrote commemorative essays in the *Musical Quarterly*, musicians Kurt List, Lou Harrison and Ernst Křenek contributed articles in his honor to *Modern Music* and Roger Sessions paid him a tribute in the journal *Tempo*. Schoenberg's life still left much to be desired. He was forced to retire from UCLA at the age of seventy and therefore had to take on many more private pupils during 1944 and 1945. ASCAP increased his royalties, friends raised funds in order to help out, but it was not until Schoenberg sold several manuscripts to the Library of Congress that he felt he received any financial aid.

In January, 1945, Schoenberg applied to the Guggenheim Foundation for a grant to enable him to give up his pupils and complete *Moses und Aron, Die Jakobsleiter* and several theoretical works. He specified that his pension from UCLA was $38 a month and that he had a wife and three children, aged thirteen, eight and four, to support. The Guggenheim Foundation rejected his request; of the works mentioned in the application, he finished only the *Structural Functions of Harmony*.

Schoenberg did not turn the other cheek. He was as vocally bitter about his treatment in the United States as he had been about his treatment in Vienna. In a letter to Henry Cowell he wrote:

> It seems as if I have to celebrate a comeback in New York. It is time. It's a comeback because I have never been there, you know. I was so seldom performed in New York that nobody knows whether my music is worth hearing or not.
>
> It is worse here in Los Angeles. Mr. Wallenstein is six years here in Los Angeles and has not yet played one piece of mine.

And, in a letter to Kolisch, Schoenberg sums up his accurate assessment of the U.S. situation:

> They (la Boulanger's pupils, the imitators of Stravinsky, Hindemith and Bartók as well) have taken over American musical life lock, stock and barrel. The only person who can get an appointment in a university department is one who has taken his degree at one of them, and even the pupils are recruited and scholarships awarded to them in order to have the next generation in the bag. The

tendency is to suppress European influence and encourage nationalistic methods of composition constructed on the pattern adopted in Russia and such places.

Perhaps because of his disenchantment with this situation, Schoenberg spent a great part of his last years compiling his writings for a book, *Style and Idea*, published in 1950. From time to time he turned to composition. In 1946 he became seriously ill. After he recovered he wrote to his biographer, H. H. Stuckenschmidt: "I have risen from real death and now feel very well." During the five weeks of the summer that followed, Schoenberg wrote the String Trio, Opus 45. It is short, dodecaphonic, in one movement, and utilizes unusual registers and varying tone colors with harmonics, pizzicati, bowed and struck col legno. Thomas Mann spoke about Schoenberg's own view of the Trio: "One must bear in mind here a meeting with Schoenberg at which he told me of his new, just completed Trio, and of the experiences of life that he secreted in this composition; this work in a certain sense is a repetition of them. He declared that he described his medical treatment including his 'male nurse' and the rest in it."

During 1947 Schoenberg finally received an official accolade, $1,000 from the American Academy of Arts and Letters. Schoenberg wrote a letter of acceptance:

. . . That you should regard all I have tried to do in the last fifty years as an achievement strikes me as in some respects an overestimate. My own feeling was that I had fallen into an ocean of boiling water; and as I couldn't swim and knew no other way out, I struggled with my arms and legs as best I could. I don't know what saved me, or why I wasn't drowned or boiled alive—perhaps my own merit was that I never gave in. Whether my movements were very economical or completely senseless, whether they helped or hindered my survival, there was no one willing to help me and there were plenty of people who would have gladly seen me go under. I don't think it was envy—what was there to envy?—and I doubt whether it was lack of good will, or worse, positive ill will on their part. Perhaps they just wanted to get rid of the nightmare, the agonizing disharmony, the unintelligible thinking, the systematic lunacy that I represented, and I must admit that those who thought in that way were not bad men—though, of course, I could never understand what I had done to them to make them so malicious, so violent, so aggressive. . . . Please don't call it false modesty if I say that perhaps something was achieved, but that it is not I who deserves the credit. The credit must go to my opponents. It was they who really helped me.

The letter, in which Schoenberg diagnoses his own "systematic lunacy," reveals that the suspicious nature that prompted the imposition of stringent regulations in his private society almost thirty years before was still very much part of his personality.

It has been publicly claimed that Schoenberg and Freud never met. This is incorrect. An interview was arranged by a member of the Schoenberg family during the 1920's. After it was over—the meeting was characterized as friendly, polite, respectful, cool, focusing on art and music—Schoenberg turned to his relative and said: "Freud is certainly an interesting man but what has that got to do with me?"

In 1947, Schoenberg composed the dramatic cantata, *A Survivor from Warsaw*. Scored for speaker, male chorus and orchestra, the work deals with the heroic episode of the Polish Jews during the last days of the Warsaw ghetto. Hebrew songs are heard against the cacophonous sounds of the murderers. Schoenberg's use of different languages—the narrator's English and German juxtaposed with the chorus intoning the Hebrew chant—contributed a terrifying naturalism. *A Survivor from Warsaw*, first performed at the University of Mexico in 1948, made a thunderous impact on the audience. It was dramatic, expressive, rhetorical music, not far removed from the Romantic tradition into which the composer had been born.

During the last months of his life he worked on both text and music to a religious work, *Modern Psalms*, scored for speaker, chorus and orchestra. The work is addressed to God, the "unimaginable (*Unvorstellbaren*) of whom I cannot and must not make an Image." The text includes a discussion of prayer, a request to God to punish all offenders, a description of the Chosen People, an essay in praise of superstition, a treatment of the miracle as a calculated chess maneuver on the part of God, and several statements concerning racial identity.

The *Modern Psalms* reveals Schoenberg's thoughts at the end of his life. The setting remains unfinished in precisely the same textual context as that point at which Schoenberg stopped composing *Moses und Aron*. The words "And nevertheless, I pray," are set, but the rest of the sentence, "because I do not want to lose the rapturous feeling of oneness, of unity with you," remains unset. *Die Jakobsleiter*, *Moses und Aron*, and the *Modern Psalms* are the only major works that Schoenberg began and did not complete.

The clearest expression of the composer's inner life is in the

Arnold Schoenberg
RICHARD FISH

libretto for *Moses und Aron*. Moses (Schoenberg) sees and understands everything but he cannot convey his vision. (Moses had a speech impediment in the Bible.) Aron, glib, articulate, able to sway the people, claims that the tablets containing the Ten Commandments are images, "just part of the whole idea." "Then," says Moses, "I shall smash to pieces both these tablets and I shall also ask Him to withdraw the task given to me." At the end of the second act (Schoenberg never wrote the third), Moses falls to the ground in total despair. It is not that he doubts the existence of one God; it is that he despairs of ever being able to communicate his vision to the world: "O word, thou word, that I lack."

Moses is a speaking-voice part; Aron is a bel canto tenor. The entire score of *Moses und Aron* realizes the compelling musical idea for which Schoenberg lived: the whole opera is based on a single row. Schoenberg began it in Germany in 1930, when the Prussian government considered his music degenerate. He continued to work on it in the United States during a period in which Americans rejected his music for the same reason. But Schoenberg's vision persisted; in reply to a South African correspondent he wrote in 1949:

> The kind of tonality which is preferred today, which uses all kind of incoherent dissonances and returns without any reason to a major or to a minor triad, and rests then for a time and considers this the tonality of the piece, seems to me to be doomed. I cannot believe that this will last very long. . . . May I add that I believe, when the movement of the reactionaries has died away, that music will return to composing with twelve tones.

His letter was prophetic: the method of composing with twelve tones related only to each other was to be the impetus behind virtually everything that followed in art music during the 1950's and 1960's.

Chapter 7

The Viennese composer Ernst Křenek once characterized Schoenberg's students as docile men who displayed "sectarian fanaticism and spineless devotion to their master." All the evidence supports his claim. After 1910, when Schoenberg began to make carbon copies of his letters and to demand high fees for his paintings ("even now my name belongs to the history of music"), his personal manner and perfectionistic demands resulted in a paralysis of creativity among many of his pupils.

In 1933, Marc Blitzstein, a former Schoenberg pupil, wrote in an American music journal of Schoenberg's anticipated arrival in the United States: "A danger for his pupils lies in his insistence on genius, on perfection, in his ruthlessness with the near-perfect; the danger of paralysis and despair. Most of Schoenberg's Berlin and Vienna pupils have given up composing, convinced the master is right, composing is too hard, it is hopeless; one can never reach the goal and so on." Lois Lautner, one of Schoenberg's first American pupils, confirmed Blitzstein's fear. In an article published in the

Winter, 1967, issue of the Michigan *Quarterly Review* she wrote: "Although Schoenberg offered to teach me free of charge wherever he was, I had decided that I was not creating 'new beauty' for this century or any other. I would teach, after all."

Most of his pupils did exactly the same thing. But two musicians of great stature did emerge—Viennese composers Alban Berg and Anton Webern—whom Schoenberg began to teach in 1904. Berg's music sprang from the world of German Romanticism; his ties to the tonal world, like Schoenberg's, were never severed. Webern, on the other hand, looked directly into the future. In a strikingly passionate article published in 1952, Pierre Boulez, a prime mover of the "new music," expressed his disdain for Schoenberg and reverence for Webern:

> . . . We can see why Schoenberg's 12-tone music was bound to come to a dead end. In the first place he explored the new technique in only one direction. Rhythm was neglected, and even such questions as intensity, dynamics etc. considered in a structural sense. Perhaps it would be better to dissociate Schoenberg's work altogether from the phenomenon of the tone row. The two have been confused with obvious pleasure—sometimes with unconcealed dishonesty—and a certain Webern has only been too easily forgotten.
>
> Perhaps we might convince ourselves that the tone row is a historical necessity. Perhaps, like Webern, we might succeed in writing works whose form arises inevitably from the given material. Perhaps we could enlarge the field of 12-tone compositions to include other intervals than the semi-tone: micro-intervals, irregular intervals, complex sounds. Perhaps the principle of the tone row could be applied to the five elements of sound: pitch, duration, tone production, intensity and timbre. Let us, then, without any wish to provoke indignation, but also without shame or hypocrisy, or any melancholy sense of frustration, admit the fact that SCHOENBERG IS DEAD.

Stravinsky supported Boulez's judgment. In 1955, commemorating the tenth anniversary of Webern's death in the avant-garde German journal, *Die Reihe*, Stravinsky wrote:

> The 15 of September 1945, the day of Anton Webern's death, should be a day of mourning for any receptive musician.
>
> We must hail not only this great composer but also a real hero. Doomed to a total failure in a deaf world of ignorance and indifference he inexorably kept on cutting out his diamonds, his dazzling diamonds, the mines of which he had such a perfect knowledge.

As late as 1961, Stravinsky still had only praise for Webern: "He is the discoverer of a new musical distance between the musical

Anton Webern
THE BETTMANN ARCHIVE

object and ourselves, and therefore of a new measure of musical time."

Anton von Webern was born in Vienna in 1883, the year that Wagner died and nine years after Schoenberg was born. Early in his career he discarded tonality, which Wagner had extended to its ultimate limits.

Webern's father was a mining engineer and administrator in the Austrian Imperial regime. By the time Anton was eighteen, he had studied piano, cello and music theory, and was composing constantly. His early songs, written before he met Schoenberg, indicate that even at that time he never chose easy solutions to compositional problems: not one of them, written between 1899 and 1904, is strophic or constructed in the traditional a b a pattern.

Webern was thoroughly educated in music history, one of the first composers to pursue such studies. In 1902 he began to study musicology at the University of Vienna under the scholar, Guido Adler. He completed his dissertation in 1906; it treated Heinrich Isaac's *Choralis Constantinus*, a monumental work written at the beginning of the sixteenth century. Isaac's use of a Gregorian chant as a *cantus firmus* for these fifty-eight pieces bears some similarity to the perpetual variation of a single idea that characterizes 12-tone music.

As soon as Webern began to study with Schoenberg, in 1904, the results showed in his work. One of his earliest pieces, *Im Sommerwind*, reveals a careful study of *Pelleas und Melisande*; both works introduce melodic ideas that are later combined, four and five at a time. His String Quartet, written in 1905, shows a similar debt to *Verklärte Nacht*; both are built on the principle of perpetual variation and are based on traditional tonal harmonies. A major theme in the Webern quartet is, in fact, derived from a subsidiary motive in the Schoenberg work.

The significant interplay between teacher and student is revealed in a lecture Webern delivered in the early 1930's in which he described the effect that Schoenberg's Chamber Symphony had on him:

> In 1906 Schoenberg came back from a stay in the country, bringing the Chamber Symphony. It made a colossal impression. I'd been his pupil for three years and immediately felt "You must write something like that, too." Under the influence of the work I wrote a sonata movement the very next day. In that movement I reached the farthest limits of tonality.

At that time Schoenberg was enormously productive. Every time we pupils came to see him something else was there. It was frightfully difficult for him as a teacher; the purely theoretical side had given out. By pure intuition, amid frightful struggles, his uncanny feeling for form told him what was wrong.

Both of us sensed that in this sonata movement I'd broken through to a material for which the situation was not yet ripe. I finished the movement—it was still related to a key—but in a very remarkable way. Then I was supposed to write a variation movement, but I thought of a variation that wasn't really in a key at all. Schoenberg called on Zemlinsky for help, and he dealt with the matter negatively.

Now you have an idea of how we wrestled with all of this. It was unendurable. Indeed, I did go on to write a quartet in C Major —but only in passing. The key, the chosen key note, is invisible— so to speak—"suspended tonality."

It was thus shortly after Webern's "keyless" movement that Schoenberg wrote his own keyless movement in the Second Quartet, and soon after that that he composed his first "atonal" works, the Piano Pieces, Opus 11, and the *Georgelieder*, Opus 15. In these works the harmony is free from all tonal ties and the melody contains notes "foreign" to the harmony. In numbers 2 and 5 of the *Georgelieder*, Schoenberg does not return to the tonic. In his lectures Webern said why: "Everyone feels the end anyway."

The work that appears to have had an even more crucial effect on Webern than the Chamber Symphony is Schoenberg's Five Pieces for Orchestra. The composition had sprung from a discussion with Mahler in which Schoenberg held that it was possible to create an actual melody by sounding a single tone on different instruments. This was his initial application of the idea that "a note is perceived by its color, one of whose dimensions is pitch. Color, then, is the great realm, pitch one of its provinces. . . ."

The effects of economy and concentration of the orchestral pieces reached their zenith in Schoenberg's Three Pieces for Orchestra, written in 1910 and only discovered after his death, as well as in the Opus 19 Piano Pieces, written in 1911 after the trauma of Mahler's death. But these compositions represent the end of the road for Schoenberg. Robert Craft has written: "After his Opus 19 Pieces, Schoenberg was to return to the rhetoric and time-scale of Brahms, whereas Webern inhabited ever after a completely new time-world begotten only with the materials of 12-tone composition. However close Webern was to Schoenberg, their paths had already diverged."

The story that Webern tells of his particular path during a lecture on February 12, 1932, is a fascinating one:

> About 1911 I wrote the Bagatelles for String Quartet Opus 9, all very short pieces, lasting a couple of minutes—perhaps the shortest music so far. Here I had the feeling "When all twelve notes have gone by, the piece is over." Much later I discovered that all this was part of the necessary development. In my sketchbook I wrote out the chromatic scale and crossed off the individual notes. Why? Because I had convinced myself, "This note has already been there." It sounds grotesque, incomprehensible and it was incredibly difficult. The inner ear decided quite rightly that the man who wrote out the chromatic scale and crossed off individual notes *was no fool*. Josef Matthias Hauer, too, went through and discovered all this his own way. In short, a rule of law emerged; until all twelve notes have occurred, none of them may occur again. The most important thing is that each "run" of twelve notes marked a division within the piece, idea or theme.
>
> My Goethe song, "Gleich und Gleich" (Four Songs, Opus 12, No. 4, composed in 1917), begins as follows: G-sharp A D-sharp G, then a chord E C B-flat D, then F-sharp B F C-sharp. That makes twelve notes: none is repeated. At that time we were not conscious of the law, but had been sensing it for a long time. One day Schoenberg intuitively discovered the law that underlies twelve-note composition. An inevitable development of the law was that one gave the succession of twelve notes a *particular order*. . . .
>
> Today we've arrived at the end of the path, i.e. at the goal; the twelve notes have come to power and the practical need for this law is completely clear to us today. We can look back at its development and see no gaps.

Schoenberg's response to the Six Bagatelles is contained in a curious mystical Preface, published in June, 1924:

> Though the brevity of these pieces is a persuasive advocate for them, on the other hand that very brevity itself requires an advocate.
>
> Consider what moderation is required to express oneself so briefly. You can stretch every glance out into a poem, every sigh into a novel. But to express a novel in a single gesture, a joy in a breath—such concentration can only be present in proportion to the absence of self-pity.
>
> These pieces will only be understood by those who share the faith that music can see things which can only be expressed in music. These pieces can face criticism as little as this—or any—belief. If faith can move mountains, disbelief can deny their existence. And faith is impotent against such impotence.
>
> Does the musician know how to play these pieces, does the

listener know how to receive them? Can faithful musicians and listeners fail to surrender themselves to one another?

But what shall we do with the heathens? Fire and sword can keep them down; only believers need to be restrained.

May this silence sound for them.

Schoenberg's pupil Erwin Stein made the following comment about Webern: "Ecstasy was his natural state of mind. His compositions should be understood as mystical visions." Not only did Schoenberg and Webern share a mystical view of the world; they also had in common the instinct to adore. As Schoenberg adored Mahler, so Webern adored Schoenberg. Hans Moldenhauer, director of the Webern Society, writes that Webern had an "almost fanatical regard" for Schoenberg, and a letter that Berg wrote to Webern in 1910 testifies to the love both pupils felt for their imposing master:

> How despondent you must be again, far away from all those divine experiences, having to forego the walks with Schoenberg and miss the meaning, the gestures, the cadence of his talk. Twice a week I wait for him at the Karlplatz, before teaching begins at the Conservatory, and for the 15 to 30 minute walk, the hubbub of the city is drowned by the "roar" of his words. But to tell you all this is only to increase your sense of deprivation. . . .

Webern's adoration brought with it an identification in the most personal psychological terms. His statement, "With me things never turn out as I wish, but only as ordained for me—as I must," is strongly reminiscent of Schoenberg's frequently expressed claim that he had been driven into a painful path on "orders from the Supreme Commander."

If Webern's music had simply realized Schoenberg's principles, his path would have been an easier one, the challenge nullified, the identification with the ever-rejected Schoenberg destroyed. But instead of following in Schoenberg's footsteps, Webern chose a new, highly individual path and forged altogether new routes for the evolution of music in this century.

Webern's works were unprecedentedly short and incredibly quiet. Boulez has written that Webern's unique rhythmic innovation is "this conception whereby sound and silence are linked in a precise organisation directed toward the exhaustive exploitation of our powers of hearing. The tension of sound is enriched to the extent of a genuine respiration, comparable only with Mallarmé's contribution to poetry."

Webern filled the few measures of his pieces with the uncomfortable intervals of the major seventh and minor ninth and placed enormous expressive value on each sonority. Each tone was assigned its special function in the overall scheme; no note was ever wasted. The instruments, used at the extremes of their registers, play only one note at a time, with the dynamics and tempi frequently changing from note to note. Webern, the composer of the *ppp* sixteenth note, often used crescendo and diminuendo on one tone. The instructions that accompanied the score were usually "Like a whisper" or "Dying away." Webern created a distilled and lonely lyricism that was not understood for years, awaiting a postwar generation of musicians.

His Symphony, Opus 21, written after Schoenberg had published a number of 12-tone works, was more tightly constructed than anything composed by Schoenberg himself. Scored for clarinet, bass clarinet, two horns, two harps, violins, violas and cellos, the work lasts only ten minutes. Webern describes the second movement:

> The row is F A-flat G F-sharp B-flat A; E-flat E C C-sharp D B. It's peculiar in that the second half is the cancrizans of the first. This is a particular intimate unity. So here there are only twenty-four forms, since there are a corresponding number of identical pairs. In the accompaniment to the theme, the cancrizans appears at the beginning. The first variation of the melody is a transposition of the row starting on C. The accompaniment is a double canon. Greater unity is impossible. . . . In the fourth variation there are constant mirrorings. This variation is itself the midpoint of the whole movement after which everything goes backwards. So the entire movement is itself a double canon by retrograde motion.

It was later, however, in his Opus 27 Piano Variation, that other composers assert Webern extended the same tightly knit organization he had given to pitch, to other attributes of the musical tone. The work has been analyzed by musicians and theorists who claim to have discovered in it precedents for the serial organization of duration, density and register as well. Although Webern never said that he was extending the serial organization of pitch to other structural elements of the musical tone, he might have been doing so unconsciously, in much the same manner as he intuitively wrote his first 12-tone work.

Boulez has claimed that Webern was not tied to the row as "theme." Webern, himself, acknowledged that: "I can work without thematicism, that is to say, much more freely, because of the unity that's now been achieved in another way: the row ensures unity.

"Adherence is strict, often burdensome, but it's *salvation!* We couldn't do a thing about the dissolution of tonality, and we didn't create the new law by ourselves—it forced itself overwhelmingly on us. This compulsion, adherence, is so powerful that one has to consider very carefully before finally committing oneself to it for a prolonged period, almost as if taking the decision to marry; a difficult moment! Trust your inspiration! There's no alternative!"

In 1930 Webern was appointed reader and "specialist adviser" to the Austrian radio on all questions to do with new music. In April, 1931, he was honored by the first concert devoted to his own compositions, performed by Kolisch, Steuermann and others. In May, 1932, he received Vienna's Music Prize. Even after Hitler came to power, he continued to teach. Schoenberg never forgave him his sympathy with the Nazis, and after Webern's death, refused to help the family on moral grounds.

Webern's death has been recorded by Moldenhauer; the scholar spent years tracking down the story: increased bombings of Vienna had forced the composer to move to Mittersill, a small town eighty miles southwest of Salzburg where his daughter and her family lived. One evening, shortly after the end of the war, Webern stepped outside the house to smoke a cigar after dinner. American soldiers, approaching to intercept Webern's son-in-law in a black market transaction, unaccountably killed Webern by mistake.

Webern remained tied to Schoenberg throughout his life. The ambivalence Schoenberg felt for Mahler, Webern felt for Schoenberg. The younger man tried repeatedly to break away and on one occasion a quarrel persisted for three years. Such a relationship is infinitely complex; one cannot adore without deeply resenting the beloved who holds one so captive. Still, in 1944, the year before his untimely death, Webern wrote to a friend asking about plans to commemorate Schoenberg's birthday:

"How will you celebrate September 13th? Pass on my deepest remembrances, which possess me night and day, my unspeakable longing! But also my unwearying hopes for a happy future."

Chapter 8

Webern's compositional style caused a radical shift toward abstraction in music. The German journal *Die Reihe* and its American counterpart, *Perspectives of New Music*, both published by members of the post-Webern school, revealed an analytic, scientific approach that had little in common with the aesthetic discussions of the past few hundred years. Although Webern did not go nearly as far as some of his followers in the permutational ordering of his work, he too believed that art and science were one: "When one arrives at the correct conception of art, there can be no more distinction between science and inspired creation. The further one presses, the more everything becomes identical, and at last one has the impression of encountering no human work but rather a work of nature."·

The wedding of music and mathematics was not a new phenomenon in the 1950's. The earliest writers saw in music an imitation of the harmony of the spheres and the medieval university included music in its curriculum. Through the end of the Renaissance, composers and theoreticians continued to perceive a numerical order in music. The world could be understood in musical-mathematical symbols.

But in the seventeenth century, with Monteverdi and the beginnings of opera, scientific-proportional ideas were displaced by dramatic-expressive ones. Composers, newly self-conscious about expression, devoted themselves to *musica poetica*. Even purely instrumental work was affected by this shift in attitude. The dissolution of the Church modes and the emergence of tonality implemented the new aesthetic. In the sonata form—the basic musical structure of the eighteenth and nineteenth centuries—the composer presented two different but related tonalities, juxtaposed them in a state of conflict, and resolved them in favor of the tonic key. The sonata form is a dramatic one.

But after the end of World War II, a movement rose which looked at the universe in neo-Platonic terms, and sought to bring about a reunion of art and science. In the New World, music was welcomed into the American university and musicians so trained received Ph.D.'s. Ernst Křenek expressed the renewed influence of mathematics on music in a complicated work, *Sestina*, in which the last line summed up the idea of a large group of avant-garde musicians of the 1950's and 1960's: "What looks ahead subordinates itself to number."

Such a statement recalls that of the medieval architect Jean Mignot, who claimed: "*Ars sine scientia nihil.*" But a return to an old view of music does not imply a repetition of it—even in the hands of its most ardent disciples. Musicians know now, for example, that the musical tone is not as simple a property as the ancient Greeks, medieval Christians and Renaissance musicians thought it to be. During the eighteenth century, the French physicist Joseph Sauveur demonstrated that each vibrating string generates not only one fundamental tone but a subsidiary series of higher tones. Thus a sequence of tones is heard when one tone is produced by a conventional instrument or the human voice. This "harmonic series" prevents the listener from grasping the "pure" tone itself.

The electronic generation of sound, developed in the early 1950's, made it possible to produce a pure "sine" tone, a tone without any overtones. With the new instruments that became available to composers in the fifties and sixties, it was possible to realize serial music of such complexity that it would have staggered the human performer. The contemporary theorist Roman Vlad wrote that if we believe that the evolution of music cannot come to a full stop, then it is only through electronic means that it can progress further than Webern. At the time of this pronouncement—1955—much of the musical world agreed. Karlheinz Stockhausen articulated the tone for the movement: "All music must start with Webern; there is no other choice."

Thus it was via the post-Webern serialists that music arrived at electronically generated sound. Although the means of producing it were revolutionary, the principles on which it was based derive from an old and distinguished tradition.

The new technology did not dictate its own aesthetic. Musicians in different countries absorbed it in a manner consistent with their own national styles.

During World War II the tape recorder was perfected and almost immediately became a medium for tonal manipulation. With it, composers could superimpose existing sounds and create complex and interesting sonorities. France was the original center for tape recorder work. But Webern's followers, working in Germany, concentrated on the sine tone, a single frequency generated by electronic means. Experimenting in an electronic studio under the sponsorship of Cologne Radio, they had as their mentor Dr. Werner Meyer-Eppler of the Institute of Communication Theory at the University of Bonn. Dr. Meyer-Eppler, together with Herbert Eimert and Robert Beyer, gave the first demonstration of electronic music in Germany. He also introduced the word "parameter" into music, borrowing it from mathematics where it means a quantifiable variable. The parameters of a musical tone are frequency, duration, intensity, timbre, attack and decay.

At Cologne, the sine tone was the raw material, produced by an electronic generator and then manipulated on tape. In contrast to other electronic studios, those in Paris and New York, Cologne concentrated on generating sound electronically immediately after the end of the war. The production of electronically generated sound was discussed at Cologne as early as 1949 by Robert Beyer, who had been engaged in such speculation since the 1920's. In 1951 the Phonetic Sound Institute of Bonn University produced an electronic instrument, the Bode Melachord, which had two organ-like keyboards that simulated primary sound sources. Stockhausen studied there and became, with G. M. Koenig, one of the staff composers at Cologne. But the studio offered its facilities to others; Křenek and Boulez were among those who used them in the early years.

The 12-tone aesthetic prevailed at Cologne. Whereas the technique had gradually evolved in the United States through the influence of Schoenberg and Křenek, who were teaching there, it had been forced to go underground in Europe because of the crises of the 1930's and World War II.

But after World War II, Germany came to life musically, and the serial idea provided the impetus. Stockhausen's analysis of Webern's Concerto, Opus 24, which appeared in the journal *Melos*, became as famous as the concerto itself and influenced scores of young composers. In it Stockhausen articulated the manner in which Webern utilized the serial principle not only in relation to pitch, but in relation to the other parameters. Works produced at Cologne were not, of course, limited to a scale of twelve equal semitones; any interval was now possible. But the serial idea prevailed.

Stockhausen's study of physics and acoustics at the University of Bonn prepared him to cope with the new technology. At the studio he had at his disposal three different generators. One produced sine tones; a second produced electrical impulses; and a third produced "white noise," which includes all the sounds and their overtones. The composer was then free to mix the sounds from the three generators to provide whatever result he had in mind. Thus the musical creator suddenly found himself able to manipulate his own material, that of sound, much as the painter was more than ever conscious of the physical properties of his own tools.

As editor of the avant-garde *Die Reihe*, as a prime mover of the international school at Darmstadt, and as staff composer at Cologne, Stockhausen played a crucial role in focusing world attention on German music. Boulez was one of several composers who left their native countries to live in Germany. The reasons were apparent: the Germans organized festivals, holiday study courses, and many critical journals. They performed, published and recorded more new music than any other nation.

In 1955, in the United States, a machine appeared that was originally designed for commercial purposes but turned out to be ideally suited to the electronic realization of serial composition. The RCA Olson-Belar electronic sound synthesizer, first installed in a studio in Princeton, New Jersey, and then at the Columbia-Princeton Electronic Music Center, produced almost total electronic sound synthesis. Milton Babbitt, music professor at Princeton and one of the directors of the Columbia-Princeton center, focused his attention on this machine.

The music synthesizer is an elaborate device controlled by means of coded input tape. The instrument builds up sounds of conventional instruments or even primitive vocal sounds. In addition, fundamental tones produced by the synthesizer can be combined in novel ways.

Two paragraphs from an article published by Milton Babbitt indicate how far music had traveled since Schoenberg tried to communicate the Word of God:

> The Mark II synthesizer provides for the production of any measurable control of these components of the musical event: frequency, envelope, spectrum, intensity, duration, and of the mode of progression from such an event to the following event. This control resides in the programming input of the Synthesizer, where the properties of these components are specified in the form of binary instructions, holes punched in a fifteen inch wide paper roll by keys, mounted on a keyboard and arranged in ten vertical columns of four keys each. . . .
>
> The first column of keys—representing sixteen binary choices—selects, under the usual and simplest conditions, what the designers term "frequency," actually one registral element of a frequency class, while the second column usually selects "octave," that is, any registral number of the octave determined frequency class of which the selected frequency is a representative. The "frequency" and "octave" selections together determine what the musician usually signifies by the term "frequency." The third column selects "envelope," the growth, steady rate (if any) and decay characteristics of the event. The fourth column usually selects the spectrum and the fifth the intensity.

Babbitt says that he uses the word "usually" to emphasize that "nothing is pre-fixed" in this machine. "Any set of keys, and this means, of course, the instruction conveyed by the hole punched by any member of the set, can be made to determine values within any of the five categories of the components." Thus, with the synthesizer, the composer is still physically in touch with the sound-making process; he manipulates switches to test his results before punching the code on the paper tape that controls the oscillators, filters and other electronic mechanisms that produce the sounds he wants.

Babbitt, who played the violin at six, is a musician who grew into technology. In this sense, he may be at the end of his line. Many of the younger computer musicians are technologists from the start

*RCA Electronic Sound Synthesizer at Columbia–Princeton
Electronic Music Center, New York City (MARK II)*
MANNY WARMAN

experimenting with electronic sound. These young men and women, trained in the complex language of computer technology, are less involved with the traditional concepts of music than Babbitt and the electronic musicians of his generation. Those working at the Bell Laboratories in New Jersey illustrate the point; their looks, manners and conversation have more in common with engineers than with the highly charged, formerly long-haired artist.

The project at Bell Labs began in 1957 when Max V. Mathews, a Ph.D. in electrical engineering and director of the behavioral research department of Bell Laboratories, attended a concert of Schoenberg's 12-tone works. What he heard provoked him to consider generating such sounds with the computer. Mathews set up this system: A computer memory is fed instructions by the composer. These instructions describe the various parameters of a musical tone and cause the computer to transmit a series of numbers from the computer memory to a converter. They become a series of electrical pulses that vary according to the original values that the computer generated. The pulses are smoothed by a filter and come out as sound through an ordinary loudspeaker.

Some composers have successfully crossed the bridge into technology. Iannis Xenakis, a Greek composer working with computer Sigma V, succeeds in his stated objective that "new music should use science and mathematics but not be dominated by them." Nevertheless, it is probable that if Schoenberg had lived to hear electronically generated sound, he would not have been happy with it. Even at the height of the electronic excitement—in 1955— one of its prime proponents, Roman Vlad, articulated the fear that many felt: "The danger," he wrote in *The Score and IMA*, "is that man will lose his freedom and become a slave to the machine that he has created with his own hands."

Webern, the shy son of an engineer, was the pivotal figure in the transition. What Schoenberg considered an effective device for hiding emotions and actual events became, in the hands of many of Webern's immediate followers, the basis for a new grammar in music in which "theme," "idea," "the Word of God" played little if any role at all. Schoenberg used to say: "A Chinese philosopher speaks, of course, Chinese. The question is what does he say?" Many of the post-World War II serialists would have replied that the message was irrelevant.

Despite some recent anti-serial events, Schoenberg achieved one of his primary goals: the 12-tone technique succeeded in shifting the balance of power away from Stravinsky and his American disciples back to the Austro-German domain where it had prevailed from Bach through Wagner.

"I claim," Schoenberg wrote in 1931, "the distinction of having written truly new music which, based on tradition, is destined to become tradition."

II. STRAVINSKY AND THE FRANCO-RUSSIAN STYLE

People always expect the wrong thing of me.
They think they have pinned me down and then
all of a sudden—au revoir!

IGOR STRAVINSKY
Modern Music, 1946

Chapter 9

In *Moses und Aron* Schoenberg pits the two brothers against one another. Moses, who understands the God of the Jews, cannot communicate his vision. Aron, who has no vision, can articulate and sway the people. Writers generally agree that Schoenberg identified with Moses and that Aron served as a symbol of the performer—the attractive bearer of someone else's message.

But there may also be something of Igor Stravinsky in this Aron. For Stravinsky, like Aron, is as uncommitted a theoretician as he is a great musician.

Stravinsky's attitude toward Schoenberg's commitment to the "idea" is revealed in a conversation between Mallarmé and Degas related in Stravinsky's autobiography, which he wrote when he was fifty-two years old:

> Degas, who, as is well known, liked to dabble in poetry, one day said to Mallarmé: "I cannot manage the end of my sonnet and it is not that I am wanting in ideas." Mallarmé, softly, "It is not with ideas that one makes sonnets but with words." So it is with

Beethoven. It is in the quality of his musical material and not in the nature of his ideas that his true greatness lies. It is time that this was recognized, and Beethoven was rescued from the unjustifiable monopoly of the "intellectuals" and left to those who seek in music for nothing but music.

Schoenberg and Stravinsky were locked in a power struggle that began before the onset of World War I and lasted until Schoenberg's death. Schoenberg saw the once securely entrenched hegemony of the Austro-Germans threatened by the *Sacre du Printemps*. He was correct in his assessment of Stravinsky's threat, although few shared his perception of the event. Boris de Schlœzer, an eminent Stravinsky authority, has written that the real significance of the *Sacre*, not generally grasped at the time, lay in the reaction the work created against chromaticism and atonality.

Between 1940 and 1951 Schoenberg and Stravinsky lived only ten miles apart from one another in Hollywood, California. It is no accident that they met only once—at the funeral of a mutual friend. Both avoided each other conscientiously and visitors to one never mentioned having paid a visit to the other. The two giants of early twentieth-century music were not only recipients of altogether different national characteristics and artistic gifts; they also were strikingly different men.

In contrast to the extraordinary secrecy that always surrounded Schoenberg and the resulting paucity of material about him, Stravinsky is accessible in the extreme. The bibliography in *Stravinsky*, by Eric Walter White, published in 1966, lists forty-nine books and more than three hundred recent articles. In addition, Stravinsky has written eleven books and published numerous articles in magazines and newspapers throughout the world.

Whereas Schoenberg's relatively few words represent his deepest convictions about the most serious matters, Stravinsky's many verbal expressions reflect a restless, changeable, volatile figure who accepts the fluctuating nature of his personality apparently without difficulty. In the Foreword to his autobiography he acknowledged his infidelities: "As I call my recollections to mind, I shall necessarily be obliged to speak of my opinions, my tastes, my preferences, and my abhorrences. I am but too well aware of how much these feelings vary in the course of time. This is why I shall take great care not to confuse my present reactions with those experienced at other stages of my life."

And, at sixty-two, in the American journal *Modern Music*, the composer wrote:

> I do not have any ultimate viewpoint of composition and when I write my next symphony it will be an expression of my will at that moment. And what that will is going to be I do not know. I wish people would let me have the privilege of being a little bit unconscious. It is so nice, sometimes, to go blind, just with the *feeling* for the right thing.

Still later, in *The Observer* (London) on the occasion of his eightieth birthday:

> My agenbite of inwit is that I do not know, am not aware, while composing, of any question of value. I love with my whole being whatever I am now composing, and with each new work I always feel that I have just found the way, just begun to compose. I love all my children, of course, and like any father I favor the backwards and imperfectly formed ones. But I am excited only by the newest— Don Juanism—and the youngest—nymphetism.

Unlike the conflicted, visionary Schoenberg, Stravinsky has always responded with instinct, deftness and musicianship to the musical matter at hand. When the famous Russian ballet master Serge Diaghilev asked him to string together a number of eighteenth-century pieces, he complied and wrote *Pulcinella*. When his friend and colleague, Ernest Ansermet, returned from the United States with some jazz material, Stravinsky responded to this impetus with *Ragtime*. When, in the 1930's, Stravinsky made his first contact with a commercial recording company, he produced the Serenade in A, in which the length of each movement corresponded to one side of a 78-r.p.m. disc. And when Ringling Brothers commissioned him to write a Polka for a group of elephants wearing tutus in the Barnum and Bailey Circus, he did just that. Finally, in 1952, when his devoted young friend and amanuensis, Robert Craft, introduced him to large doses of Anton Webern, he repudiated his hostile attitude to "the three Viennese" (Schoenberg, Webern and Berg) and embraced the serial procedure.

Stravinsky's essentially receptive nature has been commented upon by Craft, who lived as a member of the Stravinsky family for much of the period that followed their meeting in 1948: "The initial agony [of composition] could be softened by imposition from without. Stravinsky seemed to seek imposition." This was true not only of his musical composition but of his prose writing as well. The composer readily acknowledges that his autobiography and the *Poetics of Music* were written with other men, and, since 1957, he has spoken through Craft.

None of the stylistic changes which Stravinsky has made during his long and productive life affected the nature of his working habits. Unlike Schoenberg, he finished just about everything he began. And unlike Schoenberg, he suffered no long periods when he couldn't create music. Writing of the sketchbooks, Craft points out: "Most sketch entries are dated and it is possible to determine in them exactly what was composed on what date. The dates show that Stravinsky has been able all his life to produce about the same amount of music each day."

Stravinsky was as rooted in Russia as Schoenberg was rooted in Vienna and Berlin. Although he left St. Petersburg in 1914 and, as he declared in 1966, "fled every reminder of my past until a decade ago," he obviously maintained very deep ties to his native land.

He never repudiated his Russian forefathers. According to White's biography, Stravinsky's first teacher, Rimsky-Korsakov, "became a sort of father-figure in Stravinsky's life following the death of his own father in 1902." Stravinsky's affection for Rimsky is supported by Erik Satie, who wrote in 1923: "Stravinsky remembers Rimsky very kindly and always speaks of him with great affection and filial gratitude."

Stravinsky's feeling for Rimsky was not only matched but exceeded by his admiration for Tchaikovsky, who was as revered in Russia as Wagner was revered in Germany. In 1921, Stravinsky praised Tchaikovsky's *Sleeping Beauty*:

> It is a great satisfaction to me as a musician to see produced a work of so direct a character at a time when so many people, who are neither simple, nor naive, nor spontaneous, seek in their art simplicity, "poverty," and spontaneity. Tchaikovsky in his very nature possessed these three gifts to the fullest extent. That is why he never feared to let himself go, whereas the prudes, whether raffiné or academic, were shocked by the frank speech, free from artifice, of his music.

The letter to Tchaikovsky, written just after Stravinsky completed his "neoclassic" Octet, quickly became notorious. People had assumed that the composer would be against everything emotional and subjective, everything for which Tchaikovsky stood. But

Stravinsky's respect for the older composer remained intact. He dedicated his comic opera, *Mavra*, to the three Russian artists he most admired—Pushkin, Glinka and Tchaikovsky, and dedicated *Le Baiser de la Fée* to Tchaikovsky, many of whose melodies he quoted in the piece.

In the 1936 *Autobiography*, Stravinsky wrote of his first and only contact with Tchaikovsky, which occurred at a gala performance of Glinka's *Russlan and Ludmilla* at the Imperial Opera in St. Petersburg in 1893:

> Besides the excitement I felt at hearing this music that I already loved to distraction, it was my good fortune to catch a glimpse in the foyer of Peter Tchaikovsky, the idol of the Russian public, whom I had never seen before and was never to see again. He had just conducted the first audition of his new symphony, the Pathetic, in St. Petersburg. A fortnight later my mother took me to a concert where the same symphony was played in memory of the composer, who had been suddenly carried off by cholera. Deeply though I was impressed by the unexpected death of the great musician, I was far from realizing at the moment that this glimpse of the living Tchaikovsky—fleeting though it was—would become one of my most treasured memories.

In 1962 Stravinsky returned to Russia for a brief visit. In *Newsweek* he was quoted as saying: "My wish to go there is due primarily to the evidence I have received of a genuine desire or need for me by the younger generation of Russian composers. No artist's name has been more abused in the Soviet Union than mine, but one cannot achieve the future we must achieve with the Russians by nursing a grudge." Mrs. Stravinsky implied that her husband masked considerable feeling under these cool words. She said that he hestitated before accepting the Russian invitation because he was worried that "he would become too emotional" when he returned to his country. In a speech delivered before the Soviet Ministry of Culture on October 1 of that year, Stravinsky declared himself to be more a Russian than a Frenchman or American:

"The smell of Russian earth is different; and such things are impossible to forget. . . . A man has one birthplace, one fatherland, one country—he *can* have only one country—and the place of his birth is the most important factor in his life. I regret that circumstances separated me from my fatherland, that I did not bring my works to birth there, and, above all, that I was not there to help the new Soviet Union create its new music. But I did not leave Russia by my own will, even though I admit I disliked much in my Russia and in Russia generally. But the right to criticize Russia is mine, because Russia is mine and I love it. I do not give any foreigner that right."

That evening Craft entered the following note in his diary: "I am certain that to be recognized and acclaimed as a Russian in Russia, and to be performed there, has meant more to him than anything else in the years I have known him."

The Russia into which Stravinsky was born had only recently developed an art music tradition. Perhaps because of its relative geographic isolation, Russia fathered a rich and varied folk idiom, a wealth of liturgic song, but virtually no art music. Before the middle of the nineteenth century, such music was a foreign commodity, imported from other countries for the pleasure of the upper classes.

Modish, Western European art and thought first began to intrude upon Russian life at the end of the seventeenth century. During the eighteenth-century reigns of Empresses Anne, Elisabeth and Catherine, Italian music was performed at the court with Italian composers Galuppi, Paisiello and Cimarosa supervising operatic productions. Architects Quarenghi and Rastrelli added their imprint to the Italianate color of St. Petersburg, and when Catherine II became Empress in 1762, she brought with her a snobbish but infectious love for everything French. A pandering sympathy with French culture persisted in Russia well into Stravinsky's own lifetime.

By the nineteenth century nationalistic concerns began to displace the international musical idiom of the century before. Everywhere people wanted to hear their own sounds in artistic settings. Smetana appeared in Bohemia, Grieg and Sinding in Scandinavia, and Mikhail Ivanovich Glinka in Russia (1804–1857). Glinka incorporated Russian folk tunes into the classical and early grand opera forms he had learned while he was living in Paris, Berlin and Italy. His first work, A Life for the Czar, was composed in 1826. This first significant musical work written by a Russian composer was created less than sixty years before Stravinsky's birth.

Soon after the appearance of A Life for the Czar, it became apparent that two philosophies of music were emerging which reflected the general age-old division of Russian thought on everything ranging from art to politics. One group was committed to a Panslavic orientation that precluded Western influences; the other was in favor of assimilating all the wealth of the West. Supporting the former premise a group of men known as "The Nationalist Five" rose to prominence: Alexander Borodin (1834–1887), professor of chemistry at the medical academy, Modest Moussorgsky (1839–1881) army officer, César Cui (1835–1918) military engineer, Nikolai Rimsky-Korsakov (1844–1908) naval officer, and Mili Balakirev (1837–1910) who organized and taught the others. Moussorgsky was the most original musician in the group. Responding to the inspired nationalism of the 1860's, he sought to make art the servant of the people: "To seek assiduously the most delicate and subtle features of human nature—of the human crowd—to follow them into unknown regions, to make them our own: this seems to me the true vocation of the artist . . . to feed upon humanity as a healthy diet which has been neglected—there lies the whole problem of art."

Throughout his life, Moussorgsky refused to submit to the discipline of a European musical education, which the Westernized Russian composers actively sought. This second group of musicians was headed by Anton Rubinstein (1829–1894) and Peter Ilich Tchaikovsky (1840–1893). Rubinstein, a brilliant pianist, was trained in Germany and contributed immeasurably to the musical growth of his own country by setting up conservatories that disseminated musical knowledge and trained brilliant instrumental virtuosi. Tchaikovsky was one of Rubinstein's first pupils and became professor of harmony at the Moscow Conservatory. Tchaikovsky was the only Russian composer of the nineteenth century to receive worldwide acclaim; the manner in which he incorporated Russian sentiment and Russian folk melodies into European musical forms carried his art across national boundaries.

Even Rimsky-Korsakov, a leading figure in the Nationalist Five, was not immune to the pull from abroad, and in 1864 he wrote the very first Russian "symphony." In Rimsky's case the form provided him with a shell into which he inserted a literal or sequential repetition of folk melodies. He never developed his material in the generic "symphonic" sense.

The Russian Revolution, in 1917, deprived Stravinsky of his property and he no longer received an income from his estate. It was at this time that the composer built on his sympathy with French culture and crystallized a pro-Western identification. In the autobiography he argues for the Western approach and writes of his admiration for Pushkin who was in that same tradition:

   . . . By his nature, his mentality, and his ideology, Pushkin was the most perfect representative of that wonderful line which began with Peter the Great and which, by a fortunate alloy, has united the most characteristically Russian elements with the spiritual riches of the West.

   Diaghilev unquestionably belongs to this line, and all his activities have only confirmed the authenticity of that origin. As for myself, I have always been aware that I had in me the germs of the same mentality only needing development and I subsequently cultivated them.

Thus the basic ingredients of Schoenberg's and Stravinsky's musical diet were as strikingly different as German and Russian food. The most apparent difference lies in the fact that, during his student years, Stravinsky was completely under Rimsky-Korsakov's control, and Rimsky was oblivious to the Germanic idea that underlay Schoenberg's creative life: the perpetual variation of a single melodic idea.

But the more profound difference may well be this: Schoenberg was born at the end of a long and distinguished Austro-German musical tradition which, based on the sonata form, gave birth to an enormous literature for symphony, chamber and solo instruments. When Schoenberg reached his artistic maturity, tonality, the language on which the tradition was based, appeared finally to be exhausted. Schoenberg thus attempted to forge ahead and create a new musical language which would respectably uphold a very lengthy tradition.

Stravinsky, on the other hand, was born into a country during a period when his idol, Tchaikovsky, and his teacher, Rimsky-Korsakov, both borrowed melodies from popular sources and musical forms from Western Europe. It is no wonder, then, that throughout the course of his life, Stravinsky adopted exactly what he chose to and imbued the adopted form with his own dazzling, individual sounds.

> My real answer to your questions about my
> childhood is that it was a period of waiting for
> the moment when I could send everyone and
> everything connected with it to hell.
>
> IGOR STRAVINSKY,
> *Memories and Commentaries*, 1960

Chapter 10   In his recollections, Stravinsky is a weak child suffering perpetual humiliation and loneliness, a child depreciated by his parents in favor of an older brother. He was the third of four children, all boys:

> I was baptized by a prelate of the Russian Orthodox Church in Oranienbaum (a suburb of St. Petersburg) a few hours after my birth, which occurred at noon (June 17, 1882). My parents summoned a religious to say prayers for me, to sprinkle my head with anointed waters, and to draw a cross on my forehead in anointing oil. . . . According to custom in the Russian Church, frail babies were sometimes baptized summarily in this fashion. (The fact of my frailty, thus established at my first hour, was insisted upon throughout my youth, until it became a way of thinking about myself; and even now, as a healthy octogenarian leading an active and strenuous life, I sometimes remind myself that, in fact, I am much too frail and had better stop.)

Stravinsky describes his father, Feodor Ignatievich, as nervous and irritable and his mother, Anna Kholodovsky, as cold and unloving. His assessment of his mother gains support from this incident: In 1938, when Anna Stravinsky was about to attend her first performance of her son's *Le Sacre du Printemps* on the occasion of its twenty-fifth anniversary, she told a friend that she did not expect to enjoy it, because it was not "her kind of music." The composer George Antheil, a friend of Stravinsky during his early days in Western Europe, reports that Stravinsky's mother frequently chided her son about his lack of appreciation of the advanced, chromatic Scriabine, saying that he was obviously not capable of "recognizing his betters."

Despite the lack of warmth in such a setting, Stravinsky enjoyed some advantages in being a child of this cultivated, musical couple. On both sides the families had been landed gentry or artists, and Stravinsky's father possessed a library of between 7,000 and 8,000 books, including many first editions. Feodor was a famous bass singer at the Imperial Opera House in St. Petersburg, where the Stravinsky family lived. Tchaikovsky gave him an inscribed photograph and wrote a letter to a friend in which he lavishly praised Feodor's talent. Indeed, Feodor Stravinsky was so admired by Tchaikovsky that he served as a pallbearer at the great Russian composer's funeral.

Igor grew up in large, comfortable, glamorous surroundings. Tchaikovsky's photograph stood on a table in his father's studio, Rimsky-Korsakov visited from time to time, and the child was allowed the run of his father's library. But Stravinsky also recalls the sounds of his city. And it is sound, not idea, that is at the core of his creative life:

> The first such sounds that record themselves on my awareness were those of the drushkis on cobblestones or blackwood parquetry pavements. Only a few of those horse-carriages had rubber tires, and those were doubly expensive; the whole city crackled with the iron hoops of the others. The loudest diurnal noises of the city were cannonades of bells from the Nikolsky Cathedral . . . but I recall with more nostalgia the sound of an accordion in a suburban street on a lonely Sunday afternoon, or the trilling of wires of the balalaika orchestra in a restaurant café.

Stravinsky writes that he first became conscious of himself as a musician when he was two years old: "My nurse brought me home from the village where we had been perambulating one afternoon, and my parents, who were then trying to coax me to talk asked me what I had seen there. I said I had seen the peasants and heard them sing, and I sang what they had sung. Everyone was astonished and impressed at this recital, and I heard my father remark that I had a wonderful ear."

His musical gifts were supplemented by a continuous exposure to serious music. In his infancy and early childhood, Stravinsky heard his father, whose study was near the nursery, rehearse roles from the Russian repertory—Glinka, Rimsky-Korsakov, Tchaikovsky, Dargomizhsky, Borodin and Moussorgsky—as well as from the standard Italian works. At seven, Igor made his first trip to the Maryinsky Theater, across the street from his apartment, to attend a performance of Tchaikovsky's *Sleeping Beauty*; he cites that occasion as the one at which he developed a lifelong attachment to both ballet and Tchaikovsky. A year or so later his mother took him to *A Life for the Tsar*, an opera he was already able to play on the piano:

> It was then that I heard an orchestra for the first time. And what an orchestra—Glinka's! The impression was indelible, but it must not be supposed that this was due solely to the fact that it was the first orchestra I ever heard. To this day [1936] not only Glinka's music in itself, but his orchestration as well, remains a perfect monument of musical art. . . .

At nine, Igor began to study piano with a pupil of Rubinstein's, who refused him permission to improvise. Although he was unhappy at this, he learned to play the piano well enough to cope with the standard European literature: Mendelssohn's G Minor Piano Concerto, and a number of works by Mozart, Haydn, Beethoven, Schumann and Schubert. In his early teens, an uncle, an avid music lover and Russian liberal, took him under his wing and introduced Igor to the works of the Russian Five. It was through this uncle and his enlightened circle of friends that the young musician's horizons widened; the lines of communication were open between Russian nationalism and German academicism:

> Was it Glazounov, adopted son of the Five, with his heavy German academic symphonies, or the lyrical symphonies of Tchaikovsky, or the epic symphonies of Borodin, or the symphonic poems of Rimsky-Korsakov, that imbued this group with its taste for symphonism? Who can say? But however that may be, all these ardently devoted themselves to that type of music. It was thanks to this environment than I got to know the great German composers.

He also learned about German music through his private lessons with Vassily Kalafaty, who worked with him on counterpoint, invention, fugue and the harmonization of chorale melodies. Stravinsky reports that Kalafaty was very suspicious of any "new" chords but adds that he is grateful to him for teaching him to appeal to his ear as the first and last test.

But the most crucial foreign influence on Stravinsky was French. At fifteen, he met Ivan Pokrovsky, then twenty-three: "I was still in the Gymnasium when we met and he was already being graduated from the university. My life at home was unbearable (even more unbearable than usual, that is) and Pokrovsky appeared to me as a kind of shining Baudelaire versus the *esprit Belge* of my family."

Pokrovsky introduced Stravinsky to Charles Gounod, Georges Bizet and Emmanuel Chabrier and, through playing four-handed arrangements at the piano, to Offenbach's *Tales of Hoffmann* and Delibes's *Lakmé* and *Coppélia*. It was at this time that Stravinsky recognized his attraction to French music:

> I found in [it] a different type of musical writing, different harmonic methods, a different melodic conception, a freer and fresher feeling for form. This gave rise to doubts, as yet barely perceptible, with respect to what had up till then seemed unassailable dogma. That is why I am eternally grateful to Pokrovsky; for from my discussions with him dates my gradual emancipation from the influences that, all unknown to myself, the academicism of the time was exercising over me.

Thus, in his late teens, Stravinsky was an able pianist, an educated musician, and a connoisseur of musical style. But he had not yet begun to compose.

When he was twenty, during a vacation with his family at Heidelberg, Stravinsky met Rimsky-Korsakov and showed him a few pieces he had just written. He was enrolled in law school at the time; his parents never took seriously his interest in music:

> During this visit I showed Rimsky my compositions, short piano pieces, "andantes," "melodies," and so forth. I was ashamed of myself for wasting his time but I was also extremely eager to become his pupil. He looked at these tender efforts of mine with great patience, and then said that if I would continue my work with Kalafaty I might also come to him two times a week for lessons. I was overjoyed, so much so, in fact, that not only did I apply myself to Kalafaty's exercises, but I also filled several note books with them by the end of the summer.

Shortly after this meeting, Stravinsky's father, who had been suffering from cancer for over a year, died. Rimsky-Korsakov stepped quickly into the parental role and proved to be no more loving and encouraging than Feodor had been. Stravinsky never criticized this attitude, attributing it to some hidden effort to spur him on to do better things. He writes that Rimsky was always very careful not to encourage him with the loose use of the word "talent." But Rimsky went even further than avoiding complimentary words; he made public unfavorable opinions of his student's work. In 1907 one Russian critic wrote: "In the opinion of Rimsky-Korsakov, the talent of Igor Stravinsky has not yet taken clear shape. Rimsky thinks that the fourth part of his symphony imitates Glazounov too much and Rimsky himself."

It is not surprising that the Stravinsky of that time sounded a little like Rimsky. Just consider Rimsky's method of teaching Stravinsky:

> Rimsky adopted the plan of teaching form and orchestration side by side, because in his view the more highly developed musical forms found their fullest expression in the complexity of the orchestra. . . . My work with Rimsky-Korsakov consisted of his giving me pieces of classical music to orchestrate. I remember that they were chiefly parts of Beethoven sonatas, and of Schubert's quartets and marches. . . . A year and a half later I began the composition of a symphony. As soon as I finished one part of a movement I used to show it to him, so that my whole work, including the instrumentation, was under his control.

Thus Stravinsky's early work shows a classical, international orientation with touches of Rimsky in the instrumentation. He composed his first Piano Sonata, not given an opus number, in the traditional four movements: Allegro, Andante, Scherzo and Finale. His first published work, Symphony in E Flat, opens with a theme borrowed from Richard Strauss and a polyphonic texture reminiscent of Wagner's. In *Faun and Shepherdess*, Opus 2, written during 1906–7, Stravinsky set verses of Pushkin for mezzo-soprano and orchestra in a French, impressionistic way; Debussy and Ravel had obviously affected him.

In 1905, when he was twenty-three and had just finished his studies at law school, he married his first cousin, Catherine Nossenko, who was one year older than he. He describes their relationship as being "like sister and brother." In the fall of 1908, Stravinsky visited Rimsky-Korsakov to tell him he was working on a new piece to celebrate the approaching marriage of Rimsky's daughter. He took the work with him on a vacation with his wife and finished it within six weeks, but between the time Stravinsky sent off the score and it arrived in St. Petersburg, Rimsky-Korsakov died.

Almost immediately, Stravinsky abandoned the German and French influences and assumed a most pronounced Rimsky-like sound. His teacher had, on occasion, complained of plagiaristic tendencies on Stravinsky's part. And even after he died, Rimsky's family persisted in this complaint. Their attitude was succinctly expressed by Mme Rimsky-Korsakov. On seeing Stravinsky in tears at her husband's funeral, she made a remark which Stravinsky later characterized as the cruelest ever made to him: "Why so unhappy? We still have Glazounov."

But Stravinsky's next aesthetic mentor was not to be Glazounov. The winter that followed Rimsky's death, *Fireworks* was performed on the same program with another Stravinsky dazzler, *Scherzo Fantastique*. Serge Diaghilev was in the audience. *Fireworks*, scored for triangle, cymbals, big drum, campanelli, two harps and string quartet, impressed the ballet master of the newly formed Russian Ballet. He asked Stravinsky to arrange two piano pieces by Chopin for his ballet, *Les Sylphides*, for the Paris Opera during the spring of 1909. The ballet was to open with the Chopin/Stravinsky Nocturne in A Flat and close with the Valse Brillante in E Flat.

At the time Stravinsky was also working on *The Nightingale*, an opera he had started while still with Rimsky. With the help of his friend Stepan Mitusov, he had written a libretto based on a Hans Christian Andersen story about a sick Chinese Emperor who could be cured only by the song of the nightingale. The first act was completed in 1909. But because of Diaghilev's other commissions, Stravinsky could not finish the work until 1914.

Stravinsky abandoned the development of a motive, in the traditional symphonic sense, in *The Nightingale*. The fishermen repeat their air frequently from the beginning with no change. The nightingale's motive doesn't change either. And the Three Chinese Marches are really one march and two echoes rather than three distinct musical pieces. This nondevelopmental aspect of his work persisted throughout the composer's life. Béla Bartók described the basis of Stravinsky's style: "He seldom uses melodies of a closed form consisting of three or four lines but short motives of two or three bars and repeats them *á la ostinato*. These short, recurring, primitive motives are very characteristic of Russian music of a very certain category." And, referring to Stravinsky's *Perséphone*, composed in 1934, Bartók pointed out that a five-bar phrase is repeated four times. "We perceive that the repetitions are only incidents in a continuous line which, because it is not directed to any climax and is devoid of all harmonic tension, seems endless. Such melodies, undramatic in structure, are rare in other composers." Repeating melodic fragments in this way, avoiding the development of a single idea, Stravinsky, quite naturally, separated himself from Schoenberg as early as 1909, before each of the men recognized and coped with the threat of the other.

After *Les Sylphides*, Diaghilev commissioned Stravinsky to write a full-length ballet, *The Firebird*. Diaghilev originally wanted Liadov, then a more famous composer, to do it, but he was afraid that Liadov would not deliver it on time. Stravinsky was frightened by the nature of the commission—it was his first with a deadline—but he could not resist the glamour:

"It was highly flattering to be chosen from among the musicians of my generation, and to be allowed to collaborate in so important an enterprise side by side with personages who were generally recognized as masters in their own spheres."

Following the practice of Rimsky-Korsakov, Stravinsky took his literary theme from an old Russian legend. He wrote the music in the form of a *ballet d'action*, in which the music followed the stage action bar by bar. Stravinsky's arrival in Paris to participate in rehearsals put him in daily contact with the exciting world of French impressionistic music. Although he had been attracted to French culture while still in St. Petersburg, his taste for it was heightened by close association with Debussy, Ravel, Satie and Florent Schmitt. At close to fifty, Debussy epitomized French culture and specifically the French challenge to Wagner. Stravinsky has touched on his relationship with Debussy in *Expositions and Developments*, written with Craft in 1960:

I was called to the stage to bow at the conclusion [of *Firebird*] and was recalled several times. I was still on stage when the final curtain had come down, and I saw coming toward me Diaghilev and a dark man with a double forehead whom he introduced as Claude Debussy. The great composer spoke kindly about the music, ending his words with an invitation to dine with him. Some time later, when we were sitting together in a box during a performance of *Pelléas*, I asked him what he had really thought about *Firebird*. He said, "Que voulez-vous, il fallait bien commencer par quelque chose." Honest, but not extremely flattering. Yet shortly after the *Firebird* premiere, he gave me his well-known photo (in profile) with a dedication: "à Igor en toute sympathie artistique." I was not so honest about the work we were then hearing. I thought *Pelléas* a great bore as a whole, and in spite of many wonderful pages.

Despite the carping words on both sides, Stravinsky adopted French Impressionism, absorbing it into his own personal style. Virgil Thomson has written that by the time he was thirty, Stravinsky had "so firmly proved himself a master of French Impressionism that he scared the daylights out of Claude Debussy."

Although Stravinsky's additive, nondevelopmental form is related to Debussy's, there are striking differences in style between the works of the two composers. Stravinsky discussed these differences in an interview published in 1968: "Debussy referred to me as a 'primitive' and 'instinctual,' rather than a 'schooled' composer. And he was right. Like Ramanujan, who did his mathematics without any formal mathematical education, I have had to depend on natural insight and instinct for all the learning I would have acquired if I had taken a Ph.D. in composition. . . ."

Thus, at the start of his career, without a set of intellectual premises, Stravinsky created an altogether new kind of continuity in music. Despite manifold changes throughout his career, he never abandoned this mosaic structure that came so unself-consciously to him.

Although Debussy composed *Pelléas* in 1902 and his works were performed throughout Europe during the first decade of the twentieth century, the French composer failed to dispel the Wagnerian mystique. In a lecture at Harvard in 1939, Stravinsky described the situation that prevailed at that time:

> Even the admirable music of *Pelléas et Mélisande*, so fresh in its modesty, was unable to get us out into the open, in spite of so many characteristics with which it shook off the tyranny of the Wagnerian system. . . . I am not without motive in provoking a quarrel with the notorious *Synthesis of the Arts* [Wagner's *Gesamtkunstwerk*]. I do not merely condemn it for its lack of tradition, its nouveau riche smugness. What makes its case much worse is the fact that the application of its theories has inflicted a terrible blow on music itself. . . . We can speak of these things all the more freely in view of the fact that the halcyon days of Wagnerism are past, and that the distance which separates us from them permits us to set matters straight.

The halcyon days of Wagnerism were past because, between 1910 and 1914, Stravinsky succeeded in shifting the focus of the musical world away from the German Romantic agony to Paris and the Diaghilev Ballet.

Chapter 11

Like Stravinsky, Diaghilev studied music while enrolled in law school at the university and then drifted into journalism. He founded a journal, *Mir Isskustva*, against academicism and for the avant-garde: Moussorgsky, Rimsky-Korsakov, Prokofiev, Stravinsky, as well as contemporary French composers and painters. Diaghilev went to Paris in 1908 and organized a series of concerts of Russian music including a performance of *Boris Godunov* with Chaliapin playing Boris. The following year, he formed the Ballet Russe. Diaghilev's impeccable taste and formidable powers of organization produced a new kind of ballet that made dance, music, theater and scenic design equally crucial to the overall production.

The Ballet Russe never performed in Russia, but it did play most of the great cities of the West: Madrid, London, Rome, Berlin, Monte Carlo, Buenos Aires, New York, Philadelphia and Paris. Its dancers and choreographers included Pavlova, Karsavina, Lopokouva, Balanchine, Fokine, Massine, Bohm, Lifar, Nijinsky and Nijinska. Its scenic designers were Picasso, Braques, Utrillo, di

Chirico, Juan Gris, Rouault, and the Russians (Bakst, Benois, Larionov, Goncharova, among others). Its composers also were the major talents working outside the German domain, and included Debussy, Ravel, Satie, Poulenc, Milhaud, de Falla, Rieti, Schmitt, Prokofiev and Stravinsky. Stravinsky wrote more music for the company than any other composer, including his three major ballets—*Firebird*, *Petrushka* and *The Rite of Spring*.

During the winter of 1909–10, before he even received the contract, Stravinsky began *Firebird*. As soon as he finished, he left St. Petersburg for Paris to attend the rehearsals with Fokine, scenarist and choreographer for *Firebird*. Alexander Benois has described his impressions of the composer: "In those days he was a very willing and charming 'pupil.' He thirsted for enlightenment and longed to widen his knowledge. . . . But what was most valuable in him was the absence of the slightest dogmatism."

Based on a Russian legend in which a good fairy comes into conflict with an ogre, *Firebird* became an immediate success. Parisians loved its driving motor rhythms, so different from Debussy, as well as its lush Rimsky-like orchestration. The composer later said the orchestra was "wastefully large," with its triangulo, tamburo, campanelli, tamtam, piatti, xylophone, celesta, piano, three harps, sixteen first violins, sixteen second violins, fourteen violas, eight cellos, eight double basses, three trumpets, two tenor tubas and two bass tubas. Stravinsky dedicated the work to Andrey Rimsky-Korsakov, son of his late teacher, as though to compensate the family for what he had borrowed from the father. Eric Walter White notes that Stravinsky here adopts a technique Rimsky had used in his last work, *Le Coq d'Or*, of associating human elements with diatonic themes and magical elements with chromatic material. In *Firebird*, Stravinsky writes diatonic music for Ivan Tsarevich and the Princesses while he concentrates on the interval of the augmented fourth for the Firebird and the wizard Kastchei.

The Ballet Russe performed *Firebird* for the first time on June 25, 1910, at the Paris Opera House, with Karsavina in the leading role. (Pavlova refused to dance it, criticizing the music as complicated and meaningless.) The audience applauded loudly, Debussy came backstage to compliment the composer and the publishing house of Jorgenson hastily printed the score. Unlike Schoenberg, Stravinsky did not have to wait long for worldwide acclaim.

"One day when I was finishing the last pages of *Firebird* in St. Petersburg," Stravinsky writes, "I had a fleeting vision which came to me as a complete surprise, my mind at the time being full of other things. I saw in imagination a solemn pagan rite: sage elders, seated in a circle, watched a young girl dance herself to death. They were sacrificing her to propitiate the God of Spring. Such was the theme of the Rite of Spring. . . .

"Before tackling [it] . . . I wanted to refresh myself by composing an orchestral piece in which the piano would play the most important part—a sort of *Konzertstück*. In composing the music I had in mind the distinct picture of a puppet, suddenly endowed with life, exasperating the patience of the orchestra with diabolical cascades of arpeggios. The orchestra, in turn, retaliates with menacing trumpet blasts. The outcome is a terrific noise which reaches its climax and ends in the sorrowful and querulous collapse of the poor puppet."

Surprised that Stravinsky had not proceeded with the *Sacre du Printemps*, Diaghilev was nevertheless delighted with the imagery for *Petrushka* and decided to make a ballet of it. He chose Benois to work with Stravinsky on the scenario and Fokine to choreograph the piece. *Petrushka* is organized according to classical symphonic structure. It is in four movements: Allegro, Andante, Scherzo and Trio, and Rondo.

Stravinsky worked on the score in Switzerland, the Riviera, St. Petersburg and Rome. Diaghilev presented it in Paris a year after the *Firebird*, with Nijinsky and Karsavina dancing and Pierre Monteux conducting. The composer scored it for a Firebird-like orchestra but this time he created a special effect, that of a mechanistic, soulless world. Bubbling flutes set the first scene. Dolls and barrel organs on stage are accompanied by angular melodies and short, repetitive rhythms. Piano passages for Petrushka's movements suggest watches and other ticking things. The story of love, murder and resurrection could not fail in Paris. One critic wrote that it treated human material as "inextricable and precise as a dream," and in Rome the futurist poet Marinetti carried a banner: "Down with Wagner, Long Live Stravinsky!"

Petrushka's major musical innovation lay in the bitonal effect which represented the mechanical and human elements of Petrushka's personality. The now-famous Petrushka chord is an F sharp Major arpeggio juxtaposed over a C Major arpeggio—a black note chord over a white note chord. Stravinsky knew exactly what he was doing:

> I had conceived of the music in two keys in the second tableau as Petrushka's insult to the public, and I wanted the dialogue for trumpets in two keys at the end to show that his ghost is still in-

sulting the public. I was, and am, more proud of these last pages than of anything else in the score.

Diaghilev wished to have me change the last four pizzicato chords in favor of a "tonal ending," as he so quaintly put it, though, two months later, when *Petrushka* was one of the Ballet's greatest successes, he denied he had ever been guilty of his original criticism.

Bitonality was new to the audience, and the rhythmic innovations surpassed those in *Firebird*. But the melodies in *Petrushka* were familiar. The score quotes heavily from folk tunes (at least they sound like folk tunes), from barrel organ pieces and from lilting waltzes. White specifies their origins: the first hurdy-gurdy tune is from a Russian *chanson*; the second from the French pop song, "Elle avait un jambe en bois"; the first theme of the waltz in Scene Three from Joseph Lanner's *Tanze*, Opus 165; and the waltz's second theme from Lanner's Opus 200. Stravinsky obviously had nothing against borrowing. He has always acknowledged that his theatrical ideas, like the one behind the *Rite of Spring* or the one that prompted *Histoire du Soldat*, appeared to him through dreams or in visions but that his melodic material was derived from folk songs or the music of other composers.

Petrushka was Stravinsky's first score to be published by Russischer Musik Verlag, the publishing house that had been established by Serge and Natalie Koussevitzky.

Stravinsky has written that the "primus inter pares" of the musical world between 1906 and 1912 was Arnold Schoenberg. But by 1914 it was Stravinsky whom Sir Osbert Sitwell matter-of-factly identified as "the master of the epoch." Thus, between 1912 and 1914, the center of the new musical universe had apparently shifted from Schoenberg to Stravinsky. The *Rite of Spring* made the difference.

All that began with *Firebird* and developed in *Petrushka* culminated in the *Rite of Spring*. Its spontaneity, bitonality, unconventional rhythms and irregular balance established the work as one of the artistic landmarks of its time.

The *Rite* is divided into two major sections: "The Adoration of the Earth" and "The Sacrifice." Stravinsky scored it for his largest orchestra, particularly heavy on percussion instruments: four kettledrums, small kettledrum, bass drum, tambourine, cymbals, antique cymbals, triangle, tamtam and rape guero (scratcher). The composer collaborated in the scenario with Nicolas Roerich, the painter and archeologist. In a letter to Diaghilev, Roerich wrote:

In the ballet of the *Rite of Spring* as conceived by myself and Stravinsky, my object is to present a number of scenes of earthly joy and celestial triumph as understood by the Slavs. . . . My intention is that the first set should transport us to the foot of a sacred hill, in a lush plain, where Slavonic tribes are gathered together to celebrate the spring rites. In this scene there is an old witch who predicts the future, a marriage by capture, round dances. Then comes the solemn moment. The wise elder is brought from the village to imprint his sacred kiss on the new-flowering earth. During this rite the crowd is seized with a mystic terror. . . . After this uprush of terrestrial joy, the second scene sets a celestial mystery before us. Young virgins dance in circles on the sacred hill and enchanted rocks; then they choose the victim they intend to honor. In a moment she will dance her last dance before the ancients clad in bearskins to show that the bear was man's ancestor. Then the greybeards dedicate the victim to the God Yarilo.

Many critics attribute the scenario to Stravinsky's love for the Russian spring, for the composer once said to Craft that spring, in Russia, "seemed to begin in an hour and was like the whole earth cracking." But there is another dimension to the *Rite of Spring*; it picks up where *Petrushka* left off in treating the dehumanization of man. The music suggests physical action rather than a reflective spirit. Rhythms of an intensity never heard before in Western music attempt to convey the instinctual forces forging ahead unimpeded by man's intellect and reason. The rhythm is everywhere revolutionary: when the victim dances herself to death at the close of the work, she does so in bars originally marked 3/16, 5/16, 3/16, 4/16, 5/16, 3/16, 4/16. (The score has subsequently been revised for easier readings.)

But in retrospect the most striking aspect of the *Rite of Spring* was Stravinsky's adherence to a diatonic idiom at a time when the Schoenberg school was thoroughly atonal. Stravinsky's score, generated by rhythm, uses a harmonic bass; the final cadence of the sacred dance moves from dominant to tonic, the essence of classic tonality.

The Ballet Russe first performed the *Rite of Spring* at the Théâtre des Champs Elysées on May 29, 1913. But Stravinsky says that Nijinsky choreographed it inappropriately. It is difficult to determine whether the choreography—Nijinsky's first attempt—or the music caused the commotion that night. The following account of the disturbance is taken from Stravinsky's *Expositions and Developments*:

Mild protests against the music could be heard from the very beginning of the performance. Then, when the curtain opened on the group of knock-kneed and long-braided Lolitas jumping up and down (Danse des Adolescents), the storm broke . . . I heard Florent Schmitt shout "Taisez-vous garces du seizième"; the "garces" of the sixteenth arrondissement were, of course, the most elegant ladies in Paris. The uproar continued, however, and a few minutes later I left the hall in a rage; I was sitting on the right near the orchestra and I remember slamming the door. I have never again been that angry. The music was so familiar to me; I loved it, and I could not understand why people who had not yet heard it wanted to protest in advance. I arrived in a fury backstage, where I saw Diaghilev flicking the house lights in a last effort to quiet the hall. For the rest of the performance I stood in the wings behind Nijinsky holding the tails of his *frac*, while he stood on a chair shouting numbers to the dancers, like a coxswain.

The review in *Figaro* was as negative as the response of the audience:

Bluffing the idle rich of Paris through appeals to their snobbery is a delightfully simple matter. Take the best society possible, composed of rich, simple-minded, idle people. . . . By pamphlets, newspaper articles, lectures, personal visits and all other appeals to their snobbery, persuade them that hitherto they have seen only vulgar spectacles, and are at last to know what is art and beauty. Impress them with cannibalistic formulae. They have not the slightest notion of music, literature, painting and dancing; still, they have heretofore seen under these names only a rude imitation of the real thing. Finally assure them that they are to see real dancing and hear real music. It will then be necessary to double the prices of the theater, so great will be the rush of shallow worshippers at this false shrine.

But Stravinsky's score was vindicated within a year. The discordant complexity of the harmonic texture set against the simplest themes, the artful, sophisticated instrumentation used to create the most primitive effects, the profoundly original rhythm and meter were revealed clearly at the Casino de Paris in April, 1914, when Pierre Monteux conducted *Le Sacre* again in a concert version. Without the distraction of sets and dancing, the *Rite of Spring* scored a tremendous success. Stravinsky writes:

At the end of the Danse Sacrale the entire audience jumped to its feet and cheered. I came on stage and hugged Monteux, who was a river of perspiration; it was the saltiest hug of my life. A crowd swept backstage. I was hoisted to anonymous shoulders and carried into the street and up to the Place de la Trinité. A policeman pushed his way to my side in an effort to protect me, and it was this guardian of the law Diaghilev later fixed upon in his accounts of the story: "Our little Igor now requires police escorts out of his concerts, like a prize fighter."

During the 1912–13 season, Stravinsky went to Berlin for a performance of *Firebird* and *Petrushka* which the Kaiser and Kaiserin were scheduled to attend. It was during this visit that he met Schoenberg for the first time and heard his *Pierrot Lunaire*. Stravinsky recalls in his *Dialogues*: "I was aware that this was the most prescient confrontation of my life." He met that confrontation with the *Rite of Spring*; with the triumph of this work, music with a tonal center prevailed over music that was without one. Schoenberg felt the effect immediately; after Monteux's celebrated performance he set Rainer Maria Rilke's "Vorgefühl": "I cast myself forth and remain all alone—in the greatest of storms."

In a lecture delivered at Harvard in 1939, Stravinsky acknowledged the promotional aspect of his role: "Whatever field of endeavor has fallen upon our lot, if it is true we are intellectuals, we are called upon not to cogitate but to perform."

In 1965, Stravinsky's price for conducting half a performance and part of a rehearsal was $10,000. In a letter to a friend his wife commented: "I have noticed that few people listen with attention to the music in these concerts and that, in fact, few seem to have come for that purpose. What they want is to be in his numinous presence. And although $10,000 may be a lot of money, so is Igor a lot of numen."

Chapter 12

In the years between 1914 and 1923 while Schoenberg was working out the 12-tone technique, Stravinsky was dealing with a more diffuse problem: his national identity. With the outbreak of World War I, while living comfortably in Switzerland, he composed several works based on Russian ritual and legend. Then, after the 1917 Russian Revolution, which deprived him of the income from his estates, he dissociated himself from his country altogether and committed his art to the traditions of Western Europe. Stravinsky then led the development of the neoclassical movement. Schoenberg crystallized dodecaphony and Stravinsky neoclassicism at precisely the same time. The difference between them was the fundamental one of direction: Schoenberg plunged into the future, declaring the twelve tones to be equal, while Stravinsky drew from the past, reexploring tonality as a viable language. Even so, both composers aspired to a common end: order in place of anarchy and cliché.

And both explored their paths by dramatically reduced means.

Schoenberg's gigantic orchestra for *Gurrelieder* was matched by Stravinsky's for the *Rite of Spring*. Yet before Schoenberg finally finished orchestrating *Gurrelieder* in 1911, he wrote slenderly conceived works like the Chamber Symphony, the *Georgelieder*, and several groups of piano pieces. Similarly, before Stravinsky finished the *Rite of Spring*, he composed the Three Japanese Lyrics for Soprano and Piano.

In the autobiography, Stravinsky writes that "the Three Japanese Lyrics were very close to my heart. . . . The graphic solution of problems of perspective and space shown by their art incited me to find something analogous in music." The brevity of these pieces—the longest poem is only 40 syllables and each syllable gets only one quarter note—is reminiscent of the Schoenberg and Webern pieces of the time. And in the Japanese Lyrics, Stravinsky clearly moves toward atonality. The first is tonally ambiguous although it is written with a key signature of four flats while the other two have no key signatures at all. It may well have been these pieces, as well as the similarly treated *Le Roi des Étoiles*, that prompted Debussy to comment: "One wonders into whose arms the music of our time is going to fall. The young Russian school holds out its arms; but in my view they've become as little Russian as possible. Stravinsky himself leans dangerously in the direction of Schoenberg." But Stravinsky did not proceed in that direction at this time.

Just before the war, Stravinsky returned to Russia in search of folk sources for a grand *divertissement*. In Kiev he located the Kireievsky and Afanasiev collections of folk poetry and brought them with him to Switzerland. The poetry served as a source for his wedding cantata, *Les Noces*, and for *Pribaoutki, Les Berceuses du Chat*, and *Renard*, all composed during the following few years.

Stravinsky attributes his reassertion of his Russianness, after the involvement with French Impressionism, to political events: "My profound emotion on reading the news of war, which aroused patriotic feelings and a sense of sadness at being so distant from my own country, found some alleviation in the delight in which I steeped myself in Russian folk poems."

The Stravinsky family, now including two sons and two daughters, moved into a house in Clarens, Switzerland. There the composer began to work on *Les Noces*. The ideational theme is similar to that of the *Rite of Spring*: both works focus on public ritual and away from matters of heart and mind. *Les Noces* celebrates a peasant wedding, but only in the most abstract, ritualized terms.

Stravinsky never identifies any single voice with a particular character on stage; singers and chorus continually change roles. The listener grasps bits of ritual and clichés but nothing that would individualize the characters in the ceremony. The involvement he once had with Petrushka is missing in the piece composed a few years later.

In *Les Noces*, Stravinsky's involvement is with Russia, and he captures the spirit of the Russian folk song with one pervasive motif: a minor third and a whole tone within the interval of a fourth. Four three-note figures form the skeleton of almost all the themes in *Les Noces*, a compositional principle similar to that which Schoenberg was working on at the same time.

Stravinsky's avoidance of human material continues in *Renard*, a ballet about a cock, cat, fox and goat, as well as in other works of this time which treat sparrows, geese, swans and more cats (*Les Berceuses du Chat*). Stravinsky's ultimate removal from things human is epitomized in his interest, in 1917, in the player piano. He wrote a Study for Pianola and followed that with many pianola transcriptions of his works. In an interview in the *New York Herald Tribune* in 1925, Stravinsky expressed his unbound admiration:

> There is a new polyphonic truth in the player piano. There are new possibilities. It is something more. It is not the same thing as the piano. The player piano resembles the piano but it also resembles an orchestra. . . . The soul of it is the soul of an automobile. Besides the piano, it is practical. It has a future, yes. It has its utility. Men will write for it. But it will create matter for itself.

Although the themes of his post-1914 work continue to be similar to the *Rite of Spring*, the music takes a very different turn. It is elegant, subtle and contrapuntal, and no longer depends on a stage. His rhythms grow increasingly intricate. In place of a large orchestra he chooses tones that are stark and lean.

This economy was partly due to artistic considerations—where could he go after the *Rite of Spring*? But it was also caused by financial conditions: Stravinsky wanted his music performed. (Even the Ballet Russe had serious financial problems during World War I.) The composer began to score his pieces for unusual combinations of instruments and to use these instruments in novel ways. For *Les Noces* he chose four pianos and percussion and for *Les Berceuses du Chat* a contralto and clarinets. In *Renard* he treated the voice in an unconventional buffo manner, and in *Histoire du*

Soldat called for violin, double bass, clarinet, trombone, bassoon and percussion. A single percussionist played two side drums of different sizes without snares, one side drum with snares, a bass drum, cymbals, tambourine and triangle.

Perhaps stimulated by the successful concert performance of the *Rite*, and certainly stimulated by lack of money, Stravinsky immersed himself in the folk material he brought out of Russia. Writing about the appeal of the poetry, he voiced the belief that music had no expressive powers, a concept that shocked the musical world:

"What fascinated me in this verse," he wrote in the autobiography,

> was not so much the stories, which were often crude, or the pictures and metaphors, always so deliciously unexpected, as the sequence of words and syllables, and the cadence they create, which produces an effect on one's sensibilities very closely akin to that of music. For I consider that music is, by its very nature, powerless to *express* anything at all, whether a feeling, an attitude of mind, a psychological mood, a phenomenon of nature etc. . . . *Expression* has never been an inherent property of music. This is by no means the purpose of its existence. If, as is nearly always the case, music appears to express something, this is only an illusion and not a reality. It is simply an additional attribute which, by tacit and inveterate agreement, we have lent it, thrust upon it, as a label, a convention—in short, an aspect unconsciously or by force of habit, we have come to confuse with its essential being.

Despite the fact that Stravinsky drew from the tonal past, in articulating this nonexpressive function of music he looked farther into the future than Schoenberg did during his entire life. And Stravinsky was on this path as early as 1914–15. In Three Pieces for String Quartet, he does not call the work a string quartet to emphasize a break with the traditional quartet form. (Stravinsky is reported to have said that if he had his way, he would cut out the development sections of Mozart's symphonies.) The *Pribaoutki* also avoid development; the Russian title means "Say it quickly," a game in which one person says one word, a second says another and a third still another—all very rapidly. In writing down these verses no attention is paid to the traditional rules of prosody, and Stravinsky plays with the rhythmic variety that results. In the Three Easy Pieces for Piano Duet, written for his two older children to play, a simple, unchanging ostinato in the left hand accompanies extended figurations in the right. These pieces represent the composer's first excursion, since his student days, into a non-Russian, international idiom. Later he identified them as the moment at which "neoclassicism was born."

However artistically productive the time was, Stravinsky had many trying days. Financial problems precipitated a crisis with Diaghilev. The Ballet Russe was signed for an American tour and scheduled to play the Metropolitan in New York. Stravinsky wanted to conduct his own ballets there, but although he insists that the Met wanted him, the management never sent him a contract. Just before the company's second American tour, which was marked by the same neglect, Stravinsky asked Diaghilev to boycott the engagement but Diaghilev refused. Nijinsky's new wife reports a Stravinsky visit:

> He insisted that if Vaslav [Nijinsky] were a real friend he would make it a condition to go to America only if Stravinsky was asked also. I thought this rather stretching the bonds of friendship. Stravinsky talked, raged, cried; he paced up and down the room cursing Diaghilev: "He thinks that he is the Russian Ballet himself. Our success has gone to his head. What would he be without us, without Bakst, Benois, you, myself? Vaslav, I count on you."

Nijinsky sent a wire to New York, asking for Stravinsky to be included in the arrangement, but nothing ever came of it. The Ballet Russe left for New York, with Diaghilev, Nijinsky and Ansermet, but without Stravinsky. Despite his bitterness at this, Stravinsky went to Spain to greet Diaghilev on his return; the composer has always swallowed abuse when it was practical to do so—whether it came from his father, his mother, Rimsky, Debussy or Diaghilev. On that score he was far different from Schoenberg.

The 1917 Revolution deprived Stravinsky of his property. In the same year the nurse who tended him and his children died. His favorite brother died in Russia and Nijinsky retired from dancing because of increasing insanity. The composer says:

> This period, the end of 1917, was one of the hardest I have ever experienced. Overwhelmed by the successive bereavements that I had suffered, I was also now in a position of the utmost pecuniary difficulty. The Communist Revolution, which had just triumphed in Russia, deprived me of the last resources that had still, from time to time, been reaching me from my country and I found myself, so to speak, face to face with nothing, in a foreign land and right in the middle of war.

Stravinsky enlisted the help of the Swiss writer Charles Ferdinand Ramuz, who had translated for him the Russian texts to *Renard*, *Pribaoutki* and *Les Berceuses du Chat*, to collaborate in the creation of a miniature mobile theater which would produce works accessible to people in all different countries. Stravinsky found a patron, and Ramuz agreed to write the libretto for the first work, *Histoire du Soldat*, a Faustian tale of a soldier who trades his violin for material wealth and is subsequently destroyed for having made the choice.

Just before he started work on the score, inspired by the piano reductions of jazz that Ansermet brought back from the United States, Stravinsky wrote *Ragtime* for cimbalon, nine solo instruments and percussion in 1918, and *Piano Rag-Music* for Rubinstein in 1919. And *Histoire* exhibits specifically American jazz effects. In this self-consciously non-Russian work, the composer not only makes musical reference to the United States, but quotes South American tangos, Swiss brass bands, Spanish pasadobles, Lutheran chorales and Viennese waltzes.

Although *Histoire* proved to be one of the composer's most popular works, it did not serve its original purpose. Stravinsky attributes its failure to the great influenza pandemic that attacked performers, agents and managers. He was still in financial trouble the following year; this notice appeared in *Musical America*: "Word has just come to this country that Igor Stravinsky, composer of *Petrushka* and *The Nightingale* etc., is in dire need. A cable just received from an American attaché of the embassy reads: 'Cable money to Stravinsky in desperate circumstances—care of American consul in Geneva.'"

But very soon his luck improved. Diaghilev, who had delivered Stravinsky from anonymity in 1909 by providing him with a theatrical base, came to the rescue once again. He commissioned him to string together a number of pieces then thought to be by the eighteenth-century Italian composer Giovanni Pergolesi. Diaghilev thus pointed to a rich and varied source of material, distinct from indigenous art, from which Stravinsky was to derive inspiration for the next thirty years.

Stravinsky's neoclassicism, his use of material from the past, was not an original device in music. Roman Vlad, one of Stravinsky's biographers, specifies the old *Missae Parodiae*, Bach's transcriptions of Vivaldi and Marcello, Liszt's paraphrases, and the innumerable classic theme and variations as other occasions on which musicians borrowed from the past. And in 1962, Stravinsky mentioned T. S. Eliot in this context in an interview in *The Observer* (London):

> Were Eliot and myself merely trying to refit old ships while "the other side," Webern, Schoenberg, Joyce and Klee sought new forms of travel? I think that distinction, much traded on a generation ago, has disappeared. Our era is a unity of which we are all a part. Of course, we seemed, Eliot and myself, to have made art out of the *disjecta membra*, the quotations of other poets and composers, the references to earlier styles (hints of earlier and other creation), the detritus that betokened a wreck. But we used it and anything that came to hand to rebuild. We did not invent new conveyors, new means of travel. But the true business of the artist is to rebuild old ships. He can say, in his way, only what has been said.

Although Stravinsky did not refer to Picasso in this article, the great Spanish painter also played a major role in the classicism of the 1920's. Picasso has said: "The artist is a receptacle for emotions from all over the place, from the sky, from the earth, from a scrap of paper, from a passing shape, from a spider's web. . . . Where things are concerned there are no class distinctions. We must pick out what is good for us where we find it. . . . When I am shown a portfolio of old drawings, for instance, I have no qualms about taking anything I want from them."

Stravinsky first met Picasso in 1917 when the painter came to join the Diaghilev Ballet to make sets for Satie's *Parades*. Cocteau, the librettist, introduced him into the company. It was then that he drew the first of his famous Stravinsky portraits and designed the cover for *Ragtime*.

Diaghilev's idea for *Pulcinella* was a practical one. It grew out of his success with two similar ballet projects, for he had commissioned Respighi to arrange Cimarosa for the *Astuzie Femminili* and Tommasini to arrange Scarlatti for *The Good-Humored Ladies*. The "Pergolesi" manuscripts, which included two three-act operas and twelve trio sonatas, were found in the Naples Conservatory and the British Museum.

In the autobiography, Stravinsky explains what brought him back to Diaghilev:

> The proposal that I should work with Picasso, who was to do the scenery and costumes and whose art was particularly near and dear to me, recollections of the walks together and the impressions of Naples we had shared, the great pleasure I had experienced from Massine's choreography in *The Good-Humored Ladies*—all this

combined to overcome my reluctance. For it was a delicate task to breathe new life into scattered fragments and to create a whole from the isolated pages of a musician for whom I felt a special liking and tenderness.

Not only was the score eighteenth-century; the scenario was eighteenth-century as well. Diaghilev and Massine created it from a Neapolitan manuscript dating from around 1700, which involved impersonations, mistaken identities and other devices common to opera buffa. In *Pulcinella*, several men conspire to kill the protagonist out of jealousy, but he tricks them by having a double stand in for him. At the end Pulcinella miraculously emerges, marries off all the possible couples, and keeps the lovely Pimpinella for himself.

The work consists of eight tableaux. It begins with an Overture for orchestra. The tableaux that follow adhere to the traditional eighteenth-century binary forms and are marked according to tempo: Allegro, Andantino, Scherzino, etc. Stravinsky retained the original melodies and bass lines and introduced his own tissue between, a tissue basically diatonic. There is virtually no chromatic writing and polytonal passages are equally rare. *Pulcinella*, the first Stravinsky/Diaghilev production since the *Rite of Spring*, breaks with both Romanticism and Impressionism. The public was not to be treated to rich colors and sensuous effects but to the precise lines associated with eighteenth-century music and thought.

The Russian Ballet performed *Pulcinella* at the Paris Opera House in 1920. Stravinsky was delighted by the results: "Pulcinella was one of those productions—and they are rare—where everything harmonizes, where all the elements—subject, music, dancing and artistic setting—form a coherent and homogenous whole. . . . As for Picasso, he worked miracles and I find it difficult to decide what was most enchanting—the coloring, the design, or the amazing inventiveness of this remarkable man."

Thus, in 1920, when Schoenberg wrote his first 12-tone movement, Stravinsky produced his first "neoclassic" work, a work nourished by the eighteenth-century. As with dodecaphony, the neoclassical idea in music was certainly in the air. As early as 1912, Busoni, in Berlin, had composed his *Fantasia Contrapuntistica*, a bold attempt to complete Bach's *Art of the Fugue*, and in 1920 Busoni followed his own lead in a call for a "young classicism." In a letter to music critic Paul Bekker, he demanded that the "results of all earlier experiments should be classified, exploited and mastered, and should be converted into lasting, beautiful forms."

Thus, it was reasonable that Stravinsky, separated both physically and spiritually from Russia and in close contact with artists from Western Europe, should borrow their musical forms and ideas. Ingesting melodies and utilizing structures from the past, Stravinsky went on to compose many masterpieces of the neoclassic movement.

Chapter 13

"Neoclassicism" implies an objective, detached musical style that depends on a diatonic idiom—an idiom based on the seven-note scale. The movement was anti-Romantic, repudiating the emotional, subjective music of the past, and anti-dodecaphonic as well. Composers who considered themselves part of neoclassicism revived opera buffa, with its set arias, and the oratorio, too, while avoiding grand opera and program music.

As Hauer and Webern anticipated Schoenberg's composition with twelve tones, so Ravel and Satie anticipated neoclassicism. Ravel, with his *Tombeau de Couperin*, used the old dance forms *forlane*, *rigaudon* and *minuet*, while Satie's *Socrate*, a "drame-symphonie," anticipated Stravinsky's "opera-oratorio," *Oedipus Rex*.

But Hauer, Webern, Ravel and Satie did not establish schools of musical thought. To do that required the unbridled narcissism of Schoenberg or Stravinsky. Stravinsky could not have followed Schoenberg's lead, despite several pieces that indicate he considered that direction, because Schoenberg's personality allowed room only for followers, not colleagues. Determined, therefore, to stake out his own territory, Stravinsky moved from Switzerland to France, where he "felt the pulse of the world beating most strongly."

Soon after his arrival in Paris, he met Vera de Bosset, the actress-wife of Russian painter Serge Sudeikine. Hastily, the composer asked Ramuz to send her chocolates from Switzerland, and he admits in his *Dialogues* that, in 1923, he secretly dedicated his *Octuor* to her.

In his 1918 Diary, Nijinsky writes that Stravinsky did not love Catherine as she loved him. Stravinsky's increasing estrangement from his wife, particularly after meeting Mme Sudeikine, may have motivated his new career, that of conductor and pianist. During the 1920's and 1930's, the composer spent at least half of each year on tour and spread neoclassicism throughout Europe and the United States.

His last musical ties to Russia were the folk tunes quoted in the *Symphonies of Wind Instruments*, written in 1920 in memory of Debussy. The following year, 1921, Stravinsky proclaimed his identification with the Russian artists of Western European sympathies in a letter published in *The Times* (London). The letter was prompted by Diaghilev's production of *The Sleeping Beauty* in which Vera Sudeikine appeared in the nondancing role of the Queen. Stravinsky followed his praise of Tchaikovsky with a comic opera, *Mavra*, dedicated to the Westernized Russian artists. In his dedication, Stravinsky described *Mavra* as an attack on the Wagnerian music-drama, "which represented no tradition at all and fulfilled no necessity at all from the musical point of view." But forty years later, in *Expositions*, he recalled that the major motivation for the piece came not from his opposition to the *Gesamtkunstwerk*, but from his distaste for the Russian nationalists. Calling *Mavra* a "piece of propaganda," Stravinsky told Craft:

> I wanted to show a different Russia to my non-Russian, and especially to my French, colleagues who were, I considered, saturated with the tourist office orientalism of the *maguchia kuchka*, the "powerful clique," as Stassov used to call the Five. I was, in fact, protesting against the picturesque in Russian music and against those who failed to see that the picturesque is produced by very small tricks. Tchaikovsky's talent was the largest in Russia, and with the exception of Moussorgsky's the truest.

Mavra, a one-act opera based on Pushkin's *Little House in Kolomna*, is set for soprano, mezzo-soprano, contralto, tenor and orchestra, and contains melodies from both Tchaikovsky and

Glinka. The story revolves around a Russian girl who disguises her lover as a maid and brings him into her parents' house. One day, when the parents are out, the young man shaves. Surprised by the reentry of the mother, he quickly flees. *Mavra* is divided into arias, duets and quartets in the traditional Italian style and includes bits of jazz, gypsy music and Italian bel canto. It is scored for an unusual combination of instruments, particularly heavy on winds: four clarinets, three trombones, tuba, small percussion section, two violins, viola, three cellos and three double basses.

Mavra was first produced at the Paris Opera House in June, 1922, and failed completely. Stravinsky attributed the poor reception to its having been squeezed between *Petrushka* and the *Rite of Spring*, two spectacular, romantic ballets. But he writes that he was pleased with it himself: "For my own part, I was glad to see that I had completely succeeded in realizing my musical ideas, and was, therefore, able to develop them further—this time in the domain of the symphony. I began to compose my *Octuor pour Instruments à Vent*."

The composer Alfredo Casella has singled out the *Octuor* as the quintessence of neoclassicism. It is indeed cool and intellectual in the extreme, exactly what Stravinsky himself had in mind:

> I remember what an effort it cost me to establish an ensemble of eight instruments, for they could not strike the listener's ear with a great display of tone. In order that this music should reach the ear of the public, it was necessary to emphasize the entries of several instruments, to introduce breathing space between phrases (rests), to pay particular attention to the intonation, the instrumental prosody, the accentuation—in short, to establish order and discipline in the purely sonorous scheme to which I always give precedence over elements of an emotional nature.

Such intellectuality was nowhere present in *Petrushka* or the *Rite of Spring*, where the protagonists had danced themselves to death. With *Octuor*, Stravinsky promoted the cool and heady at the expense of the warm and passionate. By 1923 an emphasis on form prevailed: dodecaphony—based on a twelve-note scale—and neoclassicism—based on a seven-note scale—were both sides of the same anti-exuberant coin.

Although Stravinsky chose an ensemble of flute, clarinet, two bassoons, two trumpets and two trombones for *Octuor*, he writes that he composed the work without any instrumentation in mind. In the *Dialogues* he tells Craft that the instrumentation only came to him later in a dream. Thus the composer had arrived at a point where abstraction engaged him above all else. No longer involved in stage spectacle or body gesture, Stravinsky made music in the purest, most intramusical terms.

In 1923, for the first time, Stravinsky conducted his own work at the Paris Opera House. Press and public attacked the piece, but Satie, in an issue of *Vanity Fair*, was among those who defended him vigorously:

> I love and admire Stravinsky because I perceive that he is a liberator. More than anyone else, he has freed the musical thought of today which is sadly in need of development.
>
> I am glad to have to recognize this, I, who have suffered so much from the Wagnerian oppression, or rather, from that of the Wagnerians. For, a few years ago, the genius of Wagner was miserably admired by the combined Mediocrity and Ignorance of the crowd. . . .
>
> Wagner's dictatorship was the sole power and odiously dominated the general taste. An era of desolation, during which the classics themselves seemed blasted. . . . Today things have changed: a happy sunlight illumines the recesses of our souls.

The year in which Stravinsky conducted *Octuor* in Paris, 1923, Diaghilev presented the ballet *Les Noces*. Although Stravinsky had begun this work almost ten years earlier, he finished orchestrating it only several months before the premiere. A grand dinner for Stravinsky held on a barge in the Seine attracted as guests many luminaries of high society and art, including Picasso, Diaghilev, Cocteau and the Princesse de Polignac. With *Les Noces*, Stravinsky could bring the world to his feet; with *Octuor* he received silence or disdain. But the composer did not change his route: a sober intellectualism displaced the Romanticism of an earlier time.

In 1923 Stravinsky became the center of considerable attention. *La Revue Musicale* devoted an entire issue to him, with famous musicians attacking or defending him. And Stravinsky began to justify his old works on the basis of the new ideology. It is interesting to see that, in this journal, Michel Georges Michel quotes the composer as saying that when he wrote the *Rite of Spring*, the musical idea preceded the theatrical vision: "Note well that this idea came from the music, the music did not come from the idea. My work is architectonic, not anecdotal; objective, not descriptive construction."

And in 1924, in *The Arts*, Stravinsky again emphasized form:

> I turn to form because I do not conceive or feel the true emotive force except under coordinated musical sensation. This sort of music has no other aim than to be sufficient in itself. In general, I con-

sider that music is only able to solve musical problems, and neither the literary nor the picturesque can be in music of real interest. The play of musical elements is the thing.

At this time, Stravinsky began a new career as a pianist. For his first work he composed the Concerto for Piano and Wind Instruments, which uses the piano percussively in a three-part toccata-like theme reminiscent of Scarlatti and Bach. The winds, supplemented by double basses and timbals, borrow and adapt the toccata theme. The composer introduced the piece at a Koussevitzky concert in Paris during the spring of 1924 and played it forty times during the next five years.

After the Piano Concerto, Stravinsky wanted another touring piece. He composed a piano sonata, of which he wrote, "I gave it that name without, however, giving it the classical form such as we find it in Clementi, Haydn and Mozart. . . ." Bach, not Mozart, pervades the piece. Stravinsky played the sonata at a 1925 festival in Venice sponsored by the recently formed International Society for Contemporary Music, an outgrowth of Schoenberg's defunct private concerts. Although Schoenberg attended the event, the two musicians did not meet. The Piano Sonata's eighteenth-century contrapuntal style provoked much talk of a "return to Bach."

Schoenberg responded with his *Three Satires*, written during 1925–26. The second, "Vielseitigkeit," is a mirror canon ridiculing Stravinsky:

> But who's this beating the drum?
> It's little Modernsky!
> He's had his hair cut in an old fashioned queue,
> And it looks quite nice,
> Like real false hair—
> Like a wig—
> Just like (at least Little Modernsky thinks so)
> Just like Father Bach!

Stravinsky has confided to friends that Schoenberg's attack hurt him deeply, far more than any attack from the press. To the press attacks, Stravinsky responded with a now-famous manifesto, "L'Avertissement," published in the journal *The Dominant*, in which he discussed neoclassicism:

> There is much talk nowadays of a reversion to classicism, and works believed to have been composed under the influence of the so-called classical modes are labeled neoclassic. . . .
> It is difficult for me to say whether this classification is correct

or not. With works that are worthy of attention, and have been written under the obvious influence of the music of the past, does not the matter consist in a quest that goes deeper than in a mere imitation of the so-called classical idiom? . . .

If those who label as neoclassic the works belonging to the latest tendency in music mean by that label that they detect in them a wholesome return to this formal idea, well and good. . . .

Many American composers embraced the Stravinsky aesthetic. In 1921, Aaron Copland began to study composition at the Fontainebleau in Paris under Nadia Boulanger, a formidable proponent of Stravinsky's ideals. In 1925 Stravinsky toured the United States and appeared in New York, Boston, Chicago, Philadelphia, Cleveland, Detroit and Cincinnati. Within a few years, Leopold Stokowski, under the auspices of the League of Composers, conducted the *Rite of Spring* and *Les Noces.* The Metropolitan Opera produced *Petrushka* and *The Nightingale.* During the tour Stravinsky made contact with a commercial recording company and arranged to write his Serenade in A, the divertimento in which each movement would be the length of one 78-r.p.m. disc.

In 1927, Roger Sessions paid tribute to the now thoroughly Westernized Stravinsky in *Modern Music*:

> Younger men are dreaming of an entirely different kind of music —a music which derives its power from forms beautiful and significant by virtue of inherent musical weight rather than from intensity of utterance; a music whose impersonality and self-sufficiency preclude the exotic; which takes its impulse from the realities of a passionate logic; which, in its authentic freshness of mood, is the reverse of the ironic, and, in its very aloofness from the concrete preoccupations of life, strives rather to contribute form, design, a vision of order and harmony.

Neoclassicism attracted composers in all countries. Hindemith, earlier a follower of Schoenberg, adopted the neotonal, neoclassic idea. Bartók incorporated his Hungarian folk material into a neoclassic frame, and in the United States, Copland and Sessions were only two of the growing anti-dodecaphonic school. Stravinsky went on to create the major, mature pieces of his second period: *Oedipus Rex, Apollon Musagète, Le Baiser de la Fée,* the *Symphony of Psalms* and *Perséphone,* all written between 1927 and 1934. Each was composed for a practical purpose. He wrote *Oedipus* in collaboration with Cocteau to celebrate Diaghilev's twentieth year in the theater. The American patron Elizabeth Sprague Coolidge commissioned *Apollon Musagète,* French impresario Ida Rubinstein *The Fairy's Kiss* and *Perséphone,* and Koussevitzky, then conductor of the Boston Symphony Orchestra, the *Symphony of Psalms* in commemoration of the orchestra's fiftieth anniversary. The pieces were all characterized by restraint: stage effects were static and many musical ideas were derivative. A Capriccio for Piano and Orchestra, written during the same period to provide himself with another piece to perform, not only brings to mind the seventeenth-century composer Praetorius, who used the same title, but also Beethoven, Tchaikovsky and Carl Maria von Weber.

Stravinsky sought a static quality in all of these works. In *Oedipus* he uses Latin, a "monumental" language, and a narrator to tell the audience just what is going to happen—in the style of the classical Greek chorus, reducing the stage action to a minimum. His harmony often rests on a single chord for many measures and the rhythmic alterations are not more ambitious than moving from 3/4 to 4/4. In *Apollon Musagète,* the language is predominantly diatonic and the orchestra is limited to strings. For the *Symphony of Psalms,* Stravinsky uses another unusual orchestra, devoid of violins and violas, and adds a chorus to balance it. *Perséphone,* based on Gide's "Hymn to Demeter," imposed an additional limitation: the title role was to be assumed by Mme Rubinstein herself, who could not sing and would not dance. Stravinsky had her speak and mime the role.

Although these works were among the most lyrical and spiritual of Stravinsky's career, the initial response was primarily negative. Diaghilev agreed with the cool audience and branded *Oedipus* as "un cadeau très macabre." The other works did not fare much better. In 1934, when European commissions were about to run dry, Stravinsky issued the following "Manifesto," a defensive Introduction to *Perséphone*:

> This score, as it is written and as it must remain in the musical archives of our time, forms an indissoluble whole with the tendencies repeatedly asserted in my previous works. . . . It is a sequel to *Oedipus Rex,* the *Symphony of Psalms* and to a whole progression of works whose musical autonomy is in no way affected by the absence of a stage spectacle. . . . Nothing of all this originates in a caprice of my own. I am on a perfectly sure road. One does not criticize anybody or anything that is functioning. A nose is not manufactured: a nose just is. Thus too, is my art.

Nevertheless, *Perséphone* received only three performances, plus an official rejection for its composer: the Institut de France appointed Florent Schmitt to the post of director (vacant since the death of Paul Dukas). Stravinsky had made it clear that he wanted the job; he and his wife even became French citizens, a requirement for the position.

In Russia, Stravinsky's reception was even worse than in France. During the 1920's, when the artistic life of the Soviet Union had been bold and experimental, the composer was still held in high regard. The chief music theorist, Boris Asafiev, promoted him with enthusiasm. But the situation changed radically in 1932 when Stalin became increasingly distrustful of foreigners, an attitude that gave rise to the Moscow purges. The political xenophobia affected art: the Union of Soviet Composers took over Russian music and began its own music journal, *Sovietskaya Muzyka*, the following year. Its premise was socialist realism and its musicologist, Arnold Alshvang, repudiated Asafiev on Stravinsky, calling the expatriate "an important and near comprehensive artistic ideologist of the imperialist bourgeoisie."

Stravinsky was hurt by this and all the other criticism. Samuel Dushkin, a young violinist for whom the composer wrote the Violin Concerto and the *Duo Concertante* during the early 1930's, said: "I sensed very soon something tense and anguished about him which made one want to comfort and reassure him."

But this aspect of himself Stravinsky rarely showed to the world. His haughty manner continued unabated and was given full expression in the *Perséphone* manifesto. Nevertheless, he seemed to have lost his way; Diaghilev's death, in 1929, may have led to a lessening of his creative energy. The fact that at the end of 1934 Stravinsky could find the time to write his autobiography indicates that neoclassicism had ceased to provide much impetus for him.

Stravinsky often said of himself: "I am a Maker. I am a Doer. I am an inventor of music." But turning to a book of memoirs did not sound as if he meant that any more.

Chapter 14

By the mid-1930's, composers everywhere were classicizing. After Aaron Copland, other American musicians flocked to Boulanger. During 1935–36, Stravinsky himself taught one class a month at the École Normale, where Boulanger presided over two classes a week. A pupil, Maurice Perrin, recalls that

> under the influence of Nadia Boulanger, nearly all of us admired Stravinsky with an almost religious fervor. . . . What struck us most was his air of intense seriousness. . . . Sometimes he would sit at the piano and try to improve a certain passage. It was at such moments that he would astonish me most. He did not say: do this, use this or that chord; no: he would play a chord, listen to it, change a note, listen again, change another note, go back to the earlier chord, alter a different note etc., all the time listening with the utmost attention. . . . The result of these essays at the piano left us amazed; the fourth or fifth attempt would produce an admirable chord, of such surprising beauty that none of us could have invented it. (Stravinsky used to speak, in such cases, precisely of inventing a chord.)

Walter Piston, Elliott Carter, Virgil Thomson and Marc Blitz-stein were among the famous Boulanger pupils. Their accessible, melodic music, unencumbered by harsh dissonance, drowned out dodecaphony in the United States. The Boulanger school had its counterparts in New England: Harold Shapero, Irving Fine and Arthur Berger taught at Harvard where Leonard Bernstein was a student. At Tanglewood, in Lenox, Massachusetts, Aaron Copland led the "neoclassic" school, and Howard Hanson was director of the Eastman School of Music in Rochester, New York. Vladimir Ussachevsky has said that a student at Eastman could not hear any Schoenberg, Webern or Berg during the late thirties and early forties.

Stravinsky was delighted with the Americans' attention and, in the autobiography, complimented their taste:

> The serious interest of the Americans in music is displayed, among other ways, in the judicious selection of those to whom they apply for instruction. A large number of young people have come to France to complete their musical education—indeed, since the War, this has been almost a tradition. . . .

In 1935, with a sympathetic public awaiting him, Stravinsky returned to the United States to undertake a second American tour; *Time* magazine covered the story. In 1936, the composer began negotiations with Lincoln Kirstein and Edward Warburg for a ballet, *The Card Party*, for the newly formed American Ballet Company. And in 1937, *Jeu de Cartes* was produced at the Metro-politan Opera House with Balanchine choreographing and Stra-vinsky conducting. *Jeu de Cartes* was accompanied by *Apollon Musagète* and a newly choreographed production of *Le Baiser de la Fée*, both also by Balanchine.

In 1938, millionaire Robert Bliss paid Stravinsky $1,000 to write a concerto, the *Dumbarton Oaks*, to celebrate Bliss's thirtieth wedding anniversary; Bliss followed this with an even more hand-some commission, $2,500, to commemorate the fiftieth anniversary of the Chicago Symphony Orchestra, a work to be ready for the 1940–41 season. Stravinsky's last European commission had been in 1933.

In 1939, before he began work on the Symphony in C for Bliss and Chicago, Stravinsky received the Charles Eliot Norton profes-sorship at Harvard, given annually to men who have achieved high international distinction in the arts. Stravinsky, the first musician to be so honored, received $10,000 to deliver six lectures.

Stravinsky with American Composers during a rehearsal for Les Noces.
(From left to right: Samuel Barber, Stravinsky, Lukas Foss,
Aaron Copland, Roger Sessions)
DON HUNSTEIN

The late 1930's, attractive years for the composer in the United States, were especially grim for him in Europe. Not only had commissions stopped flowing, but in 1939 *La Revue Musicale* devoted an issue to him which was harshly critical. And personal tragedy struck in incredible profusion: between November, 1938, and June, 1939, Stravinsky's mother, wife and daughter died. With few meaningful ties left in Europe, Stravinsky moved to the United States. Vera de Bosset joined him a few months later. They married and settled in Los Angeles, in the heart of the movie community, just a short distance from Arnold Schoenberg.

Stravinsky writes that the Symphony in C reminds him of the unhappiest period of his life. He had been in poor health when he accepted the Bliss commission and did so to pay the medical bills for his wife and daughter, both of whom were in a tuberculosis sanitarium near Paris. The composer, too, became ill. Shortly after *The Card Party*'s premiere, doctors discovered a lesion in his left lung and ordered him to join his family in the sanitarium. But he refused and worked on the *Dumbarton Oaks* piece and the Symphony in C. Although Stravinsky borrows nothing specifically from Franz Josef Haydn, the musicologist Edward Cone has demonstrated, in an analysis published in 1963, how the spirit of Haydn pervades the work. Cone points out that the traditional framework is retained, with diatonic melodies, metric regularity, harmonic simplicity and typical patterns. But he adds that Stravinsky injects sudden harmonic shifts, persistent but mild dissonances and his own distinctive instrumental sound.

American commissions for Stravinsky dried up during World War II, so he turned to the film industry; but all his efforts there failed. A score for a film, *The Moon Is Down*, based on a short novel by John Steinbeck, about the Nazi invasion of Norway, was rejected; so he converted it to *Four Norwegian Moods*. Another with a Russian setting had to be converted to *Scherzo à la Russe*. Still another for Orson Welles's *Jane Eyre* became the middle movement of the *Ode*, and the music he wrote for Franz Werfel's *Song of Bernadette* was salvaged as the second movement of the Symphony in Three Movements.

But Stravinsky kept hammering away because he needed money: "I have never regarded poverty as attractive," he writes. "I do not want to be buried in the rain, unattended as Mozart was. . . . The very image of Bartók's poverty-stricken demise, to mention only one of my less fortunate colleagues, was enough to fire my ambition to earn every penny from a society that failed in its duty to Mozart."

Stravinsky arranged the *Firebird* as a love ballad, "Summer Moon," so that it would turn up on juke boxes and deliver him large royalties. He wrote a circus polka for Barnum and Bailey and the *Ebony Concerto* for Woody Herman among other efforts to tap Tin Pan Alley.

But even Stravinsky became enmeshed in the production of "meaningful" and "relevant" music. The Symphony in Three Movements, which he conducted at Carnegie Hall in 1946, shows the power that socialist realism exerted on one so committed to Western formalism. Stravinsky writes that the first movement was inspired by a documentary film of "scorched earth tactics in China," and the episode for clarinet, piano and strings was conceived "as a series of instrumental conversations to accompany a cinematographic scene showing the Chinese people scratching and digging in their fields." The second movement came from the rejected *Song of Bernadette* score, and the third, the composer continues, was partly a "musical reaction to the newsreels and documentaries that I had seen of goose-stepping soldiers," while the latter part of the movement was associated "with the rise of the Allies after the overturning of the war machine."

In 1945, Stravinsky became an American citizen and signed a contract with the firm of Boosey and Hawkes, who took over all of his works published by Édition Russe de Musique. The composer was bitter about the lack of a U.S./Russia copyright agreement which prevented him from collecting royalties on his earlier, popular pieces. To rectify this, he re-orchestrated these frequently played compositions in order to collect payment on the revised versions. Among them were *Petrushka, Symphonies of Wind Instruments, Apollon Musagète, Pulcinella, Oedipus Rex, Symphony of Psalms, Le Baiser de la Fée, Octuor* and *The Nightingale*. But the sparer orchestrations of the 1940's did not compete with the lusher treatments of his younger days and conductors generally preferred to use the original scores. That he devoted his time to re-orchestrating old pieces indicated the artistic bankruptcy threatening him at that time.

In 1946 Stravinsky received his first European commission since *Perséphone*; Paul Sacher asked for a concerto for orchestra. Stravinsky's letter to Sacher about the Concerto in D reveals his depression at that time: ". . . What can be said other than that the work is composed for a string orchestra (that—one will see immediately), that it is in three movements (that—one will read in your programs in any case), that it is not in the least atonal (but that—don't you think that the public should have the pleasure of discovering this for themselves?)" Thus, in 1946, Stravinsky appeared to be in an aesthetic impasse. In 1969, Lukas Foss described his own impasse in similar circumstances: "Neoclassicism—the pouring of new musical wine into old formal bottles—was a dead end."

But before Stravinsky found the solution, he wrote a work which represents the culmination of his interest in eighteenth-century music. In 1947, at the Chicago Art Institute, Stravinsky saw Hogarth's prints depicting *The Rake's Progress* and thought he might use them as a series of tableaux for his first opera in English. His neighbor, Aldous Huxley, recommended W. H. Auden as librettist and Auden asked his friend the poet Chester Kallman to collaborate with him. Boosey and Hawkes agreed to finance the project and Stravinsky began work in 1948. In an interview before the premiere in September, 1951, the librettists said that they considered operatic tradition had been carried by Verdi, Puccini and others to a point at which it had exhausted itself and thus they had retreated to the eighteenth century for inspiration. So did Stravinsky. During the entire period of the composition of the work, he listened repeatedly to Mozart's *Così fan Tutte*.

The premiere in Venice was a star-studded event. Mme Stravinsky, in a charmingly malicious tone, reports that Boulanger was there carrying Stravinsky's valises and the rest of the world seemed to share Boulanger's adoration. But the glitter could not hide the failure that many saw in *The Rake's Progress*. Even Virgil Thomson, an ex-pupil of Boulanger's, has described the story as "an incredible mélange of *Little Red Riding Hood, Dr. Faustus* and *Oedipus Rex* . . . in which the hero murders not his father but the woman in his motherly sweetheart and marries, in the form of a bearded lady, his father's image." Thomson suggests that the score did not compensate for the libretto.

In 1948, still revising old works, Stravinsky met his new Diaghilev, the bright, young conductor Robert Craft, and the composer's life took a turn. As Diaghilev had pointed him to Pergolesi and the eighteenth century, so Craft directed the sixty-six-year-old musician to Schoenberg and his disciples Webern and Berg.

Just after Stravinsky crystallized his plans for *The Rake's Progress*, Craft wrote to him asking him for the then unobtainable score for the *Symphonies of Wind Instruments*. Stravinsky replied that he was finishing a new version of the piece and would like to have the pleasure of conducting it himself. Craft, director of a small chamber ensemble, the Chamber Art Society, wrote that he had no money to offer him. But Stravinsky—obviously anxious for some musical action—uncharacteristically answered that he would do it for nothing. They first met in Washington, D.C., where Stravinsky was introduced to Craft by Auden. Craft, according to his own testimony, was overwhelmed:

> On the subject of Stravinsky I lived and breathed a mimiety, as Coleridge would call it, enough to perturb anyone of my acquaintance. I must have been guilty of displaying my admiration to Stravinsky, but I also must have shown genuine knowledge of his music, for he invited me to come to Hollywood to stay in his house, and to accomplish certain tasks for him. I did go there, I became famulas. . . .
>
> When I first moved there Los Angeles was divided, like the rest of the musical world, into twin hegemonies of Stravinsky and Schoenberg. The dividing line was Los Angeles' and the world's doing, of course, not the masters . . . the fact remains that they were kept separate and isolated. Paris and Vienna had crossed the world with them, establishing small and exceedingly provincial Viennas and Parises separated by only ten miles of Hollywood no man's land, but as far apart as ever. Musicians came from all over the world to visit them, not mentioning to one composer their meetings with the other. . . .

And so a curious relationship began between Stravinsky, his wife and Robert Craft, in which identities spilled over onto one another: the writings of all three seem to emerge from the same pen. Friends have reported that Craft will anticipate what Stravinsky will say and that Stravinsky will consider an idea to be his when Craft articulated it only moments before. The Craft/Stravinsky conversations, published in the late 1950's and through the 1960's, reveal the extraordinary intimacy of this union. (Stravinsky had used other people as media before: the autobiography and *Poetics of Music* were both written through other men.)

Thus Stravinsky made use of a virtuoso in the English language—Robert Craft—to express his thoughts to the American public. But it is wrong to conclude from this fact that the young and erudite Craft played the sole and controlling role in Stravinsky's shift from neoclassicism to serialism.

On Friday, June 13, 1951, shortly before *The Rake's Progress* premiere, an event of enormous consequence occurred: Arnold Schoenberg died.

Schoenberg's death set into motion a chain of events which led Stravinsky to abandon neoclassicism and to embrace what he refers to as "seriality," just as almost half a century before, Rimsky-Korsakov's death had led him to abandon a Germanic structure and adopt the style of the Rimsky orchestra. While the prime innovator of a technique is alive, Stravinsky seems unable to adopt that man's idea; hubris prevents him from doing so. But once that formidable figure is dead, Stravinsky can readily incorporate and assimilate his technique without the slightest loss of identity. The adoption of the serial idea by the giant of the neoclassic movement has been characterized by Hans Keller as "the most profound surprise in the history of music," and by others as a form of prostitution.

A surprise, perhaps, but not prostitution. It is important to note that Stravinsky never deprecated either Schoenberg or dodecaphony. As early as February, 1913, in an interview in London's *Daily Mail*, he attacked Vienna for ignoring Schoenberg, "one of the greatest creative spirits of our era." And, as late as 1939, when neoclassicism was at its peak and dodecaphony anathema everywhere, Stravinsky spoke highly of Schoenberg at Harvard:

> Whatever opinion one may hold about the music of Arnold Schoenberg (to take as an example a composer evolving along lines essentially different from mine, both aesthetically and technically), whose works have frequently given rise to violent reactions or ironic smiles—it is impossible for a self-respecting mind equipped with genuine musical culture not to feel that the composer of *Pierrot Lunaire* is fully aware of what he is doing and that he is not trying to deceive anyone. He adopted the musical system that suited his needs and, within this system, he is perfectly consistent with himself, perfectly coherent. One cannot dismiss music that one dislikes by labelling it cacophony.

Stravinsky's motivating artistic credo does not lie in "impressionism," "neoclassicism" or "serialism." "Rape," he has claimed, "may be justified by the creation of a child." Thus Stravinsky, a great polyphonist and profoundly original creator of rhythms and new sounds, "raped" Schoenberg and Webern in the early fifties. He even raped their heritage. In a 1966 film produced by Leacock and Pennebaker, Stravinsky pointed out a photograph of Wagner in his studio and said: "I have Wagner in my head. I have Wagner in my ears. I think very much more of Wagner today than I did twenty years ago."

But his musical identity has never been in question. The serial works are as Stravinskyan as the impressionist and neoclassic pieces. Jean Cocteau recognized this as early as 1922 when writers and musicians attacked the composer for his conversion from the grand impressionistic works to the spare, lean, neoclassic sound: In *La Revue Musicale*, Cocteau wrote:

> There is no disorder in this Slavic genius. He sounds his organs, takes care of his muscles and never loses his head. He knows that an artist who spends his whole life in the same costume ceases to interest us. Consequently he transforms himself, changes his skin and emerges new in the sun, unrecognizable by those who judge a work from its outside.

Stravinsky did not effect either change overnight. In *Themes and Episodes* he describes what happened:

> I have had to survive two crises as a composer, although as I continue to move from work to work, I was not aware of either of them as such, or indeed, of any momentous change. The first—the loss of Russia and its language of words as well as of music—affected every circumstance of my personal no less than my artistic life, which made recovery more difficult. Only after a decade of samplings, experiments, amalgamations, did I find the path to *Oedipus Rex* and the *Symphony of Psalms*. Crisis Number Two was brought on by the natural outgrowing of the special incubator in which I wrote *The Rake's Progress* (which is why I did not use Auden's beautiful *Delia* libretto; I could not continue in the same strain, could not compose a sequel to the *Rake*, as I would have had to do.) The period of adjustment was only half as long as this time, but as I look back on it I am surprised at how long I continued to straddle my "styles." Was it because one has to unlearn as well as to learn, and at seventy the unlearning is more difficult?

Some of Stravinsky's followers felt betrayed by the composer's shift to the serial idea; neoclassicism and dodecaphony had too long been promulgated as polar opposites with each side fighting for the other's annihilation. But many more composers followed Stravinsky's lead.

Chapter 15

Polyphony reasserted itself in Stravinsky's music even before he met Robert Craft. Just before *The Rake's Progress*, he composed the contrapuntal ballet *Orpheus*, and the weighty, polyphonic Mass. But the death of Schoenberg, who had arrogated to himself leadership of the 12–tone movement, and the goading of Craft precipitated his actual conversion to the serial procedure, which he treated with increasing comprehensiveness from that time on. Stravinsky's appropriation of the musical system that originated with Schoenberg did not, however, imply an appropriation of Schoenberg's expressive, Romantic style. Stravinsky repudiated the rhetoric and gesture of Schoenberg; referring to the Violin Concerto, Opus 36, he told Craft:

> The pathos is last century's and since pathos is created by language, the language in essence must be last century's too; harmonize the second movement in a purely Brahmsian manner—you have only to move a few notes over a bit—and the theme is happily

restored to its true habitat. Schoenberg is the evolutionary center but only up to a period many years before this concerto.

So Stravinsky by-passed Schoenberg in favor of Webern.

Craft attributes what he refers to as Stravinsky's "deep impression" of the serial technique to his hearing Webern's Quartet, Opus 22, several times in January and February, 1952. In April the composer began the Cantata for Soprano, Tenor, Female Chorus and Orchestra, in which he first used the row technique but limited his row to less than twelve notes. Stravinsky's self-conscious adoption of the serial technique is not only apparent from the structure of the work but from the highly technical language he uses in the program note; this excerpt describes one of the ricercars:

> . . . the piece begins with a one-bar introduction by the flutes and cello, the statement of the canonic subject which is the subject of the whole piece. This subject is repeated by the tenor over a recitative style accompaniment of oboes and cello, in original form, retrograde form (or cancrizans, which means that its notes are heard in reverse order, in this case, in a different rhythm), inverted form and finally, in retrograde inversion. . . .

But the new technique did not interfere with the old sound: Stravinsky's interest in sonority continued to compete with his interest in pitch, and the repetition of small phrases, brought about by the use of vocal works with repeated refrains, motivated the repetition of small phrases of music, a feature that Bartók noted in early Stravinsky scores. In *In Memoriam Dylan Thomas*—Stravinsky was planning to write an opera with Thomas when he died—the composer set the line "Rage, rage against the dying of the light" almost identically four different times. In addition to the repeated refrain, a two-bar instrumental phrase occurs seven times: as Introduction, Ritornelli between each verse, and Coda. The non-developmental, mosaic-like structure of the *Rite of Spring* and *The Nightingale* persists in Stravinsky's late serial work.

In Memoriam Dylan Thomas, the Septet, and *Three Songs from William Shakespeare*, written just after the Cantata, are all based on a row limited to fewer than twelve notes. But in the *Canticum Sacrum* of 1955, Stravinsky adopted the entire chromatic scale in his first comprehensive 12-tone work.

Based on the Old Testament and scored for tenor, baritone, chorus and orchestra, the *Canticum Sacrum* was commissioned by and heard at the ISCM Festival in Venice, the same auspices under which Stravinsky introduced his "Bach-like" Sonata in 1925. The first movement of the *Canticum Sacrum* pronounces God's commandment and the last His fulfillment. The last is treated by a cancrizans of the first, making the piece not only cyclical in its form but suggestive of a literal reversal of time. Rhythms and pitch flow backward as easily as forward.

In a speech celebrating Stravinsky's eightieth birthday, Babbitt referred to the significance of the *Canticum Sacrum* and Stravinsky's use of the 12-tone row:

"There is little point, in the name of discretion, in attempting to minimize the results of the appearance of an incontrovertibly 12-tone work by Stravinsky. . . . That Igor Stravinsky should now be creating works which were instances of a musical system originally associated with the name of Arnold Schoenberg, appeared to destroy a fundamental preconception of how the activity of contemporary music has long since been compartmentalized and assigned, and how the issues had been patly and permanently drawn. Composers, presumably, are competitors, and never colleagues; their primary activity is that of consolidating their holdings while attempting to depreciate the value of the holdings of other composers."

One musicologist maintained that Stravinsky's use of dodecaphony was a way to mourn Schoenberg's death, while another ridiculed the serialists: "There is great swagger about this conversion which the partisans celebrate in the musical equivalent of 'from log cabin to the White House motif.'" But Stravinsky was not deterred; he confirmed his allegiance to 12-tone writing with his next work, *Agon,* written in close collaboration with Balanchine. *Agon* begins diatonically, turns chromatic and 12-tone, and then returns to the original diatonic bars. Stressing his interest in the number 12, Stravinsky arranged twelve movements in four groups of three and prescribed the choreography for twelve dancers. The New York City Ballet presented the piece in 1957; it has remained popular in the repertoire ever since.

Despite the fact that the same popularity does not hold for Stravinsky's nonchoreographed serial pieces—they still receive strikingly few performances—serialism won the battle in Stravinsky's mind. *Threni: Id Est Lamentationes Jeremiae Prophetae* no longer presents the serial portion framed between diatonic passages, as did *Canticum Sacrum* and *Agon.* In *Threni* the original thematic idea is sung by the soprano in the Introduction with the alto's theme the inversion of the original theme. The whole work is based on a series derived from this thematic idea.

Stravinsky has identified his next work, *Movements for Piano and Orchestra*, as the "cornerstone" of his late period, as *Oedipus* was the cornerstone of his middle period. With *Movements* he extends the serial principle into the other elements of music: "My polyrhythmic combinations," he told Craft, "are meant to be heard vertically," and he cited as a parallel the second Agnus Dei in Josquin's *Missa l'homme armé*. Babbitt celebrated Stravinsky's *Movements*: "Never before have his linear—and above all—his ensemble rhythms been so intricate. . . . Never before have registral, timbral—and resultingly—dynamic elements been so manifestly ordered and organized."

After *Movements*, Stravinsky wrote a few very short, concentrated pieces: the *Epitaphium für das Grabmal des Prinzen Max Egon zu Furstenberg*, the patron of the Webern-inspired Donaueschingen Festival, and a Double Canon in memory of Raoul Dufy. Each is serial and lasts only one minute and sixteen seconds. Even the weightier work that followed, *A Sermon, A Narrative and a Prayer*, one of Stravinsky's most lyrical serial works, lasts only sixteen minutes. The piece is divided into two sections, both of which are followed by the same refrain: "And the substance of things hoped for, the evidence of things not seen, is faith. And our Lord is a consuming fire."

In 1961 Stravinsky received a commission by NBC to write a musical play with choreography by Balanchine. He spoke to Craft about writing music for television:

> Visually it offers every advantage over stage opera, but the saving of musical time interests me more than anything visual. This new musical economy was the one specific medium which guided my conception of the Flood. Because the suspension of visualizations can be instantaneous, the composer may dispense with the afflatus of overtures, connecting episodes, curtain music. I have used only one or two notes to punctuate each stage in the Creation, for example, and so far, I have not been able to imagine the work on the operatic stage because the speed is so uniquely cinematic.

Stravinsky wove a strong tonal feeling into this serial score through the use of certain "harmonic" intervals. He did the same in his next work, *Abraham and Isaac*, a sacred ballad in Hebrew for the Israel Festival Committee. In his notes he defends these harmonic intervals: "Octaves, fifths and double intervals can be found but they are not in contradiction to the serial basis of composition, being the result of concordances from the several serial forms, or what I call serial verticals."

With *Variations*, written in memory of his friend Aldous Huxley, Stravinsky attacks his unresponsive listener in much the same manner as he did in connection with *Perséphone* ("I am on a perfectly sure road. One does not criticize anything or anybody that is functioning."): in referring to the density of the extraordinarily complex *Variations*, he touches on the question of musical information and reasserts his strong anti-Romantic attitude:

> The question of length (duration) is inseparable from that of depth and/or height (content). But whether full, partly full, or empty, the musical statements of the *Variations* are concise, I prefer to think, rather than short. They are, whatever one thinks, a radical contrast to the prolix manner of speech of our concert life: and there lies the difficulty, mine with you no less than yours with me.

During the middle and late 1960's, Stravinsky continued to write in memory of many dead: the *Elegy for JFK*, an *Introitus for T. S. Eliot*, and the *Requiem Canticles* for several friends. And for his wife, he composed *The Owl and the Pussycat*. In 1967, he served as the subject of *Bravo Stravinsky*, written by Craft in collaboration with photographer Arnold Newman. Craft asked the composer:

> R.C. Having composed with series for so many years now, are you aware of any compulsiveness in certain combinations of numbers?
> I.S. All composers eventually become obsessed with numbers, I suspect, that rapport expressed between them being so much greater than expressions of rapport in reality. I cannot explain this to non-musicians. . . . It may be that my love of combining twos, threes, fours and sixes is compulsive, and that I am behaving in music like the man who has to lock his door three times or step on all of the cracks of the sidewalk. . . .

Craft's question and Stravinsky's reply bring the reader back to Schoenberg's magical use of numbers and to the impetus behind his treatment of the twelve notes of the chromatic scale.

Since the mid-1960's, much new music has been produced that has little to do with numbers or order. In interviews published in *The New York Review of Books*, Stravinsky depreciates the new trends; referring to the work of Karlheinz Stockhausen, he says he is bored with these "note-clumps and silences." Suggesting that the resources of serial writing have not yet even been tapped, Stravinsky has maintained that "those younger colleagues who already regard 'serial' as an indecent word, in their claim to have gone far beyond, are, I think, greatly in error."

Stravinsky and Robert Craft
DON HUNSTEIN

An anti-Stravinsky cynic might ask: If Stravinsky were to outlive Stockhausen, might he not create "note-clumps and silences" just as he appropriated Rimsky's orchestra after Rimsky's death and Schoenberg's series after Schoenberg's death? There is little doubt that he would not. Stravinsky's need to control his material is too great to allow him to embrace the "aleatoric" idea. The importance of chance in music, probably initiated by John Cage and adopted by Stockhausen and many others, has culminated in an approach to art in which significance lies only in what the spectator perceives, because the only meaning found in the work is that imposed upon it by the outside. But Stravinsky's self-conscious commitment to form is diametrically opposed to the negation of it. Always striving for the ultimate in form, Stravinsky lent added weight to the serial procedure with the choice of many sacred subjects for his serial compositions.

In *The Observer*, on his eightieth birthday, Stravinsky remarked:

> I was born to causality and determinism and I have survived to probability theory and chance. I was educated by the simple "fact": the trigger one squeezed was what shot the gun; and I have had to learn that, in fact, the universe of anterior contributing possibilities was responsible. . . .
>
> I do not understand the composer who says we must analyze the evolutionary tendency of the musical situation and go from there. I have never consciously analyzed any musical "situation" and I can "go" only where my musical appetites lead me.

III. VARÈSE AND OTHER MUSICAL CURRENTS

Chapter 16

The revolution Edgard Varèse began in music was ahead of anything dreamed of by his contemporaries: "Scientists are the poets of today. 'Art' means keeping up with the speed of light." Varèse was born in 1883, nine years after Schoenberg, one year after Stravinsky, and the same year as Anton Webern. While those around him concerned themselves with the problems of handling total chromaticism, Varèse moved onto a completely different track. In 1917 the composer described the quest that was to pervade his entire life: "I dream of instruments obedient to my thought and which, with their contribution to a whole new world of unsuspected sounds, will lend themselves to the exigencies of my inner rhythm." Varèse began his career by questioning the principles that underlay Western music. He did not accept the fact of twelve equal semitones; he regarded it as an arbitrary division of the octave. Nor did he accept the tempered fifth. He repudiated the physical principles on which his art was based, and thus made a clean break with the past. Varèse pointed the way to a pitchless music, with an

Edgard Varèse
DON HUNSTEIN

emphasis on pure sound and rhythm, and thus led the move toward the current preoccupation of serious composers with electronic music. It is significant that Varèse, unlike Schoenberg and Stravinsky, did not wait until he was driven from Europe. He came to the United States well before that, arriving in New York in 1915. Varèse considered *Amériques*, which he completed in 1922, his first truly representative work. He wrote it when Schoenberg was composing his first dodecaphonic movements and Stravinsky his first neoclassic compositions.

Varèse enjoyed America. "The people here," he said, "have a sense of optimistic realism. In Europe they bellyache." But even the United States, with its preoccupation with technology, did not finally met Varèse's standards. He once told an audience of Sunday afternoon concert goers: "Contrary to the general belief, an artist is never ahead of his time but most people are far behind theirs! Einstein once said, 'Our situation cannot be compared to anything in the past. We must radically change our ways of thinking, our methods of action.' Yet Einstein, who played the violin and had a predilection for Mozart, did not see that the world was standing still, that it was obstinately refusing to change its thinking or actions."

For Varèse that refusal meant that he was unable to produce many of the sounds he imagined. During the greater part of his life this composer was forced to operate within the fixed values of the tempered system and with conventional instruments that dictated the duration, dynamics and timbre of his notes.

Even so, he could still make some remarkable sounds. After World War II, Varèse received his first tape recorder and interpolated taped sounds into his orchestral work *Déserts*. The difficulty in determining when the orchestra stops and when the electronic interpolations begin testifies to Varèse's skill in producing revolutionary sounds with conventional means.

Today a composer is free to use all aural phenomena as raw material for his creative work. The current emphasis on sound per se and interest in pitchless composition can be directly traced to Varèse and his relentless pursuit of his goals.

In his speech at Princeton in 1959, Varèse said that he had often been criticized for disparaging the past and insisted that he had never done so: ". . . that [the past] is where my roots are. No matter how original, how different a composer may seem, he has only grafted a little bit of himself on the old plant. But this he should be allowed to do without being accused of wanting to kill the plant. He only wanted to produce a new flower. . . ."

But in fact Varèse's roots go no farther back than Claude Debussy, the first truly twentieth-century musician. Born in 1862, Debussy anticipated much of the new musical thought. As early as 1883, he wrote a letter to Ernest Chausson in which he humorously spelled out the future musical aesthetic: "Instead of spreading art among the public, I would suggest founding a society for Musical Esotericism." Debussy amplified his ideas in a little essay written under the name of Monsieur Croche, calling for freedom rather than a new classicism: "Discipline must be sought in freedom, and not within the formulas of an outworn philosophy only fit for the feeble-minded. Give ear to no man's counsel; but listen to the wind which tells in passing the history of the world."

An aberrant strain characterizes the recent history of French music. Committed to both letters and ideas, the French have consistently fought the mainline tradition, acting as gadfly to the established musical thought. As Rameau formulated a new theory of harmony based on root progression in 1722 (an analysis of chords based on their roots), so Debussy, in the late nineteenth century, turned away from the Wagnerian music-drama that was sweeping Europe in favor of sounds from outside Western civilization.

On his visit to the Bayreuth Festival in 1888–89, Debussy realized the necessity for a musical language diametrically opposed to the grand pathos and histrionic extroversion of the *Gesamtkunstwerk*. After successfully combatting Wagner's influence on his own musical development, Debussy composed subtle and introverted compositions. His dynamics range from the quadruple pianissimo to the mezzo forte. *Pelléas et Mélisande*, finished in 1902, anticipated developments soon to come from Vienna. Debussy used the whole-tone scale (C D E F# G# A# C) in the first pages of the score; thus he suspended tonality in Western music about five years before Schoenberg's Quartet, No. 2. Debussy turned away from the full triad in favor of the archaic-sounding fourth and fifth. The result is apparent in the opening measures of *La Cathédrale Engloutie*, where Debussy produces an effect similar to the medieval organum of the twelfth- and thirteenth-century musicians Leonin and Perotin. Debussy treated the chord as an independent sonority, as a vertical conglomerate in itself, independent of its harmonic context.

His unorthodox melodies and free treatment of rhythm (no longer did bar lines determine rhythmic units) were matched by innovations in timbre. The flute in *L'Après-midi d'un Faune* takes precedence over all other elements. Debussy scored flutes and clarinets in rarely used low registers and violins in extremely high ones. He muted his horns and trumpets, muffled his drums, and called for cymbals to be brushed lightly. In an opera (never completed) based on a story by Edgar Allan Poe, *The Devil in the Belfry*, Debussy had the protagonist whistle rather than sing. Such was the nature of the mind of the man whose ideas influenced Varèse.

Henri Varèse, Edgard's father, was, like Webern's, an engineer. The two most advanced musical figures of the first half of the century were raised with a respect for mathematics and science.

Varèse has described his father as "a kind of Prussian sergeant, the drill-master type," and his mother as retiring and frightened of her husband. When he was only a few weeks old, his parents sent Edgard to live with an aunt in the town of Villars in the province of Burgundy, where Debussy was also raised. His maternal grandfather, whom the boy loved, ran a bistro in Paris and so young Edgard spent much of his time traveling between Burgundy and the capital.

When he was nine years old, Edgard was sent to Turin to live with his parents. Henri Varèse, who had studied at the Polytechnicum in Zurich, wanted Edgard to follow in his path. He was so unnerved at any display of his son's interest in music that he locked the grand piano, covered it with a shroud, and kept the key hidden from his son. Such behavior may well have goaded the rebellious, aggressive boy into a commitment to a life in music.

In Turin, Edgard attended musical events at the Conservatory and opera house. He began secretly to visit the director of the Conservatory, Giovanni Bolzoni, who gave him harmony and counterpoint lessons. Through Bolzoni, Varèse became a member of the percussion section of the opera house orchestra and even conducted a rehearsal once when the conductor fell ill.

Edgard's mother died when he was fourteen. Varèse remained with the family for a few years after her death but left when the antagonism between him and his father became unbearable. According to Louise Varèse, the composer's widow, the father bullied Edgard in such a depreciating way that the boy grew up "not liking himself." She quotes him as saying, "I believe I have an allergy to myself." Varèse's only biographer, Fernand Ouellette, writes that the composer's attitude toward his father colored all future professional father-son relationships:

As soon as any man established a relationship with Varèse involving authority over him (Rodin or d'Indy, for example), that relationship was bound to fall apart very quickly. Behind the face of a d'Indy lurked the features of his father, hated since birth. Because of this, it took very little—a simple criticism which Varèse disliked intensely—to make all his aggressiveness, his willfullness, and his violence burst through to the surface.

Such feelings might well have contributed to the strength of Varèse's rebellion against the music of the status quo.

Varèse visited the Paris Exposition, which had so affected Debussy, when he was seventeen. Two years later he settled in Paris. Although the first performance of *Pelléas et Mélisande* had just created a scandal, there was little other musical excitement for him there. Composers performed at the Concerts Colonne during Varèse's first year in Paris included these undistinguished names: Bachelet, d'Ollone, Witkowski, Coquard, Hue, Saint-Quentin, who were supposed to represent the "new" in music. The old—d'Indy, Saint-Saëns, Lalo, Charpentier, Widor, Dukas and Chausson—were producing nothing that interested him.

Nevertheless, Varèse's exposure to science led him to think about the actual materials of music:

> When I was around 20, I became interested in a book by Wronsky, a disciple of Kant. Wronsky had written his own theories of philosophy, and while reading the book, I was struck by a phrase he coined to describe music. It was this: "the corporealization of the intelligence in sounds." I liked that phrase, and later it set me to wondering what, if anything, existed between sounds; or in other words, was there a sound between the C key and C#, or a difference between C# and D flat?
>
> The question led me to Helmholtz's *Physiology of Sounds*: I then began to think of the opposite of sound, of silence, and of how it can be used. . . . Now, to me, the climax of a crescendo can be a space of absolute silence.

In 1904 Varèse entered the Schola Cantorum, where he studied counterpoint, fugue, medieval and Renaissance music, and composition and conducting with d'Indy. Quickly, he became disenchanted with d'Indy: "The reason I left him was because his idea of teaching was to form disciples. His vanity would not permit the least sign of originality, or even independent thinking, and I did not want to become a little d'Indy. One was enough."

After one year at the Schola Cantorum—which Debussy described as the "citadel of the mandarins who made music into a pedantic science," Varèse changed to the Conservatoire. But the Conservatoire did not represent much of a change; to a man who was to consider music the true "art-science" and refer to himself as an "organizer of sounds," one established school was not very different from another.

Through the recommendations of Massenet and Widor, Varèse received the Première Bourse Artistique de la Ville de Paris when he was only twenty-three years old. During that year he married his first wife, Suzanne Bing, and set up housekeeping in an unheated room. Varèse soon became restless and depressed. Louise Varèse reports that whenever this happened, her husband would move. This time—1907—the young couple left France for Berlin.

When Varèse moved to Berlin, Ferruccio Busoni's *Sketch of a New Aesthetic of Music* had just created considerable attention in musical circles. Busoni, who preceded Schoenberg at the Berlin Academy, was not only an extraordinary pianist but also a champion of new music. In this revolutionary tract, Busoni discussed the possibility of new scale formations, microtones (tones smaller than a half step), and new instrumental possibilities. He stated that the progress of music could eventually be impeded by the physical limitations of existing instruments. Busoni applied his ideas by building a "harmonium," an instrument tuned in third tones that anticipated electronic instruments no longer tied to the halftone scale. With the whole tone divided in three, the octave C–C would be composed of eighteen third-note steps. Busoni never composed in this system.

Varèse describes Busoni's importance to him:

> I had read his remarkable little book, *A New Aesthetic of Music* (another milestone in my development), and when I came across his dictum: "Music was born free and to win freedom is its destiny," I was amazed and very much excited to find that there was someone besides myself—and a musician at that—who believed this. It gave me courage to go on with my ideas and my scores.

There were, of course, differences between the two men. Varèse explains: "It was Busoni who coined the expression 'The New Classicism' and classicism new or old was what I was bent on avoiding."

During the years 1907 to 1915, Varèse traveled between Berlin and Paris. In Berlin he was friendly with Busoni, von Hofmannsthal,

Strauss, and the conductor Karl Muck; in Paris with Romain Rolland, Debussy and Ravel. But these impressive contacts produced no practical results.

In 1910, the year his first and only child was born, Varèse did not have a single pupil. His intensity may have put students off: "I became a sort of diabolical Parsifal on a quest, not for the Holy Grail, but for the bomb that would explode the musical world and allow all sounds to come rushing into it through the resulting breach. . . ."

Varèse's first bomb exploded in December, 1910, when Josef Stransky presented his work *Bourgogne* to a conventional concert audience. Although Schoenberg's *Pelleas* was introduced that same week, *Bourgogne* created the larger scandal. Critics complained of "caterwauling" and "din"; later Varèse repudiated this early work, and destroyed it.

In 1912, in the Choralionsaal in Berlin, Stravinsky and Varèse heard the first performances of the atonal *Pierrot Lunaire*. Stravinsky did not like it; Varèse reports that he did. In 1913 Varèse attended the premiere performance of the *Rite of Spring*, the work that reaffirmed a tonal center and deified its composer the following year.

In 1914, Schoenberg stopped publishing. At the same time, Varèse turned to a conducting career; the milieu did not encourage radical musical ideas. Varèse conducted a successful concert of contemporary music in Prague, but World War I interrupted his career. Inducted into the French army, he was quickly discharged because of the difficulty he had breathing. Louise Varèse says that even in his youth, Varèse suffered from claustrophobia and gasped for breath as he walked down the rue de Rivoli.

The musical traditions of Western Europe may also have been smothering Varèse. In 1915 he left Paris alone—his marriage having broken up two years before—and arrived in the United States. Varèse found a more sympathetic milieu in New York City than he had in Paris or Berlin.

Chapter 17

In the nineteenth century, the two best-known American composers, Edward MacDowell and Horatio Parker, got their training in Europe and leaned heavily on traditional Romantic forms. But by the time Varèse came to the United States, a new American music was emerging. Musicians not bound to classic tonality, measured rhythms or conventional combinations of instruments were quietly at work in New England and New York.

Charles Ives was one of them. Born in Danbury, Connecticut, in 1874, Ives didn't struggle to overcome conventional systems; he simply ignored them. His father, George Ives, the town's bandmaster, was an extraordinary musician: arranging most of his players in the center of the town square, he placed others on roofs and still others on verandas from which they played their own refrains. Like Varèse, George Ives repudiated the tempered system. He invented new instruments; one had glasses and bells tuned in microtones.

Here is Charles Ives describing his father: "Father had a kind of natural interest in sounds of every kind, known or unknown, 'measured as such' or not, and this led him into situations that made some of the townspeople call him a crank whenever he appeared in public with some of his contraptions. . . . Once when Father was asked: 'How can you stand it to hear old John Bell bellow off-key the way he does at camp-meetings?' his answer was: 'Old John is a supreme musician. . . . Don't pay too much attention to the sounds. If you do, you may miss the music. You won't get a heroic ride to Heaven on pretty little sounds.' "

Charles Ives grew up surrounded by music: the town band, the chapel hymn, the theater tune and ragtime. He studied counter-point, harmony, sightsinging, piano, violin and cornet with his father and played the drum in the town band. For a special kind of "ear-stretching exercise," his father had him sing a piece in one key while harmonizing it in its most dissonant key. At Yale, Ives studied with Horatio Parker and produced a conventional sym-phony for his Bachelor of Arts degree. When he graduated in 1898, he moved to New York.

In Manhattan, Ives set up an insurance agency and began to compose: "You cannot set an art off in a corner and hope for it to have vitality, reality and substance. There can be nothing exclusive about substantial art. It comes directly out of the heart of the experience of life and thinking about life and living life. My work in music helped my business and my work in business helped my music."

In Ives's pieces, the listener hears singers yell slightly different versions of the same tune and four bands simultaneously play four different pieces in the town square. But American music had no place for this sort of composition, and Ives remained in a state of neglect. Although he began composing before his contemporary Schoenberg, his major works were not played until after 1930. An opportunity for early international recognition was tragically aborted in 1911: when Gustav Mahler saw the score of Ives's Third Symphony in 1910, he promised to perform it the following year. But that was the year Mahler died, and the symphony remained unperformed until the late 1940's.

After 1917 Ives wrote little music, and in late 1918, he became ill and stopped composing altogether. During his early convales-cence, he gathered together all of his material and began to publish it on his own (he could afford to do so because of the success of his insurance business). In addition to the 114 songs and the

Concord Piano Sonata, Ives also published *Essays Before a Sonata*, which he introduced with the following comment: "These prefatory essays were written by the composer for those who can't stand his music—and the music for those who can't stand his essays: to those who can't stand either the whole is respectfully dedicated."

It was easy to assume from such statements that Ives was immune to neglect. Schoenberg made this error. He first heard the American composer's work during the 1940's in Los Angeles. Schoenberg jotted down these words:

> There is a great man living in this country—a composer. He has solved the problem of how to preserve one's self and to learn. He responds to negligence by contempt. He is not forced to accept praise or blame. His name is Ives.

But Henry Cowell—the composer, and biographer of Ives—indicates that he was not nearly so self-sufficient. Cowell reports an incident in which a violinist from Germany visited Ives and while listening to the music responded with irritation. Cowell quotes Ives: ". . . he started to play the first movement of the First Sonata. He didn't even get through the first page. He was all bothered with the rhythm and notes and got mad. He kept saying: 'This cannot be played. . . . This is awful. . . . It is not music, it makes no sense.' Even after I had played it over for him several times he could not get it then. I remember he came out of the little back music room with his hands over his ears and said: 'When you get awfully indigestible food in your stomach that distresses you, you can get rid of it. But I cannot get those horrible sounds out of my ears with a dose of oil.' "

Ives did not respond with contempt:

"After he left, I had a kind of feeling which I have had, on and off, when other celebrated musicians have seen, or played, or tried to play my music. It was only temporary, but I did for a while feel that there must be something wrong with me. Said I to myself: I am the only one, with the exception of Mrs. Ives, Ryder, and Griggs, who likes any of my music—except perhaps some of the older more conventional things. Why do I like to work in this way and get all set up over what just upsets other people . . .? No one else seems to hear it the same way. Are my ears on wrong?"

But Ives, as it soon became clear, was not alone. In 1912 Cowell banged his fists and elbows on the piano and created tone clusters for the first time. And there were others: Wallingford Riegger, Carl

Ruggles, Ruth Crawford Seeger, George Antheil and Leo Ornstein. The idea that jazz is America's only musical contribution to world culture is widespread but wrong.

Varèse arrived in the United States in 1915 with ninety dollars thinking he could pick up a conducting career that had been cut off in Prague before the war. He planned to bring new music to America, and because he brought many letters of reference from European musicians, Varèse received the assignment to conduct the Berlioz *Requiem* at the gigantic Hippodrome Theater. At his disposal was the musical army that Berlioz had prescribed: 150 instrumentalists and 300 singers. Varèse was much at home with this large-scale work, so dependent upon huge masses of sound.

The performance in April, 1917, received rave notices. Paul Rosenfeld, one of the most advanced American music critics, wrote that the conductor possessed the "inspiration of genius." But even this success did not help Varèse's career. Apart from one concert, conducted in Cincinnati eleven months later, the composer-conductor was out of work.

In 1917 he met Louise Norton, then in the process of divorcing her husband. As soon as she and Varèse could, they married and lived in New York. Mrs. Varèse went on to become an outstanding French translator, but he would not use her income for family expenses. Earning a living was a continual struggle.

In April, 1919, Varèse became conductor of the New Symphony Orchestra, a cooperative in which participating musicians were to share in the profits. The idea of performing well-rehearsed contemporary works was the same as that behind Schoenberg's society, begun only months before. But the method of operation was entirely different: whereas Schoenberg limited attendance to an enlightened few, Varèse tried to reach the largest possible audience. He wanted to spread new music everywhere and to stress American works in an international context. In a press conference held to introduce the series, Varèse praised American composers who were neglected:

> There is an urgent need for an organization that shall take what *has been* for granted and lay stress upon what *is*. Until we possess and support such an organization, we are, so far as music is concerned, nothing but careless bystanders, heedlessly watching the painful growth of art without doing a thing to help it along. Musical history is being made now. American composers should be allowed to speak their messages into the ears of those for whom they are intended: the people of today.

But Varèse's plan did not materialize. No American work appeared on the initial program and the recently composed European works—by Bartók, Debussy, Casella and Dupont—did not appeal to the audience. The musicians were as unfriendly as the public; they did not want to learn new scores. After a second, unsatisfactory effort, the orchestra's council tried to get Varèse to change his approach. He refused and was replaced. Varèse told the press: "Too many musical organizations are Bourbons who learn nothing and forget nothing. They are mausoleums, mortuaries for musical reminiscences . . . the tories of art are like the tories of politics. They cling to the old and shrink from the new."

During this period Varèse began his most important work: "With *Amériques* I began to write my music and I wish to live or die by my later works." *Amériques* is written in sonata form, but is characterized by a new preoccupation with sound. Varèse's first version of the piece had Berlioz-like dimensions: 142 instruments included 2 sirens and 21 percussion instruments juxtaposed against the melodic instruments. In the *Christian Science Monitor*, Winthrop Tyron wrote: "Now this work, dispassionately regarded, may be said to mark a date in the history of art. In all reason it may be accounted the first original score for grand orchestra that has been made in America since the twentieth century began. Everything else can be referred to some European model. But here we are completely out of the field of borrowed, derived, imitated thought."

Despite his advanced ideas, Varèse was a romantic man. The day after the performance he described his work as the "interpretation of a mood . . . the portrayal of a mood in music." It is interesting to note that, in the 1950's, Varèse confided that he did not delight in the technology that had materialized. Louise Varèse reports that he was an emotional man and wanted his music to produce an "emotional effect."

Varèse's departure from the New Symphony Orchestra left him without an outlet for his work. So, with his friend the harpist Carlos Salzedo, the composer started the International Composers Guild. In July, 1921, the Guild published a manifesto in which Varèse praised composers and attacked performers:

> The composer is the only one of the creators today who is denied direct contact with the public. When his work is done, he is thrust aside and the interpreter enters, not to try to understand the work but impertinently to judge it. . . . Dying is the privilege of the weary. The present day composers refuse to die. . . . It is out of such collective will that the International Composers Guild was born.

Edgard and Louise Varèse
RICHARD SAUNDERS

The Guild attracted substantial financial and artistic support. Financier Adam Gimbel and painter Joseph Stella served on the administrative board, and Carlos Salzedo, with composers Ruggles and Casella, joined Varèse on the technical board. Mrs. Harry Payne Whitney and a friend, Mrs. Christian Holmes, backed the costly operation. For the next six years they contributed $200 to Varèse's monthly support and provided enough money for the concerts as well.

The ICG held its first concert at the Greenwich Village Theater in February, 1922, before an audience of three hundred people. During the next six years it presented works by Ruggles, Riegger, Stravinsky, Satie, Honegger, Poulenc, Milhaud, Schoenberg, Webern, Berg and the Mexican composers Chávez and Revueltas. It also presented the first American performances of such twentieth-century works as Schoenberg's *Pierrot Lunaire*, Stravinsky's *Les Noces*, Webern's *Movements for String Quartet*, Berg's Chamber Concerto for Violin, Piano, and Thirteen Winds, Hindemith's Concerto for Violin and Chamber Orchestra and Honegger's *Easter in New York*. Its conductors included Leopold Stokowski, Eugène Goossens, Fritz Reiner and Otto Klemperer. The ICG arrangement apparently gave Varèse what he needed; during these years, he wrote *Offrandes*, *Hyperprism*, *Octandre* and *Intégrales*, each of which was introduced at an ICG concert.

Varèse's style did not vary much from work to work. He tackled problems in the late *Déserts* that were similar to those in the early *Amériques*. He thought always in volumes and densities of sound, ignoring conventional harmonies and melodies; and created what has been characterized as "sonorous objects moving in a new sound-space."

Offrandes, performed in April, 1922, scored for soprano and small orchestra, was divided into two sections, each based on a poem. Although the form was dictated by the poetry, the hierarchy of musical elements anticipated much recent work. No longer did melody prevail over duration and timbre. The orchestra's balance of power shifted, with strings subservient to the percussion. In *Offrandes*, Varèse worked with the entire frequency range, scoring piccolos and high trumpets in high registers and contrabass trombones and tubas in very low ones, with passages that included notes at the extremes of the range held for relatively long periods of time. Varèse looked forward to a time when the composer would no longer be dependent upon the capacity of a human lung. After the *Offrandes* premiere, he spoke to the *Christian Science Monitor* of electronically generating instruments: "What we want is an instrument that will give us a continuous sound at any pitch. The composer and electrician will have to labor together to get it. At any rate, we cannot keep working in the old school colors. Speed and synthesis are characteristic of our epoch. We need twentieth-century instruments to realize them in music."

Varèse then wrote *Hyperprism*, a very short, tightly knit work scored for seventeen percussion instruments against nine melodic ones. The piece begins with percussion alone. A rhythmic figure with appoggiaturas resting on a single pitch generates a variety of tempi and moods. With *Hyperprism*, Varèse rejects all thematicism, and thus the work looks directly into the future. It was first performed uptown at the Klaw Theater; the ICG was attracting a larger audience. The use of the siren gave Varèse the gradation of pitch which Busoni had referred to many years before. The *New York Herald Tribune* reported:

> After the Varèse number a large part of the audience broke into laughter, which was followed by hisses and catcalls. The supporters of the musicians began to applaud and amid the uproar Salzedo jumped to his feet, and after calling to the audience to be quiet, cried: "This is serious." Apparently for the purpose of restoring order, the musicians played the Varèse number again while half the audience left the building.

A few critics praised *Hyperprism*. Subsequent performances in Philadelphia and Carnegie Hall under Stokowski's direction prompted Paul Rosenfeld to claim that "Varèse undoubtedly has done as much with the aural sensations of contemporary nature as Picasso with the purely visual ones."

Eugène Goossens conducted *Hyperprism* in London in 1924. He told a reporter from the *Musical Advance*: "Varèse is near the Schoenberg camp but a very great difference exists between the two. They have written of Schoenberg that his music emanates from a sick mind whereas, of Varèse, whatever criticism has been provoked of him, there has been no solicitude as to the state of his health."

Varèse followed *Hyperprism* with *Octandre*, composed at the end of 1923 and performed in January, 1924. Scored for flute, oboe, clarinet, bassoon, horn, trumpet and string bass, the work is divided into three general sections, characterized by an unusual use of instruments. An oboe opens the first slow movement, a low piccolo the lively second, and after a slow, subdued passage, a bassoon announces the flamboyant third. Varèse introduces an innovation in the metric markings of the flute part: 1/4 1/2; 3/4 1/2; 4/4 1/2. The extra half represents an added half beat or an eighth note at the end of the measure, but 1/4 and 1/2 is not the same as 3/4. The former is conducted by one long and one short stroke of the baton, while the latter is conducted with three even strokes. Providing his own means to get precisely the results he had in mind was characteristic of Varèse.

The composer's next work, *Intégrales*, contains high-volume screams, short shops, wild crescendi and rapid decrescendi. Scored for winds, brass and seventeen percussion instruments, the piece was composed and performed in 1925. Varèse's description of what he had in mind was strikingly clairvoyant in terms of the objectives of the present-day musician: *Intégrales*, he said, was conceived for "spatial projections" and was constructed to "employ acoustical means" which did not then exist but which he knew would do so some day.

Stokowski conducted *Intégrales* at Aeolian Hall in March, 1925. Winthrop Tyron, critic of the *Christian Science Monitor*, wrote that it was the "first original score for grand orchestra that had been made in America since the twentieth century began. Here we are completely out of the field of borrowed, derived, or imitated musical thought." But Olin Downes of *The New York Times* and Deems Taylor of the old *Herald Tribune* ridiculed Varèse's work. When Stokowski conducted *Amériques* in the spring of 1926, Downes wrote that the piece reminded him of "election night, a menagerie or two, and a catastrophe in a boiler factory."

The following winter Varèse completed a gigantic work, *Arcana*, which Stokowski conducted in 1927. On the title page of the score, the composer included a quotation from Paracelsus's *Hermetic Astronomy*. Paracelsus was a medieval physicist, alchemist and mystic; Varèse must in some measure have identified with him.

Arcana was scored for 120 players and even more instruments; Stokowski later admitted that his musicians detested the piece. The audience apparently detested it too. Hissing overwhelmed the applause. By 1927 the handwriting was on the wall: "neoclassicism," taught by Boulanger in Paris, boosted by Stravinsky on his 1925 American tour, and promulgated through the recently formed League of Composers, triumphed over Varèse and his advanced musical colleagues.

By the late 1920's the concept of socialist realism had gained momentum. Art for the social good was not best implemented by experimentation in sound and system but rather by "borrowed or derived musical thought." From this time on, neoclassicism grew in the United States, nourished by the League of Composers which was presided over by Claire Reis. Mrs. Reis had been an administrator of the ICG but broke with the parent group in 1923 because she and Varèse did not get along and because she did not agree with his "first performance only" policy. Twenty-five years later, Mrs. Reis wrote in the *Musical Quarterly*: "The new League preferred to repeat good works rather than to present compositions too immature for public performance."

The ascendancy of neoclassicism can be seen in the fact that the League flourished while the ICG died. Pitts Sanborn, a New York music critic, wrote an article in the League's official journal, *Modern Music*, in which he attacked Varèse as being prepared to "score for a bird-cage, an ash-can, or a renuncible carpet sweeper, provided any of these entities can make a desired contribution to his sonorous whole."

In the fall of 1927, Varèse dissolved the ICG and began to search for another outlet for his music. In a last attempt to provide a "new" music group, he collaborated with Ives, Riegger, Cowell, Salzedo and Nicolas Slonimsky to found the Pan-American Association of Composers. Advocating experimentation and deploring neoclassicism, Varèse explained the reason for the group:

> The Pan-American was born because I realized that Europe was drifting back to neoclassicism, or rather what is so-called, there really being no such possible thing. You can't make a classic; it has to become one with age. What is called neoclassicism is really academicism. This influence we wish to combat is an evil thing, for it stifles spontaneous expression. . . . It is not that we believe music should be limited to a passport, but rather, that today very little is alive, musically, in Europe. . . .

A few months later after setting up the Pan-American group, Varèse left New York for Paris with a $2,000 gift from Stokowski and a small income of his own. When he arrived in Paris he told the newspaper *Figaro* of his negotiations with an electric company "to do research into certain instruments which we hope will have a voice more in conformity with our age."

He was referring to machines for synthesizing sounds which he had been talking about with Harvey Fletcher, the acoustical director of the Bell Telephone Laboratories. The Bell Labs project did not materialize, however, so Varèse formulated his own ideas for a laboratory in Paris. But again he failed to attract financial backing.

Varèse's fascination with scientific phenomena appeared not only in his titles, but also in a work for which he never actually wrote the music, *L'Astronome*. Set in an observatory, it had as protagonist an astronomer who raked the sky with his telescope. In the final scene, when the astronomer is thrust into space, factory sirens and airplane propellers were to sound. The music was, he told a friend, to be "as strident and unbearable as possible, so as to terrify the audience and render it groggy."

Varèse's activities in Paris were not limited to far-out speculation. He supervised performances of *Intégrales* and *Amériques* and conducted *Octandre* and *Offrandes* at Pan-American concerts there, subsidized entirely by Charles Ives. Still limited to conventional instruments, Varèse began *Espace* and *Ionisation*.

Scored exclusively for percussion, *Ionisation* is sonority. Varèse uses instruments of definite pitch—celesta, piano, and tubular chimes—as well as instruments of indefinite pitch—gongs, cymbals, triangles, sleighbells, guiro, maracas, claves and cencerro. The work is structured according to different qualities of sound: metal, wood, heavy, light. *Ionisation*, scored for thirty-seven instruments and thirteen players, is Varèse's most familiar work. The title refers to atomic fission; scientists report that a recording of *Ionisation* was frequently played at Oak Ridge while they were at work on the atom bomb.

As the bomb symbolized a revolution in technology, so *Ionisation* symbolized a revolution in music. But the man behind these strikingly new sounds did not exude the one quality—the absolute knowledge that he possessed the only truth—that appears to be essential to gain worldwide renown. Varèse was a personable man who liked to cook, drink wine with friends, and listen to the works of others as well as to his own. His widow says that "he was egocentric but not conceited, not the egoist that Schoenberg was. Varèse had doubts; I wonder whether Schoenberg ever had doubts."

In 1933, during Varèse's last year in Paris, Nicolas Slonimsky conducted *Ionisation* at Carnegie Hall. According to the *Musical Courier*, it "moved even earnest devotees of the musical esoteric to smiles."

The response to Varèse was just as negative in Berlin and Paris. When Slonimsky conducted *Arcana* in Berlin in 1932, the critic of *Cottbuser Anzeiger* wrote that the audience was outraged. And in

Paris the situation was such that Varèse wrote to a friend: "It is disheartening to see the young school here in France becoming zealously academic. It is perhaps normal at a time of world-wide hesitancy to wish to escape into the categorical past, but life with its exigencies goes on and in the end will sweep away all that is static, all that does not move with the rhythm of life."

In the fall of 1933, Varèse and his wife returned to New York. His first large-scale work on his return was *Ecuatorial*, for which the Russian professor of electronics, Leon Theremin, created two instruments. Varèse had provided the specifications for these: they were to have keyboard control and an upward range of an octave and a half above the highest C of the conventional piano. He scored the work for percussion, brass, piano, organ and voice, in addition to the theremins. Slonimsky conducted it in April, 1934, and it was very badly received. Even his partisans turned against him, complaining that the voice was overwhelmed by the instruments and that the theremins produced only caterwauling.

Receiving increasingly few performances, Varèse turned again to electronics, and applied to the Guggenheim Foundation for help. His request stated the following objectives:

> To pursue work on an instrument for the producing of new sound. To inspect other new inventions in certain laboratories in order to discover if any of them could serve any new sound conceptions. To submit to the technicians of different organizations my ideas in regard to the contribution which music, mine, at least, looks for from science, and to prove to them the necessity of closer collaboration between composer and scientist.

Although Varèse applied several times, and had the recommendation of Harvey Fletcher, the Guggenheim characteristically denied his requests. Desperate for a laboratory, Varèse even tried to get into the Hollywood sound studios but could not interest anyone there in his ideas. The advance in musical thought that had begun in the early years of the century had come to a paralyzing halt.

In 1934, Varèse indulged in some wishful thinking: "I think that Stravinsky is finished and I believe Schoenberg is of much greater importance." Thus he anticipated neoclassicism's demise by a whole very active generation. Nationalism, the Depression, socialist realism and the WPA forced American music to become conservative if it was to be accepted and supported. Accessibility was the keynote of the age and radio its primary medium.

Varèse had helped to make New York City a mecca of contemporary music during the 1920's, challenging the life of Paris or Berlin. But that activity came to an end in the early 1930's. Apart from the beautiful *Density 21.5*, which Varèse wrote for the flutist Georges Barrère, his work of the early and mid-1930's is hardly known even today.

Through the help of a wealthy patron, Varèse went to Santa Fe in 1937 and taught several music courses there. He frequently repeated the admonition that new instruments were needed "to liberate sound and free the composer from the tempered system." But he appeared to be speaking in a vacuum.

At this time he was profoundly depressed. Continuing to produce scores, he would destroy the pages as he went along. In 1937, in the depths of despair, the composer subjected himself to an unnecessary and debilitating operation. This powerful and emotional man, desperately in need of public acclaim, then waited what must have seemed a lifetime for time and technology to catch up with him.

Chapter 18

Jean Paul Sartre, in an introduction to René Leibowitz's *The Artist and His Conscience*, poses what he views as the dilemma of music:

> By forcing music, a non-signifying art, to express predetermined meanings, it becomes alienated. But again, by rejecting the meaning you call "extra-artistic," musical liberation runs the risk of leading to abstraction and of offering the composer in question that purely formal and negative freedom which Hegel characterizes as Terror. Conceivably our era offers the artist no other alternative.

Sartre, in concluding, crystallizes the choice: "Reaction or terror? An art that is free but abstract, or an art that is concrete but indentured?"

Between the middle 1930's and the late 1940's, when Varèse was destroying his scores as he wrote them, music had become concrete and indentured. Regressive influences prevailed in the United States, Germany and the Soviet Union.

From a purely practical point of view, the American composer was better off in the early 1930's than he had been ten years before. By then, Varèse had succeeded in his original mission. The International Composers' Guild, emphasizing an eclectic international approach, gave rise to other music organizations including the Pro Musica in the Middle and Far West, the New Music Society of San Francisco, and the Pan-American Association of Composers. The League of Composers, with its neoclassic orientation, spawned the Philadelphia Music Society, the Chicago branch of the International Society of Contemporary Music, and the Copland-Sessions modern music concerts. In addition, important performances of contemporary music took place at the Coolidge and Yaddo festivals and concerts of the Eastman School of Music.

Koussevitzky and Stokowski performed and championed new scores, and Varèse, Salzedo, Ives, Bloch, Leo Ornstein and their generation were followed by George Antheil, Howard Hanson, Roger Sessions, Roy Harris, Virgil Thomson, Randall Thompson, William Schuman and Marc Blitzstein.

Henry Cowell, though a member of the younger group, allied himself to Varèse's advanced musical ideas. He described the contemporary scene in *American Composers on American Music*, published in 1933. Cowell enumerated the following groups of composers: Those Americans "working with indigenous materials and reflecting a free and independent spirit" he identified as Ruggles, Ives, Harris and himself. Those "somewhat original Americans who follow French or neoclassic tendencies" he cited as Sessions, Antheil, Blitzstein, Thomson and Copland, the last of whom, he added, "introjects jazz themes and rhythms in music that is otherwise French in conception." As for the conservative musicians, "who make no attempt to write anything departing from the general types of European music," he mentioned Hanson, Walter Piston and Deems Taylor.

Thus Cowell stated that a multiplicity of responses prevailed in 1933. But he did not specify where the balance lay. In the same years, Sessions in an article in *Modern Music* pointed to the general conservative trend:

> The reactionary tendency observable in every country during the past two musical seasons is only the latest and one of the most superficial symptoms of an underlying condition. . . . It is obviously the reaction of a public which, for the first time in music history, finds itself increasingly out of touch not with this or that contemporary music but with "modern music" itself. . . .

The music of Schoenberg and his pupils is still very inadequately known, even to musicians, and at least as much on account of its material complexity as of its emotional content, it will probably for some time continue to be so. It is *par excellence* music for the "initiated," and it is difficult to see how it will ever reach a large listening public. . . .

One may reject many of Schoenberg's ideas and modes of procedure while acknowledging not only his historical position as initiator of more contemporary music than is usually accredited to him, but also his work, and that of some of his followers, as in itself a fundamentally unassailable element in the music of this time.

Sessions's respect for Schoenberg, and his acknowledgment of the inaccessibility of his music, gives a clue to the climate of those years. Although the "difficult" musician was never completely submerged, he was, most assuredly, out of favor. The emphasis on the attractive and accessible through the use of simple techniques and the pop idiom had taken precedence over everything else.

Several composers changed their styles in accordance with the times. Unlike Varèse—who saw no connection between politics and art—Copland and Blitzstein radically altered their techniques. Copland, trained under Boulanger, had used polyphonic and chromatic devices in works composed in the 1920's. In his Piano Concerto of 1930, he employed a kind of serial technique based on a four-note row that shows familiarity with Webern's ideas. Blitzstein, before working with Boulanger, had been a student of Schoenberg in Berlin. In the 1920's and early 1930's, he composed in a complex, heavy-handed manner and publicly condemned those who appealed to the masses. As late as 1933, Blitzstein attacked the growing concept of the popular in art:

A new deification—of the savage, the child, the peasant, the artless music maker has set in. . . . Success has crowned Kurt Weill with his super bourgeois ditties (stilted Otchi Tchornayas and Road to Mandalays), harmonized with a love of distortion and dissonance truly academic; the "sonx" (sic) go over, the modernisms get sunk. This is real decadence, the dissolution of a one-time genuine article, regurgitated upon an innocent public ready, perhaps even ripe to learn.

But by 1936 both Copland and Blitzstein had reversed their positions. The Depression had brought into being the Work Projects Administration, which sponsored art among other things. The Marxist philosophy of socialist realism attracted intellectuals and artists throughout Europe and the United States. Copland wrote the popular *El Salón México,* and *Danzon Cubano,* a two-piano piece based on Cuban dance rhythms. Blitzstein delighted the nation with *The Cradle Will Rock,* one of the most popular theater pieces of the socially oriented decade. The work was a direct rebuttal of his earlier position and he confirmed his allegiance to the new commitment in another *Modern Music* article entitled "Coming —The Mass Audience." Several years later, in *Our New Music,* Copland projected his ideas in a full-length book in which he stated that the "12-tone system is the artificial product of an 'overcultured' society and lies outside the main current of music." He cited radio as the primary cause:

> What radio has done, in the final analysis, has been to bring to the surface this need to communicate one's music to the widest possible audience. This should by no means be confused with opportunism. On the contrary, it stems from a healthy desire in every artist to find his deepest feelings reflected in his fellow man.

Radio influenced German music as well. The German broadcasting system regularly commissioned composers to write new works and paid well for them. Clarity of text and simplicity of music were needed to attract a large listening public. In Germany, radio implemented the *Gebrauchsmusik* idea, music designed for the ordinary day-to-day situation, music that amateurs could play at home. *Gebrauchsmusik* was the antipode to *luxusmusik,* that music of the immediate past which Sessions described as art for the "initiated," art too complex for the bourgeoisie.

Paul Hindemith, espousing the *Gebrauchsmusik* idea, appeared at the other end of the spectrum from Schoenberg. In his first mature works, written during the early 1920's, his debt to Schoenberg was still apparent. But soon he turned to a simplified style and, by 1927, avowed his commitment to music for everyone.

Bertolt Brecht and Kurt Weill, dramatist and composer respectively, carried *Gebrauchsmusik* to its conclusion. Like Blitzstein, Weill did a complete about-face. Having joined Busoni's master class in 1921, he was closer to Mahler and Schoenberg than to any neoclassic composer. But in 1927 Weill met Brecht and was won over to his dramatic ideals. Their collaboration produced *The Threepenny Opera* and *Mahagonny.* In the notes to a 1930 performance of *Mahagonny,* Brecht wrote that the work "pays conscious tribute to the senselessness of the operatic form. The irrationality of opera lies in the fact that rational elements are employed, solid reality is aimed at, but at the same time, it is all washed out by the music.

A dying man is real. If, at the same time, he sings, we are translated to the sphere of the irrational."

Weill wrote simple ballad tunes and Brecht treated the voice in the simplest of ways, making certain that actors and actresses with no vocal training could handle all of the parts. Between them, Weill and Brecht overthrew grand opera tradition in a more striking fashion than Hindemith ever dreamed possible, delighting the new, not-so-educated bourgeois German audience.

Although Weill began to suffer from Hitler's growing rise to power in the early 1930's, Hindemith still remained in favor and continued to promote the idea that music—whether it is good or bad—is futile if it does not reach a large listening public. Trying his own hand at a comic opera, *Neues vom Tage (News of the Day)*, he used a libretto by a variety show producer; the title was borrowed from a column in the daily press.

By the middle 1930's, Hindemith used triads and tonal cadences. In *The Craft of Musical Composition (Unterweisung im Tonsatz)*, published in two volumes in 1937 and 1939, he dismissed atonality and polytonality as outmoded ideas, contrary to psychological and acoustical fact. Hindemith declared that the tone row destroyed the gravitational uprightness of traditional harmony, and he revised his early work to conform to his later theories. Preaching the then prevalent principle of art, he wrote: "People who make music together cannot be enemies, at least, not while the music lasts. . . . The proclamation of one's modernity is the most efficient cover for a bad technique, unclear formulation, and the lack of personality. . . ."

Throughout the 1920's, Schoenberg retained a small, cultist following. But those who remained faithful did so at a great price: they lost the favor of the German people. Many formerly devoted disciples followed the path of Alfredo Casella, who wrote shortly after Schoenberg announced the 12-tone technique:

> The triumph of Schoenberg is now fifteen years old. From that time to the present the technique of *Pierrot Lunaire* and *Erwartung* has not been further evolved either by the many disciples or—and this is a far graver concern—by the Master himself. What seemed at the outset to offer absolute freedom and a boundless horizon now appears to be, if not a narrow prison, then a vast park enclosed by lofty, unsurmountable walls. . . . The impassable gulf which separates the art of Schoenberg from our souls is his lack of radiance and joy. . . . In his art all is dim, with a hopeless, despairing density. The tragedy and pessimism of the great German Romanticists have

degenerated here so that they bear the grimace almost of insanity or hyperacute neurasthenia. . . .

Hanns Eisler's defection from the Schoenberg group was the most notorious. His 1926 *Zeitungsausschnitte*, scored for soprano and piano, was a caustic parody of the German Romantic spirit. In adopting the radically simplified style, also brought about through contact with Brecht, Eisler repudiated Schoenberg, who never forgave him for what he considered to be high treachery. In a letter to Zemlinsky, Schoenberg asked for precise, short answers to several crucial questions:

> Please just write your answers in besides the questions.
> I.   Did Herr E. say that he is turning away from all the modern stuff?
> II. That he doesn't understand twelve-note music?
> III. That he simply doesn't consider it music at all?

Schoenberg then angrily reminded Zemlinsky of the praise the latter had bestowed upon Eisler, "saying he was the only independent personality among my pupils, the only one who 'didn't repeat after me.'"

Schoenberg was forced to leave Germany in 1933. The Third Reich tolerated only tonal pieces composed by Aryans. Among other musicians who were compelled to leave their country were Bruno Walter, Otto Klemperer, Arthur Schnabel, Adolf Busch and Kurt Weill. Their offenses ranged from *"Kulturbolschevismus"* to non-Aryan descent to criticism of the Nazi-revered Wagner. The Mendelssohn Violin Concerto was banned from the concert halls, and opera houses lost conductors, intendents and singers.

By 1937, Hindemith was out of favor. A prototypical German musician, he still proved unacceptable to the Nazi regime. Hindemith's basically intellectual approach, his emphasis on the craft of his art, and his marriage to a Jewish woman, placed him in an unfavorable light; those in charge diagnosed his work as being "infected with Bolshevism and suspect of internationality." He could not appear as violist in any Germany city and, in 1940, moved to the United States.

By the mid-1930's, the German musician most in favor with the Nazi regime was Carl Orff, a thoroughgoing conservative. Orff wrote his most famous work, *Carmina Burana*, in 1936 and expressed his commitment to "extra-artistic" meaning in music: "Melody and speech belong together. I reject the idea of a pure music."

In reaction to the situation that was devastating the musical

culture of the country, Wilhelm Furtwängler, a conductor friendly
to the Nazis, appealed to Goebbels for moderation. But Goebbels
rejected his request with the following explanation:

> I, as a German political man, cannot recognize the line of de-
> marcation which you would establish: that between good and bad art.
> Art must not only be good; it must be conditioned by the needs of
> the people—or, to put it better, only an art which springs from the
> integral soul of the people can in the end be good and have meaning
> for the people for whom it was created. Art, in an absolute sense, as
> liberal Democracy knows it, has no right to exist. Any attempt to
> further such an art could, in the end, cause the people to lose its
> inner relationship to art and the artist to isolate himself from the
> moving forces of his time, shut away in the airless chambers of "art
> for art's sake." Art must be good, but beyond that, conscious of its
> responsibility, competent, close to the people and combative in spirit.

Goebbels, in this letter to Furtwängler, expressed the Platonic
view of art, which Blitzstein celebrated in *The Cradle Will Rock*
and the Soviet Union embraced with fervor. In Russia the shift
from the bold and experimental to music that served the purposes
of the state was more explicit than in any other country. The career
of Serge Prokofiev reflects this shift clearly. Prokofiev's early works,
written before the Russian Revolution, were imaginative and dissonant, revealing similar motor drives to those that characterized
early Stravinsky. In 1918, Prokofiev left Russia and composed and
performed in the West. In his autobiography, published in 1941,
Prokofiev tells why he continued to live abroad when Moscow
presented his work and when, in 1923, the Petrograd Philharmonic
invited him to conduct several concerts of his music:

> Why did I not return to my native land? I believe the chief and
> basic reason was that I had not yet fully grasped the significance of
> what was happening in the USSR. I did not realize that events there
> demanded the cooperation of all citizens, not only men of politics
> as I had thought, but men of art as well. . . .

Political events shaped Prokofiev's development. Lenin's death,
in 1924, precipitated the struggle between Trotsky and Stalin. In
1928 Trotsky was banished to Central Asia and in 1929 expelled
from the Soviet Union. Under Stalin's regime, art became the
servant of the state. In 1932, in a Moscow newspaper, Prokofiev—
still living in Paris—expressed his adoption of the Soviet point of
view:

What subject matter am I looking for: not caricatures of short-comings, ridiculing the negative features of our life. I am interested in subject matter that would assert the positive elements, the heroic aspect of Soviet construction. The new man, the struggle to over-come obstacles.

The next year the composer wrote to a friend of his longing for his native land. In Paris, he said, he was becoming enervated. "I risk dying of academicism."

On his return to Russia in 1933, Prokofiev began several practical projects: scores for the films *Lieutenant Kije* and *Alexander Nevsky*, for the ballets *Romeo and Juliet* and *Cinderella*, and for the propagandistic opera, *Simeon Kotko*, based on V. Katayev's story, "I, Son of the Working People." Prokofiev also wrote piano sonatas and symphonies which were simpler and less dissonant than his earlier pieces. He often spelled out his conceptual meanings. His *Symphony 1941* is divided into three major sections: In Battle, At Night, and Brotherhood of Nations. He wrote the opera *War and Peace* and the oratorio *On Guard for Peace* during the later years of his career.

In the autobiography, Prokofiev criticizes Stravinsky's neoclassicism: "For my part I did not approve of Stravinsky's predilection for Bach's method—pseudo-Bachism—or rather, I did not approve adopting someone else's idiom and calling it one's own. True, I had written a 'Classical Symphony' myself, but that was only a passing phase. With Stravinsky this 'Bachism' was becoming the basic line of his music."

Prokofiev's negative attitude toward Stravinsky was shared by others at this time. In 1929, the Soviet critic Leonid Sabaneyeff wrote that Prokofiev dominated that period in Russia because he was "more deeply rooted in the soil than Stravinsky, the rationalist who had conquered the world."

But as Hindemith's German qualities were eventually superseded by those of Orff, so Prokofiev's Russian qualities were outmatched by Shostakovich. Born in 1906, fifteen years after Prokofiev, Dmitri Shostakovich never subscribed to any artistic philosophy other than that held by the post-Revolution regime: "I consider," he wrote, "that every artist who isolates himself from the world is doomed. I find it impossible that an artist should wish to shut himself away from the people who, in the last analysis, form his audience. I always try to make myself as widely understood as possible and, if I don't succeed, I consider it my own fault."

In 1936, *Pravda* castigated Shostakovich for his enormously successful *Lady Macbeth of Mzensk*:

The listener is from the very first bewildered by a stream of deliberately discordant sounds. Fragments of melody, beginnings of a musical phrase appear on the surface, are drowned, then emerge again to disappear once again in the roar. To follow this "music" is difficult; to get anything out of it, impossible. The composer apparently does not set himself the task of listening to the desires and expectations of the Soviet public. He scrambles sounds to make them interesting to formalist aesthetes who have lost all good taste.

But Shostakovich regained the Soviet seal of approval with his next work, the Fifth Symphony, which he prefaced with the following note: "Creative reply to just criticism." *Pravda* praised the work for its "grandiose vistas" and "philosophical seeking."

In the United States, Shostakovich assumed a role of heroic proportions. *Life* magazine pointed out that it was unpatriotic not to like the Seventh (Leningrad) Symphony. And Copland identified Shostakovich as the "key figure of his time because he made the music of a living composer come fully alive for a world audience. The success of the Seventh Symphony was in large measure due to a consciously adopted musical style which is accessible to listeners everywhere."

Thus, by the late 1930's, music, a "non-signifying art," was expressing "predetermined meanings" throughout many countries of the world.

Chapter 19 In France, the simple and direct in music did not arise in response to the politics of the 1930's; rather, it had developed fifty years before in opposition to Wagner. In the 1880's, Satie began the attack on German Romanticism. His *Sarabandes* and *Gymnopédies* contained all the seeds of the neoclassic movement: nondevelopmental form, concern with sonority, and the reduction of music to its essential elements.

A direct contemporary of Satie, Debussy also turned his back on the weighty German tradition. At the turn of the century, he inaugurated the suspension of tonality, did away with the tyranny of the bar line, and raised timbre to a position of eminence among the hierarchy of musical elements.

Before World War I, Debussy was famous throughout Europe. But Satie received little attention until 1920, when Henri Collet, in an article entitled "Five Russians, Six Frenchman, and Erik Satie," compared Satie, Darius Milhaud, Arthur Honegger, Georges Auric,

Germaine Tailleferre and Francis Poulenc with the Russian nationalists. The name "Les Six" became identified with the group.

Satie wrote sardonic, witty music. "Airs to Make One Flee," "Three Pieces in the Shape of a Pear," and "Dessicated Embryos" ridiculed the pompous in German music. He also produced some large-scale works: *Parades*, for the Diaghilev Ballet, was written in collaboration with Picasso, Massine and Cocteau. Satie called for a typewriter, steamwhistle and rattle in the instrumentation.

Satie's collaboration with Cocteau led to an important liaison. In a book entitled *Le Coq et l'Arlequin*, Cocteau supported Satie's views and attacked romantic music as the "kind one listens to with one's head in one's hands." He appealed to the serious composer to bring the circus and music hall into the realm of art music.

Many composers did exactly that, spurred on by the examples of the French. In 1922, two years before Gershwin's *Rhapsody in Blue*, Milhaud, on a trip to the United States, visited Harlem and heard Negro jazz. "Its effect," he wrote in his autobiography, "was so overwhelming that I could not tear myself away. More than ever I was resolved to use jazz for a chamber work."

Thus Milhaud appropriated jazz effects for his important *La Création du Monde*. Stravinsky had made the first such amalgamation several years earlier in *Ragtime* and *Piano Rag-Music*. Inspired by both Stravinsky and Milhaud, and by the increasing pervasiveness of the American pop idiom, *Jonny Spielt Auf*, *Threepenny Opera* and *Neues vom Tage* all appeared in rapid succession.

Poulenc and Honegger also contributed to the postwar musical life of France with mildly dissonant, polytonal music. But all the efforts of Les Six could not keep it alive. By 1933, composers found nothing in Paris to nourish them. After a brief stopover in that city, Schoenberg left to teach in an unknown Boston conservatory. Prokofiev, suffering from a "stifling academicism," left Paris to return to Russia. And Varèse and his wife sailed back to New York.

In 1933, writing in an American journal, the French musicologist and anthropologist André Schaeffner diagnosed the situation: "The death of Diaghilev, no matter what has been said and what can be said about his strange conceptions, left a gap in the musical life of France. . . . Diaghilev is dead, and he was everything."

Nevertheless, the next striking advance in music came from France, where Pierre Boulez attracted worldwide attention in applying the serial principle beyond the realm of pitch.

During the early 1940's, before he was twenty, Boulez studied under Olivier Messiaen, the leader of a new group of musicians who called themselves "La Jeune France." Messiaen picked up where Debussy had stopped in his absorption of musical elements from outside the West; he enlarged the use of Gregorian and Oriental modes and went on to make a systematic study of Indian rhythms. In 1942, during the Nazi occupation, Messiaen taught at the Paris Conservatoire, introducing his students to exotic musical ideas and analyzing the rhythms of Stravinsky and Debussy.

In the *Technique de mon langage musical,* published in 1944, Messiaen wrote that the sources of his style lay in Gregorian chant and particularly in the asymmetrical rhythms of Hindu music. Concentrating on these tiny rhythmic cells, Messiaen focused on the element of duration. By revealing the possibility of treating rhythmic structures independently of sonorous ones, he engaged the interest of Boulez.

In 1945 Boulez graduated from the Conservatoire and began to study under René Leibowitz, a former student of Schoenberg. It was then that he committed himself to dodecaphony, the serial treatment of pitch. But the following year he abandoned Leibowitz and moved into uncharted spheres: to his perceptions about rhythm —made under Messiaen—he added his knowledge of the 12-tone technique. With his Second Piano Sonata, written in 1948, Boulez became probably the first European composer to extend the serial treatment of pitch to the duration of notes. The composer said that with this work he "succeeded in making a total break with the universe of classical 12-tone writing, the decisive step towards an integral serial work, that will be realized when structures of tone color and dynamics join serial structures of pitch and rhythm."

Boulez extended the serial principle to these other musical elements in 1950–51 in his *Polyphonie X* and *Structures for Two Pianos.* In the *Structures,* the smallest aspect of each musical event undergoes a perpetual transformation. Thus each pitch value never recurs with the same attack, the same intensity or the same duration. A staggering multiplicity of possible combinations occur, from which the composer makes the final choices. It was during this period—when he elevated other elements of the musical tone to the position which pitch alone had occupied—that Boulez wrote his famous article "SCHOENBERG IS DEAD."

But almost as soon as he succeeded in controlling a serial world, Boulez began to break away from it and draw on many aspects of his musical past. *Le Marteau sans Maître* (1954) is nourished by the serial idea but not confined by a strictly interpreted serial procedure. Its percussive treatment and rhythmic invention recall early Stravinsky, and the choking melodies, the tenuous balance between sound and silence, owe a very great debt to Webern. Even the ghost of Schoenberg appears: the length of the pieces and their sequence remind the listener of *Pierrot Lunaire*. Based on poems by René Char, *Le Marteau sans Maître* is scored for contralto and small instrumental ensemble in which the vibraphone plays a central role. The piece has been singled out by Stravinsky as the best composition the generation has produced. Here the composer is in full control, allowing no intrusion from the outside.

Le Marteau sans Maître is one of the last pieces of the 1950's in which the composer maintained an autocratic stance. Even Boulez, a secretive and formidable personality, moved away from the traditional concept of high art in the 1950's, having been influenced by his friendship with John Cage. In Boulez's Third Piano Sonata and *Improvisations sur Mallarmé*, later enlarged into *Pli Selon Pli*, he indicated several possibilities in the order of execution from which the performer was free to choose.

In 1959 Boulez left France for Germany. Building on his experience as founder and director of the Domaine Musical, he frequently served as guest conductor of the South-West German Radio Orchestra (Hans Rosbaud was the permanent conductor) which concentrated on presenting new scores. Later, Boulez served as director of the London BBC and the New York Philharmonic Orchestras and of the Institut de Récherche et de Coordination Acoustique/Musique in Paris. In each post his purpose was to promote his own cause, to make familiar to large audiences a modern language in which he believes, a language in which form exercises a centripetal role. However much Boulez played with freedom, he never became genuinely enamored of it.

Chapter 20

Under the influence of Milton Babbitt, the post-Webern serial idea grew more identifiably into a school of composition in the United States than it did in Europe.

Babbitt was a traditionally trained musician who grew up in Jackson, Mississippi. At four he began to play the violin and at six he performed the Bach D Minor Concerto in a public recital. In 1932, when he was sixteen, Babbitt saw his first Schoenberg score which an uncle brought back from a trip abroad; it helped form his decision to compose. After graduating from New York University, he began to study with Roger Sessions. In 1939, when 12-tone writing was the object of scorn (even the cerebral Sessions opposed it) and Stravinsky was lecturing at Harvard, Babbitt adopted dodecaphony for his own use.

Babbitt also anticipated others in the organization of duration, intensity, attack and decay, and timbre. Boulez and Babbitt, strikingly different men and musicians, began to organize musical elements along serial lines at about the same time.

Babbitt, concentrating on the technique as a language and system, preached the total organization of all musical elements and became the leader of a very influential American school. The school centered in the universities—not the conservatories; its emphasis was intellectual. Throughout the 1950's and 1960's, Babbitt persisted in a battle to win for the composer the intellectual status of the mathematician and philosopher. By the late 1960's both Princeton and Harvard were among those institutions granting a composer the Ph.D.

Babbitt attempts to control every aspect of his material. Each note in a Babbitt score contributes to several serial relations. Benjamin Boretz, a Babbitt-influenced composer and theoretician, has described Babbitt's work with words that are remarkable for the absence of traditional aesthetic notions: "Every musical event is given a multiple function, and the resulting 'syntax' is so 'efficient' that a single sound may convey as much information (i.e. musical action) as, say, a whole section of a Mozart symphony."

Because the symphony orchestra of the 1950's was unfamiliar with this complex language, performances of the music were rarely satisfactory. To get around this obstacle, Babbitt turned to technology and to synthesized sound. RCA, in its efforts to design a machine for commercial purposes that would imitate the sounds of large orchestras, inadvertently provided him with his most useful tool.

Babbitt thinks that this "new" music—the serialization of all the parameters of a tone—can be compared to the 20th-century revolution in physics. To Babbitt the content of a musical work depends on a number of developing structures. The trained musician may derive nourishment according to his recognition of the various serial patterns. Like some academicians in other fields, serial composers in the United States tend to write for one another and leave all "outsiders" behind. Babbitt articulated this attitude in an interview in *The New York Times* before a performance of his *Relata II* during the spring of 1969. (Despite the need to get past the limits of symphony orchestras, writing for a well-trained and prestigious ensemble still engaged his interest.) But his main interest remained in the electronic field: "I love going to the studio with my work in my head, realizing it while I am there, and walking out with the tape under my arm. I can then send it anywhere in the world, knowing exactly how it will sound."

As "total control" developed, so did "chance" music. Whereas Babbitt committed himself to organizing every aspect of his work, John Cage, a Californian born in 1912, so completely removed the composer from the controls that the accidents of life were allowed to prevail. Babbitt's highly structured form and Cage's negation of form—a form in itself—have a common base: both are restatements that there is no *a priori* order, no God-given frame of reference, no "natural" synthesis with melody, harmony, rhythm and timbre playing their "appropriate roles."

As early as 1937, Cage declared his commitment to unorganized sound: "I believe that the use of noise to make music will continue and increase until we reach a music produced through the aid of electrical instruments which will make available for musical purposes all the sounds that can be heard."

Cage attended Pomona College in California, studied with Schoenberg for a short time after working seriously as a painter, and came to New York in 1942. In his *Third Construction* of 1940, he used rattles, tin cans, a lion's roar and conch shells. Later, in *A Construction in Metal*, he called on seven percussionists to play on bowls, pots, tin sheets, gongs and metal bars.

In the mid-1940's, Cage extended the tone-cluster idea of his most influential teacher, Henry Cowell, to his own invention, the "prepared piano." "Preparation" meant placing bolts, nuts, strips of rubber and other foreign objects across and among the strings of the piano. Washers would clatter on the strings when certain keys were pressed; a bell-like chord could be produced by striking only one note on the keyboard if a pencil had been wedged between adjacent strings.

By 1950, Cage had stopped preparing instruments; intent had disappeared from his vocabulary. Now he turned to "accidental" or "aleatory" composition. As a student of Zen Buddhism, Cage was inspired also by the ancient Tibetan book, *I Ching*, in which he discovered that tosses of a coin could be translated into abstract patterns. Cage translated these patterns into compositional decisions. His *Imaginary Landscape No. 4* for twelve portable radios and twenty-four players is a classic aleatory work: a turn of the knob produced the next unpredictable sound. In a defined time span any sound could appear. To compose his music for *Carillon No. 2* in 1954, Cage placed a sheet of graph paper behind a piece of cardboard. Then he marked the imperfections on the cardboard —crystal glazes, discolorings and accidental marks—and punched a pin through each of them so that holes appeared on the graph paper. Cage then set up the following system: "One horizontal inch on the graph paper equals one second and three vertical inches equal any pitch range (one octave or two or three)."

The influence of aleatory music under Cage and several American sympathizers—Earle Brown, David Tudor and Morton Feldman—grew during the 1950's. Accustomed to accepting their musical cues from Europe, Americans could now take pride in Cage, who influenced both Stockhausen and Boulez in adopting a musical ideology that would burgeon in the 1960's. A new notation was needed to implement the aesthetic of chance and Earle Brown was probably the first to supply it. In his *Folio* of 1952-53, he illustrated visually the action of the music on paper and thus generated many of the recent experiments which are so far removed from traditional notation. Efforts are continually being made to persuade composers to adopt a standard, international notation, but at this date, nothing of the sort has been achieved.

Cage's influence on European music can be compared to Jackson Pollock's on painting. Both developed at about the same time. Aleatory music and action painting shared several important attributes: they elevated performance to a prime position, excerpted a "piece" from the surrounding continuum, which negated any self-contained form, and used concrete material. Most important, "chance" music and action painting celebrated the accidents that emanated from the creative act.

In 1953 Cage presented a revolutionary work, *4'33"*. The pianist walked onto the stage and sat silently in front of the piano for the length of time indicated by the title. Cage's "music" here is the collection of unintentional sounds that occur during this particular period. His point is that silence is never absolute, that even in a room designed to eliminate sound reverberation, one hears the sounds of one's own body. Cage's piece is literally that, a "piece" taken from the sound continuum, without beginning, middle or end.

In this Cage makes an aesthetic point: all sounds have value, not just those which have been willed. "A sound," he writes, "does not view itself as thought, as ought, as needing another sound for its elaboration. . . . It is inextricably synchronous with all other sounds and non-sounds, which latter, received by other sets than the ear, operate in the same manner." Cage has proclaimed that his favorite piece is "the one we hear when we are quiet."

Not all the avant-garde embraced serialism or chance. The American composer Elliott Carter has stood alone and, in the 1960's,

Boulez attacked both methods as "refusals to choose. The new music of chance is just as fetishist, except that choice is now left to the performer instead of to numbers."

Along with total control and chance, electronics determined the direction of music after World War II. Pierre Schaeffer, engineer, technician, writer and musician, and his staff at Radio-Diffusion Française, began to work with recorded sound. On October 5, 1948, the French radio broadcast a "concert of noises" which included studies of railroad trains, turnstiles and pots. In 1949, in an article in *Polyphonie*, Schaeffer coined the phrase "musique concrète" to signify the process that he had developed: music made of concrete materials.

Schaeffer began by collecting sounds: they could be superimposed; they could be mixed to produce complex sonorities. The composer was free to manipulate the material either by accelerating the speed to heighten the pitch or by slowing down and lowering it. He could play the tape backwards, reverberated or prolonged.

The composer could also cut the tape into bits whose length and duration he was able to calculate to a minute degree and loop the ends together with a "phonogène," an apparatus invented by Schaeffer. He could then put this closed circuit through the various transformations and superimpose it upon other circuits of the same kind. In place of the old concepts of tone symbolized by notes C, D, E, F and G, the complex sound patterns became norms in themselves, referred to as Sound Formation I, Sound Formation II, and so on. Filters, improved tape recorders, and devices like the phonogene contributed to the almost limitless plasticity of the process. Schaeffer, his engineer Jacques Poullin, and several members of his early group including musicians André Jolivet and Messiaen, produced works for radio, television, theater, dance and the concert hall.

Composers in the United States entered the electronic field several years later. Vladimir Ussachevsky, teaching music at Columbia University, learned about the tape recorder in 1951. His first tape recorder piece was played at a university concert in 1952 and engaged the interest of his colleague Otto Luening, who had studied with Busoni in Germany. Later that year, Stokowski programmed works by Luening and Ussachevsky at the Museum of Modern Art in what was probably the first public performance of electronic music in the United States.

An electronic laboratory, established in an engineering building on the Columbia campus, became the center of American electronic music, providing a counterpart to Schaeffer's Club d'Essai. Edgard Varèse was invited to use both.

After a silence of over a decade, Varèse began to respond to the awakening of interests in advanced music in 1947 with an Étude for Two Pianos, Percussion and Mixed Chorus. In place of a coherent choral text, he used words and phrases from different languages which bore no relation to one another. Still limited to traditional instruments, Varèse achieved something of the sound he wanted by emphasizing harsh consonants and avoiding mellifluous vowels. The first and only performance of the Étude took place at the New School for Social Research.

The following summer Varèse began to reassert his presence on the musical scene. Ussachevsky and Luening invited him to lecture on twentieth-century composition at Columbia. Later that year, in memory of Paul Rosenfeld, a staunch supporter of Varèse in the twenties, Frederick Waldman conducted *Hyperprism* at the Museum of Modern Art. Virgil Thomson wrote in the *New York Herald Tribune*: "This is real 'modern music' of twenty years back, and it still makes its point. . . . With no cue as to the work's particular meaning, your listener found it absorbing, convincing, and in every way grand. . . . I know it is great music."

Varèse spent the summer of 1950 in Darmstadt at the invitation of the International Institute of Music; at the request of the American High Commission he also gave a series of lectures at the America Houses in several large West German cities. Varèse, rich in energy and sympathy, thus transmitted his still revolutionary ideas to a receptive generation of German musicians.

During that summer, he began to compose *Déserts*, in which taped interpolations alternate with instrumental sections. Varèse conceived the work as a multi-media project: "Visual image and organized sound will not duplicate each other. For the most part light and sound will work in opposition in such a way as to give the maximum emotional reaction." But he never realized the projected film idea; *Déserts* was limited to "organized sound."

After finishing the instrumental sections in 1952, Varèse began to record the taped interpolations, which he collected from ironworks, sawmills and factories. In 1954 Schaeffer invited him to the studio in Paris to finish his tape work. Varèse carried his stored sounds with him when he went to France.

The instrumental sections of *Déserts* had been scored for two flutes, two clarinets, two horns, three trumpets, two tubas, one piano and five groups of percussion instruments. The taped interpolations Varèse recorded on two tracks to be played stereophonically. Hermann Scherchen conducted *Déserts* in a radio broadcast from the Théâtre des Champs Elysées at the end of 1954. The public response was negative. Boulez described the material as follows:

> The musical language given to the instrumental ensemble may be said to be evolving in opposing planes and volumes, the oppositions between them being manifested by the spaces maintained between the different pitches of sound, though without being founded on any fixed system of intervals, such as a mode, a tone row, or any sort of scale whatsoever. Then what is to provide them with movement, these aggregations of sound, true sound-complexes in the traditional sense of the word? Their movement will be created by the dynamics, by the tensions. . . . These "sound-objects" as it were, provided by the human potential of the orchestra, will be contrasted with the "organized sounds" of electro-acoustical links. . . .

The machinery to which Busoni had referred during the first decade of the twentieth century was finally available in the 1950's. In 1955 *Déserts* was premiered in the United States. That same year, the Olson-Belar sound synthesizer, produced by RCA, was installed at Princeton University, where Babbitt began to work with it. And at the University of Illinois, Lejaren Hiller and Leonard Isaacson began work on a project to use the Illiac computer on certain compositional tasks. This was done by letting control of the musical output be limited solely by the input instructions and leaving factors not specifically accounted for in the input instructions entirely to chance. Proponents of "total control" could work with the synthesizer; proponents of "chance" with the Illiac computer.

The Phillips Pavilion of the 1958 Brussels World's Fair testified to the erosion of all the old rules. In 1956, Le Corbusier, assigned to design the pavilion for the giant Dutch electrical manufacturer, had asked for Varèse to produce the sound. Faced with 480 seconds of time, Varèse chose several auditory "images," all different in character but heard simultaneously coming and going in different directions. Working with recorded material, which included studio-made recordings, transformed piano chords and bells, and filtered recordings of choruses and soloists, Varèse produced a three-track tape. "In the *Poème*," the composer said, "I heard my music—literally in space—for the first time."

To organize the transmission of the work, which Varèse entitled *Poème Électronique*, technicians spaced the tape over the pavilion's surfaces and along the sound paths designed into it; 150 loud-speakers amplified the sounds powered by 120-watt amplifiers. The work starts with the sound of church bells. Sirens, kettledrums, gunshots erupt from all sides of the pavilion and a voice sighs "Oh God!" with the pitch of the final vowel descending gradually into the depths of an echo chamber. While the sounds were being pro-duced, images of girls naked and dressed, of cities devastated and thriving, birds, beasts and reptiles were projected on concrete walls.

No scales, familiar rhythmic patterns or formal structures are anywhere evident in the *Poème Électronique*. Still, Varèse did not claim that the new destroys the old: "The electronic instrument is an additive, not a destructive factor. . . . Just because there are other ways of getting there, you do not kill the horse."

The pavilion brought multi-media work, electronic music and Varèse's name to the public's attention. In 1960 Columbia Records produced its first Varèse recording under the direction of Robert Craft, and in 1961 Craft conducted an all-Varèse concert at New York's Town Hall. At seventy-eight, Varèse received the first Kousse-vitzky International Award at the Plaza Hotel in the presence of such distinguished musicians of different sensibilities as Boulez, Babbitt and Leonard Bernstein. And, in 1964, in what Varèse has claimed to be the best performance of the work, Bernstein con-ducted *Déserts* at a regular subscription New York Philharmonic concert.

On November 6, 1965, Varèse died after surgery for the removal of an intestinal obstruction. In paying tribute to the composer, Boulez said: "Farewell, Varèse, Farewell! Your time is finished and now it begins."

There is something unique in the American temperament that brings formidable organization to an idea. Not only American serialists but a whole generation of electronic musicians exhibited this talent for organizing technically. Electronically synthesized sound, suited to the idea of total control, reached maturity with the RCA sound synthesizer. In the 1960's, the synthesizer was displaced by the giant digital computer. As total control and technology went hand in hand with the G.E. 645, so did chance combine with technology when Cage and Hiller, in the late 1960's, collaborated on a production which they called HPSCHD, the word harpsichord shrunken to their computer's six-letter limit. HPSCHD

Equipment for Varèse's Poème Électronique
at Brussels' World's Fair
N. V. PHILIPS' GLOEILAMPENFABRIEKEN

was premiered at the University of Illinois in its 18,000-seat field house. This noisy four-and-a-half-hour work relied on technology for its effects: 64 slide projectors, 8 movie projectors, 6,400 slides, 40 films, 52 tape machines, 59 power amplifiers and 208 computerized tapes. Mozart's "Introduction to the Composition of Waltzes by Means of Dice" provided a basis for certain harpsichord solos, and the work's entire numerical system, though computer-derived, was based on *I Ching*. Other themes were derived from the works of Mozart, Beethoven, Chopin, Schumann, Gottschalk, Busoni, Schoenberg, Hiller and Cage.

The recorded version of HPSCHD is considerably shorter than the performance, but the twenty-one-minute-long record provides an additional aleatory element: the listener is invited to participate in the work by adjusting the dials of his stereo in accordance with a computer print-out sheet provided with the album.

As composers entered the 1970's, new computers and synthesizers appeared and improved—the Moog, the Buchla and the Synket were a few—and talk abounded of systems analysis and determination of rules, using the terminology of business management. The composer who entered the 1970's was forced to remaster his tools with each creative venture that he undertook.

Epilogue In the 1950's, pop began to be taken seriously in the arts. Rock grew from a simple vehicle for a performer like Elvis Presley to a relatively sophisticated genre. The first post-atom-bomb generation provoked a wild, atavistic binge that was far removed from the music of Boulez, Babbitt or Cage.

Although art and rock shared the electronic medium, the stylistic differences between them were crucial. As art music abandoned the beat, rock revived it. And as art musicians retreated into a kind of solipsism, rock reached out into the real world, treating massive social and political events through the use of everything from Gregorian chant to techniques of the avant-garde.

Rock left its mark not only on the young but on painters, writers and advanced musicians. Was it envy of the response that rock musicians provoked or reaction to the tight control of the immediate past that led composers all over the world to accord more freedom to the performer and expect more participation from the listener? Many composers who, in the mid-1950's, had worked with the concept of total control moved away from it in the 1960's. Italian Luciano Berio, Belgian Henri Pousseur and Argentinian Mauricio Kagel—all Conservatory-trained musicians influenced by the serial idea—questioned the traditional concept of high art and the ritual of the public concert. They and a number of Americans such as Lukas Foss, Salvatore Martirano, Eric Salzman and Terry Riley— created a kind of multimedia happening with music as a primary focus.

From the sixteenth through the nineteenth centuries, artists focused their attention on man. Perspective in painting and tonality in music reflected the shift away from God's universe to the physical reality of the world. Tonality, with its built-in contrasts, was the perfect medium to express human passion.

But in the 1960's many artists turned away from man toward a more medieval-like search for that which lay behind man. The allusive total theater eschewed an enclosed form with a beginning, middle and end in favor of an unstructured openness. Composers drawn to this idea were groping toward something new, toward a symbol that could not be paraphrased or fixed in a theoretical system. This symbol had to be approached directly, in some intuitive way.

One can only dimly perceive the essence of the art of one's own time. But this much is certain: serialism, chance, and the total theater all share one denominator—they reject rhetoric and expressionism. They may also be steps in a long journey towards the crystallization of a musical language that will serve as tonality did in its own time. Max Planck, the great physicist, has described the contemporary condition of science in an essay he entitled "Where is Science Going?" He might just as well have been writing of music since *Pierrot Lunaire* and *The Rite of Spring*:

> We are in a position similar to that of a mountaineer who is wandering over uncharted spaces, and never knows whether behind the peak which he sees in front of him and which he tries to scale there may not be another peak still behind and higher up. . . .
>
> The value is not in the journey's end but in the journey itself

GLOSSARY

BIBLIOGRAPHY

INDEX

Glossary

NOTE: For nonelectronic terms, I acknowledge help from the *Harvard Dictionary of Music*, edited by Willi Apel, Harvard University Press, Cambridge, Mass., 1969. For electronic terms, I made use of a glossary prepared by Milton Babbitt and James Seawright of the Columbia/Princeton Electronic Music Center contained in an issue of the *Music Educators Journal* (November, 1968) devoted to electronic music.

aleatory music from *alea*: one of a pair of dice—music in which the composer introduces elements of chance in the composition or the performance.

atonality the absence of tonality without recourse to another system.

attack in electronic music those amplitude (volume) characteristics at the beginning of a sound.

bel canto Italian vocal technique that emphasizes beauty of sound rather than dramatic expression.

bitonality the simultaneous use of two different keys.

cancrizans a melody that reads backwards, from right to left, synonymous with crab motion or retrograde.

canon   a musical form in which a melody, stated in its entirety, is imitated exactly and in its entirety in one or more other voices, the imitating voice following at a short distance.

chromaticism   use of pitches resulting from the subdivision of the seven-note scale into a twelve-note scale in which all the tones are still "pulled" toward a focal point or tonic key. (C D E F G A B C becomes C C♯ D D♯ E F F♯ G G♯ A A♯ B C.)

decay   in electronic music those amplitude (volume) characteristics at the end of the sound.

diatonic music   music based on the seven-note scale of five whole tones and two semitones, for example, C D E F G A B C.

envelope   in electronic music those characteristics that determine the growth and decay of a signal.

filter   a device used in the electronic field that permits the transmission of only certain frequencies of the signal.

Gebrauchsmusik   utilitarian music, a term originating in the 1920's, possibly by Hindemith, that signifies music for amateurs to use at home rather than for professionals to perform in the concert hall.

Gesamtkunstwerk   collective art work, a word which Wagner designated for his all inclusive music dramas which he believed to be a new art form.

interval   distance in pitch between two tones.

ostinato   a clearly defined melodic phrase that is repeated persistently in the same voice and at the same pitch; an "obstinate" repetition.

overtones   the series of tones in addition to the pure tone that is produced by a conventional instrument or the human voice.

polyphony   the simultaneous use of different melodies.

polyrhythm   the simultaneous use of different rhythms.

polytonality   the simultaneous use of two or more different keys.

recitative   a vocal style designed to imitate ordinary speech.

ricercar   the instrumental counterpart of the vocal motet, characterized by the imitative treatment of one or more of its themes.

serial music   music based on post-1948 principles that involve more than just pitch in the structure, including duration, dynamics, tone color, etc. The name is derived from the "series" of intervals structuring 12-tone music, the technique from which serial writing stems.

sine tone   an electronically generated "pure" tone producing no overtones.

staff   five horizontal lines in and between which musical notes are written.

synthesizer   an electronic instrument system that produces sound.

timbre   tone color.

tonality   that system of seven-note scales in which one note is the focal point or tonic key.

12-tone music music which depends on a technique that originated with Schoenberg giving all twelve tones of the chromatic scale equal value.

white noise by analogy with light, a signal considered to contain all audible frequencies with amplitude randomly distributed; white noise sounds like escaping steam.

Bibliography

ADORNO, THEODOR WIESENGRUND. "Arnold Schoenberg," *Die grossen Deutschen*, IV (1957).

ARMITAGE, MERLE, ed. *Arnold Schoenberg*. New York, 1937.

———, ed. *Igor Stravinsky*. New York, 1936.

AUSTIN, WILLIAM. *Music in the 20th Century*. New York, 1966.

BABBITT, MILTON. "An Introduction to the RCA Synthesizer," *Journal of Music Theory*, VIII/2 (Winter, 1964).

BERG, ALBAN. "Society for Private Musical Performances: A Statement of Aims," in Nicolas Slonimsky, *Music Since 1900*. New York, 1949.

BORETZ, BENJAMIN, and EDWARD T. CONE, eds. *Perspectives on Schoenberg and Stravinsky*. Princeton, N.J., 1968.

BOULEZ, PIERRE. *Penser la musique aujourd'hui*. Geneva and Paris, 1964.

———. "Hommage à Webern," *Domaine musical* (1954).

———. "Schoenberg is dead," *The Score*, No. 6 (May, 1952).

CAGE, JOHN. *John Cage*. New York, 1962.

———. "For More New Sounds," *Modern Music*, XIX/4 (May–June, 1942).

———. "Indeterminacy," *Die Reihe* (1961).

———. *Silence*. Middletown, Conn., 1961.

CARPENTER, PATRICIA. "The Piano Works of Arnold Schoenberg," *The Piano Quarterly* (Spring, 1962, Fall, 1962).

CHOU, WEN-CHUNG. "Varèse: A Sketch of the Man and His Music." *The Musical Quarterly* (April, 1966).

"Contemporary Music in Europe," *The Musical Quarterly*, LI/1 (January, 1965).

COPLAND, AARON. *Our New Music*. New York and London, 1941.

CORLE, EDWIN, ed. *Igor Stravinsky*. New York, 1949.

COWELL, HENRY. *American Composers on American Music*. Stanford, Calif., 1933.

———, and SIDNEY COWELL. *Charles Ives and His Music*. London, Oxford and New York, 1955.

Domaine musical: Bulletin international de musique contemporaine. Paris.

FURTWÄNGLER, WILHELM. *Briefe*. Ed. by Frank Thiess. Wiesbaden, 1964.

GOLEA, ANTOINE. "French Music since 1945," *The Musical Quarterly*, LI/1 (1965).

———. *Rencontres avec Olivier Messiaen*. Paris, 1961.

HAUER, JOSEF MATTHIAS. *Zwölftontechnik*. Vienna, 1926.

HILLER, LEJAREN A., and LEONARD M. ISAACSON. *Experimental Music*. New York, Toronto and London, 1959.

HINDEMITH, PAUL. *A Composer's World*. Cambridge, 1952.

———. *The Craft of Musical Composition*. Tr. by Otto Ortmann. New York, 1945.

INTERNATIONAL COMPOSERS' GUILD. Collected programs of concerts.

KELLER, HANS. "Schoenberg's *Moses and Aron*" [sic], *The Score*, No. 21 (October, 1957).

LANG, PAUL HENRY. *Music in Western Civilization*. New York, 1941.

———, ed. *Stravinsky: A New Appraisal of His Work*. New York, 1963.

LAUTNER, LOIS. "On Arnold Schoenberg," *Michigan Quarterly Review* (Winter, 1967).

LEIBOWITZ, RENÉ. *Schoenberg and His School*. Tr. by Dika Newlin. New York, 1949.

MACHLIS, JOSEPH. *Introduction to Contemporary Music*. New York, 1961.

MAEGAARD, JAN. "A Study of the Chronology of Opus 23–26 by Arnold Schoenberg," *Dansk Aarbog for Musik forskning*, II (1962).

MAHLER-WERFEL, ALMA, in collaboration with E. B. Ashton, *And the Bridge Is Love*. New York, 1958.

MESSAIEN, OLIVIER. *Technique de mon language musical*. Paris, 1950.

MILHAUD, DARIUS. *Notes Without Music*. New York, 1953.

Modern Music. New York, all volumes (1924–47).

MOLDENAUER, HANS. *The Death of Anton Webern*. New York, 1961.

NEWLIN, DIKA. *Bruckner, Mahler and Schoenberg*. New York, 1947.

———. "Arnold Schoenberg's Debt to Mahler," *Chord and Dischord*, II/5 (1948).

NIJINSKY, VASLAV. *The Diary of Vaslav Nijinsky*. Ed. by Romola Nijinsky. Berkeley and Los Angeles, 1968.

OUELLETTE, FERNAND. *Edgar Varèse*. Paris, 1966.

PERLE, GEORGE. "Atonality and the 12-Note System in the U.S." *The Score*, 27 (1960).

———. *Serial Composition and Atonality*. London, 1962.

PLANK, MAX. *The New Science*. New York, 1959.

Preliminary Report on the State of Experimental Music . . . under the Rockefeller Grant to Professors Luening and Ussachevsky for Creative Research in Electronic Music. Electronic Music Center, Columbia University. Unpublished report, New York, 1957.

Princeton Seminar in Advanced Musical Studies. New York, 1962.

PROKOFIEV, SERGE. *Autobiography, Articles and Reminiscences*. Moscow, 1941 and 1946.

RAMUZ, CHARLES F. *Souvenirs sur Igor Stravinsky*. Lausanne, 1929.

Die Reihe [English ed.] No. 1. "Electronic Music." Bryn Mawr, Pa., 1957.

———. No. 2. "Anton Webern." Bryn Mawr, Pa., 1958.

RETI, RUDOLPH. *Tonality, Atonality, Pantonality*. New York, 1958.

La Revue musicale. Année 5, No. 2 (December, 1923).

———. "Igor Strawinsky," special number (May–June, 1939).

ROSENFELD, PAUL. "We Want Varèse," *Twice a Year*, 7 (1941).

RUBSAMEN, WALTER H. "Schoenberg in America," *The Musical Quarterly*, XXXVII/4 (October, 1951).

RUFER, JOSEPH. *Composition with Twelve Notes*. Tr. by Humphrey Searle. London, 1954.

SALZMAN, ERIC. *Twentieth-century Music: An Introduction*. New York, 1967.

SARTRE, JEAN-PAUL. Preface to *L'Artiste et Sa Conscience* by Rene Leibowitz, Editions de l'Arche, Paris, 1950.

SCHOENBERG, ARNOLD. *Letters of Arnold Schoenberg*. Selected and edited by Erwin Stein. Tr. by Eithne Wikins and Ernst Laiser. London, 1964.

———. *Structural Functions of Harmony*. New York, 1954.

———. *Style and Idea*. London, 1951.

———. *Theory of Harmony*. New York, 1948.

The Score and IMA Magazine. Stravinsky number. 20 (June, 1957).

SLONIMSKY, NICOLAS. *Music Since 1900*. New York, 1937.

STEIN, ERWIN. "Igor Stravinsky, Canticum sacrum ad honorem Sancti Marci Nominis," *Tempo* (Summer, 1956).

STOCKHAUSEN, KARLHEINZ. "Weberns Konzert für 9 Instrumente Opus 24," *Melos*, Heft 12/20 Jahr. (December, 1953).

STRAVINSKY, IGOR. *An Autobiography*. New York, 1936.

———. "Advertissement," *The Dominant*, I/2 (December, 1927).

———. *Poetics of Music*. New York, 1956.

———, and ROBERT CRAFT. *Bravo Stravinsky*. Cleveland, Ohio, and New York, 1967.

———. *Conversations with Igor Stravinsky*. New York, 1959.

————. *Dialogues and a Diary.* New York, 1963.

————. *Expositions and Developments.* New York, 1962.

————. *Memories and Commentaries.* New York, 1960.

————. *Stravinsky in Conversation with Robert Craft.* London, 1962.

————. *Themes and Episodes.* New York, 1966.

STUCKENSCHMIDT, HANS H. *Arnold Schoenberg.* Tr. by Edith Roberts and Humphrey Searle. London, 1959.

————. *Twentieth-century Music.* New York and Toronto, 1969.

Three Classics in the Aesthetics of Music: Debussy. Monsieur Croche the Dilettante Hater; Busoni. Sketch of a New Aesthetic of Music; Ives. Essays Before a Sonata. New York, 1962.

VARÈSE, EDGARD. "Answers by Eight Composers," *Possibilities* (Winter 1947–48).

————. "Les Instruments de Musique et la Machine électronique," *L'Age nouveau* (May, 1955).

VLAD, ROMAN. *Stravinsky.* Tr. by Frederick and Ann Fuller. London and New York, 1960.

WALDMAN, FREDERICK. "Edgard Varèse, an Appreciation," *The Juilliard Review*, I/3 (Fall, 1954).

WEBERN, ANTON. The Path to New Music. Ed. by Willi Reich. Bryn Mawr, Pa., 1960.

WELLESZ, EGON. *The Origins of Schoenberg's Twelve-tone System, A Lecture Delivered in the Whittall Pavilion of the Library of Congress, January 10, 1957.* Washington, D.C., 1958.

————. "Schoenberg and the 12-Note System," *The Listener*, London, Aug. 10, 1961.

————. *Arnold Schoenberg.* New York, 1925.

WHITE, ERIC WALTER. *Stravinsky, the Composer and His Works.* Berkeley and Los Angeles, 1966.

WILDGANS, FRIEDRICH. *Anton Webern.* New York, 1967.

WILKINSON, MARC. "An Introduction to the Music of Edgard Varèse," *The Score*, 19 (March, 1957).

Special Note: Alessandra Comini, Professor of Art History at Columbia University, showed me slides of the Gerstl paintings, alerted me to the Gerstl/Schoenberg affair, and provided the proper sources of verification.

Index

Adorno, Theodor W., 23
Ansermet, Ernest, 85, 110
Antheil, George, 92, 152, 163
Asafiev, Boris, 122
Atonality (Dodecaphony; 12-tone
    technique), *see* Schoenberg,
    Arnold; Webern, Anton von
Atonical, defined, 26
Auric, Georges, 171

Babbitt, Milton, viii, 25, 76, 134,
    175– 76, 182, 185
    Relata II, 176
Bach, Johann Sebastian, 79, 111,
    119, 133
    Art of the Fugue, 49, 113
    D Minor Concerto, 175
    Missae Parodiae, 111

Balakirev, Mili, 89
Ballet, *see* Diaghilev, Serge
Barrère, Georges, 161
Bartók, Béla, viii, xiii, xiv, 96, 120,
    126, 153
Beatles, The, xiv
Beethoven, Ludwig van, xii, 7, 10,
    14, 25, 93, 121, 184
    Ninth Symphony, 5
    String Quartet in F Major, Opus
    135, 4
Benois, Alexander, 100, 101
Berg, Alban, viii, 6, 21, 23, 40, 44,
    64, 69, 124,
    Chamber Concerto for Violin,
    Piano, and Thirteen Winds,
    155

Wozzeck, 47
Berio, Luciano, vii, viii, 186
Berlioz, Hector, 25
  Requiem, 152
Bernstein, Leonard, 124, 182
Bernstein, Martin, 53
Beyer, Robert, 74
Bitonality, 101–103
Bizet, Georges, 94
Blitzstein, Marc, 47, 63, 124, 163–65
  Cradle Will Rock, The, 165, 168
Bloch, Ernest, 54
Bolzoni, Giovanni, 143
Borodin, Alexander, 89, 93
Boulanger, Nadia, 120, 123–24, 128, 157
Boulez, Pierre, viii-ix, xiii, 64, 69, 70, 75, 172–75, 179, 181, 182, 185
  Improvisations sur Mallarmé, 174
  Le Marteau sans Maître, 173–74
  Pli Selon Pli, 174
  Polyphonie X, 173
  Second Piano Sonata, 173
  Structures for Two Pianos, 173
  Third Piano Sonata, 174
Brahms, Johannes, 3–5, 10, 15, 21, 67
  First Symphony, 5
Bruckner, Anton, 4, 15
Busch, Adolf, 167
Busoni, Ferruccio, 46, 147, 181, 184
  Fantasia Contrapuntistica, 113

Cage, John, viii, 174, 182–85
  Carillon No. 2, 177–78
  Construction in Metal, A, 177
  Folio, 178
  4'33", 178
  HPSCHD, 182–83
  Imaginary Landscape No. 4, 177
  Third Construction, 177

Carter, Elliot, viii, 178
Casella, Alfredo, 7, 44, 49, 117, 153, 155, 166
Chabrier, Emmanuel, 94
Charpentier, Gustave, 146
Chausson, Ernest, 144, 146
Chávez, Carlos, 155
Chopin, Frédéric, 96, 184
Cimarosa, Domenico, 88, 112
Clarke, Edward, 32
Clementi, Muzio, 119
Consonance, defined, 27
Copland, Aaron, 120, 123, 124, 163–65, 170
  Danzon Cubano, 165
  El Salón México, 165
  Piano Concerto, 164
Cowell, Henry, 47, 57, 151, 158, 163, 177
Craft, Robert, 21, 67–68, 85–86, 88, 97, 103, 116, 117, 128–29, 132–33, 135, 136, 182

Dargomizhsky, Aleksandr S., 93
Darwin (Charles), viii
Debussy, Claude, xii, 28, 40, 95, 97, 100, 110, 116, 148, 153, 171, 173
  Jeux, 34
  L'Après-midi d'un Faune, 144–45
  La Cathédrale Engloutie, 144
  Pelléas et Mélisande, 18, 98, 144
Delibes, Léo
  Coppélia, 94
  Lakmé, 94
Diaghilev, Serge, 85, 96, 97, 99, 110–13, 116, 118, 120–22, 172
Diamond, David, 57
Dissonance, emancipation of, 27–28
Dodecaphony (atonality; 12-tone technique), *see* Schoenberg. Arnold; Webern, Anton von
Domaine Musical, 174

Dukas, Paul, 122, 146
Dupont, Gabriel, 153

Eimert, Herbert, 74
Einstein (Albert), viii
Eisler, Hanns, 7, 49, 167
Electronic music, see Babbitt, Milton; Boulez, Pierre; Busoni, Ferruccio; Cage, John; Ives, Charles; Varèse, Edgard

Fall, Leo, 17
Falla, Manuel de, 100
Feldman (Morton), viii
Foss, Lukas, 128, 186
Freud (Sigmund), viii
Fried, Oscar, 31
Furtwängler, Wilhelm, 46, 49, 168

Galuppi, Baldassare, 88
Gershwin, George, 57
    Rhapsody in Blue, 172
Gilbert, Sir William S., 17
Glass, Philip, viii
Glazounov, Aleksandr K., 95, 96
Glinka, Mikhail Ivanovich, 88, 117
    Life for the Czar, A, 88, 93
    Russlan and Ludmilla, 87
Glossary, 189–91
Gluck, Christoph W., 5
Goehr, Rudolph, 47
Goehr, Walter, 47
Goossens, Eugène, 155, 156
Gottschalk, Louis Moreau, 184
Gounod, Charles, 94
Greissle, Felix, 13, 15
Grieg, Edvard H., 88
Gronostay, Walter, 47

Hannenheim, Norbert von, 47
Hanslick, Eduard, 4
Hanson, Howard, 163
Harris, Roy, 163
Harrison, Lou, 58
Hauer, Josef, 37–41, 115

Haydn, Franz-Josef, 14, 93, 119, 126
Herman, Woody, 127
Hiller, Lejaren, 181, 182, 184
Hindemith, Paul, viii, xiii, 45, 49, 120, 165–69
    Concerto for Violin and Chamber Orchestra, 155
    Neues vom Tage (News of the Day), 50, 166, 172
Honegger, Arthur, 171, 172
    Easter in New York, 155
Huizinga, Jan, viii

Indy, Vincent d', 146
Institut de Récherche et de Coordination Acoustique/Musique, 174
Isaac, Heinrich, Choralis Constantinus, 66
Isaacson, Leonard, 181
Ives, Charles, 149–52, 158, 159, 163
    Concord Piano Sonta, 151
    Third Symphony, 150

Jalowitz, Heinrich, 21, 58
Jazz, xiv, 111, 117, 172, 185
Jolivet, André, 179
Josquin des Près, Missa l'homme armé, 135

Kagel, Mauricio, 186
Kalafaty, Vassily, 93, 94
Keller, Hans, 9, 130
Kleiber, Erich, 47
Klemperer, Otto, 54, 155, 167
Koenig, G. M., 74
Kolisch, Rudolf, 43, 49, 58, 71
Koussevitzky, Serge, 102, 119, 163
Krasner, Louis, 57
Křenek, Ernst, 12, 50, 58, 63, 73, 75
    Jonny Spielt Auf, 50, 172

Lalo, Edouard, 146
Lanner, Joseph
  Opus 200, 102
  Tänze, Opus 165, 102
Lehár, Franz, 17
Leibowitz, René, 15, 57
Liadov, Anatoli K., 97
List, Kurt, 58
Liszt, Franz, 111
London BBC Orchestra, 174
Luening, Otto, 179

MacDowell, Edward, 149
Mahler, Gustav, 9, 14, 17, 19–22,
    25, 28, 31, 40, 67, 69, 70, 150,
    165
  Fifth Symphony, 21
  First Symphony, 21, 22
  Fourth Symphony, 21
  Kindertotenlieder, 20
Malipiero, G. F., 44
Marcello, Benedetto, 111
Martirano, Salvatore, 186
Marx (Karl), viii
Massenet, Jules, 147
Mendelssohn, Felix
  G Minor Piano Concerto, 93
  Violin Concerto, 167
Messiaen, Olivier, 173, 179
Meyer-Eppler, Werner, 74
Milhaud, Darius, xiii, 49, 57, 100,
    155, 171–72
  La Création du Monde, 172
Monteux, Pierre, 101, 104
Monteverdi, Claudio, 73
Moussorgsky, Modest, 89, 93
  Boris Godunov, 99
Mozart, Wolfgang Amadeus, 5, 14,
    93, 109, 119, 126–27, 143,
    184
  Così fan Tutte, 128
Muck, Karl, 148

Mumma, Gordon, viii

Nachod, Hans, 13, 14
Neoclassicism, *see* Stravinsky, Igor

Newlin, Dika, 19
New York Philharmonic Orchestra,
    174
Nijinski, Vaslav, 99, 101, 103, 110,
    116

Offenbach, Jacques, *Tales of Hoff-
    mann*, 94
Oliveros, Pauline, viii
Orff, Carl, *Carmina Burana*, 167
Ornstein, Leo, 152, 163

Paisiello, Giovanni, 88
Pantonality, 21, 26
Parker, Horatio, 149, 150
Pergolesi, Giovanni, 111
Perpessa, Charilaos, 47
Pfitzner, Hans, 40
Piston, Walter, 124, 163
Pokrovsky, Ivan, 94
Pop music, 172
Porter, Cole, 54
Poulenc, Francis, 100, 155, 172
Pousseur, Henri, 186
Praetorius, Michael, 121
Prokofiev, Sergei, viii, 99, 100,
    168–69
  Alexander Nevsky, 169
  Cinderella, 169
  On Guard for Peace, 169
  Lieutenant Kije, 169
  Romeo and Juliet, 169
  Simeon Kotko, 169
  Symphony 1941, 169
  War and Peace, 169
Puccini, Giacomo, 128

Rameau, Jean-Baptiste, 144
Rankl, Karl, 36
Ravel, Maurice, 95, 97, 100, 148
  Tombeau de Couperin, 115
Reger, Max, 15, 40
Reich, Steve, viii
Reiner, Fritz, 155
Respighi, Ottorino, 112
Revueltas, Silvestre, 155
Riegger, Wallingford, 151, 158
Rieti Vittorio, 100

Riley, Terry, 186
Rimsky-Korsakov, Nikolai, 86, 89, 90, 92–100, 110, 130, 137
  Le Coq d'Or, 100
Rock music, vii, xiv, 185–86
Rodriguez, José, 7, 8
Rosbaud, Hans, 174
Rosé, Arnold, 19, 20
Rosenfeld, Paul, 152, 156, 180
Rubinstein, Anton, 89, 111
Rufer, Josef, 47
Ruggles, Carl, 151–52, 155, 163
Russian Ballet, see Diaghilev, Serge

Saint-Saëns, Camille, 146
Salzedo, Carlos, 153, 155, 158, 163
Salzman, Eric, 186
Satie, Erik, 86, 97, 100, 155, 171–72
  "Airs to Make One Flee," 172
  "Dessicated Embryos," 172
  Gymnopédies, 171
  Parades, 112, 172
  Sarabandes, 171
  Socrate, 115
  "Three Pieces in the Shape of a Pear," 172
Scarlatti, Domenico, 112, 119
Schacht, Peter, 47
Schaeffer, Pierre, 179, 180
Scherchen, Hermann, 45, 46, 56, 181
Schmid, Erich, 47
Schmitt, Florent, 97, 100, 121
Schnabel, Arthur, 58, 167
Schoenberg, Arnold, viii, xii-xiv, 3–63, 141, 143, 147, 151, 152, 156, 160, 164–67, 175, 184
  Accompaniment to a Film Scene, Opus 34, 50
  Chamber Symphony, Opus 9, 8, 11, 20–22, 66, 67, 105
  Das Buch der hängenden Gärten, 9, 25–26
  Die glückliche Hand, 9, 30–32, 35
  Die Jakobsleiter, 8, 35–36, 41–43, 58, 60
  "Du lehnest wider eine Silberweide," 25
  Erwartung, 9, 30
  First Quartet, Opus 7, in D Minor, 20–21
  Five Orchestral Pieces, Opus 16, 29–30, 32, 44, 67
  Five Piano Pieces, Opus 23, 32, 41–43, 50
  Georgelieder, Opus 15, 67, 107
  Grundgestalt, 28, 29
  Gurrelieder, 7, 9, 17–19, 31, 107
  "Herzgewächse," Opus 20, 32
  Kol Nidre, 57
  Lieder Opus 1, 2 and 3, 15
  Modern Psalms, 8, 60
  Moses und Aron, 8, 52, 58, 60–61, 83
  Ode to Napoleon, 57
  Orchestral Songs, Opus 22, 34
  Orchestral Variations, 48–49
  Pelleas und Melisande, 7, 9, 18–20, 31, 53, 66
  Piano Pieces, Opus 11, 28, 30, 32, 50, 67
  Piano Pieces, Opus 33, 50
  Pierrot Lunaire ("Dreimalsieben Gedichte aus Albert Girauds Pierrot Lunaire"), 9, 32–35, 105, 148, 155, 174, 186
  Satires for Mixed Chorus, Opus 28, 47–48
  Serenade, Opus 24, 41–43
  Six Little Piano Pieces, Opus 19, 31, 67
  Six Pieces for Male Chorus, 50
  Stravinsky and, 83–86, 90, 100–103, 106–108, 113, 115, 119–20, 124, 126, 128–32, 134, 137
  String Quartet No. 2, Opus 10, in F Sharp Minor, 21–23, 25, 61

String Quartet No. 3, Opus 30, 44

String Quartet No. 4, Opus 37, 57

String Trio, Opus 45, 7, 9, 59

Suite, Opus 29, 48

Suite in G Major, 54, 57

Suite for Piano, Opus 25, 41–43

Survivor from Warsaw, A, 60

Three Pieces for Orchestra, 67

Three Satires, 119

Variations on a Recitative for Organ, 57

"Verbundenheit," 50

Verklärte Nacht, Opus 4, 9, 15–16, 18–20, 35, 66

Violin Concerto, Opus 36, 57, 132

Von Heute auf Morgen, 49–50

"Vorgefühl," 34

Webern and, 61–71, 78–79

Woodwind Quintet, Opus 26, 43, 44

Schubert, Franz, 14, 25, 93

Schumann, Robert, 4, 10, 25, 93, 184

Schuman, William, 163

Scriabine, Alexander, 28, 40, 92

Seeger, Ruth Crawford, 152

Serialism, *see* Stravinsky, Igor

Sessions, Roger, 57, 58, 120, 163–65, 175

Shostakovich, Dmitri
Fifth Symphony, 170
Lady Macbeth of Mzensk, 169
Seventh Symphony, 170

Sinding, Christian, 88

Skalkottas, Niko, 47

Slonimsky, Nicolas, 6, 42, 158–60

Smetana, Bedřich, 88

South-West German Radio Orchestra, 174

Stein, Erwin, 21, 69

Steuermann, Eduard, 32, 58, 71

Stiedry, Fritz, 57

Stockhausen, Karlheinz, viii, 74, 75, 134

Stokowski, Leopold, 57, 120, 155–58, 163, 179

Stransky, Josef, 6, 148

Strauss, Richard, 4, 15, 18, 40, 50, 95, 148
Der Rosenkavalier, 28
Elektra, 28
Salome, 28
Sinfonia Domestica, 20

Stravinsky, Igor, viii, xiv, 21, 28, 40, 47, 49, 64, 79, 82–138, 141, 143, 157, 160, 169, 173–75
Abraham and Isaac, 135
Agon, 134
Apollon Musagète, 120, 121, 124, 127
Cantata for Soprano, Tenor, Female Chorus, and Orchestra, 133
Canticum Sacrum, 133–34
Capriccio for Piano and Orchestra, 121
Concerto in D, 127–28
Concerto for Piano and Wind Instruments, 119
Dumbarton Oaks, 124, 126
Duo Concertante, 122
Elegy for JFK, 136
Epitaphium für das Grabmal des Prinzen Max Egon zu Fürstenberg, 135
Expositions, 116
Faun and Shepherdess, Opus 2, 95
Fireworks, 96
Four Norwegian Moods, 126
Histoire du Soldat, 102, 108–109, 111
In Memoriam Dylan Thomas, 133
Introitus for T. S. Eliot, 136

Jeu de Cartes (*The Card Party*), 124, 126
Le Baiser de la Fée (*The Fairy's Kiss*), 87, 120–21, 124, 127
L'Oiseau de feu (*The Firebird*), 97, 100–102, 105, 127
Le Roi des Étoiles, 107
Le Sacre du Printemps (*The Rite of Spring*), 34, 84, 92, 100–105, 107–109, 113, 117, 118, 120, 133, 148, 186
Les Berceuses du Chat, 107–108, 111
Les Noces, 107–108, 118, 120, 155
Les Sylphides, 96, 97
Mass, 132
Mavra, 116–17
Movements for Piano and Orchestra, 135
Nightingale, The, 76, 111, 120, 127, 133
Octet, 44, 86
Octuor pour Instruments à Vent, 116–18, 127
Ode, 126
Oedipus Rex, 115, 120–21, 127, 135
Orpheus, 132
Owl and the Pussycat, The, 136
Persèphone, 96, 120–22
Petrushka, 32, 100–102, 105, 111, 117, 120, 127
Piano Rag-Music, 111, 172
Piano Sonata, 95, 119, 133
Pribaoutki, 107, 109, 111
Pulcinella, 85, 112–13, 127
Ragtime, 85, 111, 112, 172
Rake's Progress, The, 128–29, 132
Renard, 107–108, 111
Requiem Canticles, 136
Scherzo à la Russe, 126
Scherzo Fantastique, 96

Schoenberg and, 83–86, 90, 100–103, 106–108, 113, 115, 119–20, 124, 126, 128–32, 134, 137
Septet, 133
Serenade in A, 85
Sermon, A Narrative and a Prayer, A, 135
Study for Pianola, 108
Symphonies of Wind Instruments, 116, 127, 128
Symphony in C, 124, 126
Symphony in E Flat, 95
Symphony in Three Movements, 126, 127
Symphony of Psalms, 120, 121, 127
Three Easy Pieces for Piano Duet, 109
Three Japanese Lyrics for Soprano and Piano, 107
Three Pieces for String Quartet, 109
Three Songs for Shakespeare, 133
Threni: Id Est Lamentationes Jeremiae Prophetae, 134
Variations, 136
Violin Concerto, 122
Sullivan, Arthur, 17
Swingle Singers, The, vii

Tailleferre, Germaine, 172
Taylor, Deems, 163
Tchaikovsky, Peter Ilich, 87, 89, 90, 92, 116, 121
Sleeping Beauty, 86, 93
Thompson, Randall, 163
Thomson, Virgil, 124, 128, 163, 180
Tommasini, Vicenzo, 112

Tonality
  abandoned, xii; *see also* Schoenberg, Arnold
  bitonality, 101–103
  defined, xi
  function of, 27
  pantonality, 21, 26
  12-tone technique (atonality; dodecaphony), *see* Schoenberg, Arnold; Webern, Anton von

Ussachevsky, Vladimir, 179

Varèse, Edgard, viii, xiii-xv, 56, 57, 141–64, 172
  Amériques, 143, 153, 157, 159
  Arcana, 157, 159
  Bourgogne, 148
  Density 21.5, 161
  Déserts, 143, 180–81
  Ecuatorial, 160
  Espace, 159
  Étude for Two Pianos, Percussion, and Mixed Chorus, 180
  Hyperprism, 155, 156, 180
  Intégrales, 155, 157, 159
  Ionisation, 159
  Octandre, 155–57, 159
  Offrandes, 155, 159
  Poème Electronique, 182–83
Verdi, Giuseppe, 128
Vivaldi, Antonio, 111
Vlad, Roman, 78, 111

Wagner, Richard, 3–4, 15, 17, 79, 86, 95, 97, 101, 130, 144, 167, 171
  Die Meistersinger, xii
  Tristan und Isolde, 5, 15, 25

Waldman, Frederick, 180
Walter, Bruno, 20, 167
Walter, Fred, 47
Weber, Carl Maria von, 5, 121
Webern, Anton von, viii, xii-xiii, 6, 21, 40, 44, 64–79, 85, 107, 115, 124, 130, 132, 141, 144, 164
  Concerto, Opus 24, 75
  Four Songs, Opus 12, 68
  "Gleich und Gleich," 68
  Im Sommerwind, 66
  Movements for String Quartet, 155
  Piano Variation, Opus 27, 70
  Quartet, Opus 22, 133
  Schoenberg and, 63–71, 78–79
  Six Bagatelles, 68
  String Quartet, Opus 9, 66, 68–69
  Symphony, Opus 21, 70
Weill, Kurt, 165–67
  Mahagonny, 165
  Three Penny Opera, 50, 165, 172
Weiss, Adolphe, 47
Wellesz, Egon, 37
White, Eric Walter, 84, 100
Widor, Charles Marie, 146, 147
Wolf, Hugo, 4
Wood, Sir Henry, 30

Xenakis, Iannis, 78

Zemlinsky, Alexander von, 14–17, 19, 20, 23, 40, 43, 49, 167
  Sarema, 15
Zillig, Winfried, 47
Zmigrod, Joseph, 47